Hong Kong Documentary Film

Hong Kong Documentary Film

Ian Aitken and Michael Ingham

EDINBURGH
University Press

© Ian Aitken and Michael Ingham, 2014

Edinburgh University Press Ltd
The Tun – Holyrood Road
12 (2f) Jackson's Entry
Edinburgh EH8 8PJ
www.euppublishing.com

Typeset in 11/13 Ehrhardt by
Servis Filmsetting Ltd, Stockport, Cheshire,
and printed and bound in the United States of America

A CIP record for this book is available from the British Library

ISBN 978 0 7486 6469 6 (hardback)
ISBN 978 0 7486 6470 2 (webready PDF)

Contents

Introduction

This book is one outcome of a programme of research that began in 2007. The research was funded by the Hong Kong Research Grants Council and took the shape of four consecutive research projects, of which I was principal investigator. The research covered areas such as Hong Kong independent documentary film, the colonial film units of Hong Kong, Singapore and Malaya, and the influence of the British official film; and all of these areas are also covered in this book to one extent or another. The research programme is also still ongoing, developing pace and changing direction, and, as I write now, in May 2013, it is outspreading to cover South-East and South Asia. An extensive set of research associations is being nurtured, and a major new website covering these areas has also been put into operation. A dedicated conference on these areas will also be held in Hong Kong in September 2013.[1] This will also be the third conference to be associated with this research programme. In many ways, therefore, the work that is represented by this book, though itself the product of considerable research activity covering a number of years, is about to reach a new level of extension and involvement.

I began to explore the documentary film in Hong Kong shortly after my arrival in the city from the UK in 2003. In order to commence, I first carried out preliminary research intended to clarify whether sufficient information and data existed to justify launching a later, large-scale research project on the subject. Initial findings proved discouraging in that it seemed there might be insufficient material to hand, and the sense of dearth which arose from these first inferences was then enlarged through subsequent discussion with local colleagues, all of whom adamantly maintained that Hong Kong did not possess a sizeable tradition of documentary film-making.

Though to some degree disenchanted, I also found this assessment plausible at the time, as I, like many others, tended to associate the Hong Kong cinema with martial arts films, melodramas, police dramas, comedies, or the art-house films of directors such as Wong Kar-wai – but not the documentary film. Existing academic publications on Hong Kong cinema also seemed to support this understanding as virtually all of these focused on the Hong Kong feature film. Academic publications on Hong Kong documentary film only began to appear from as recently as the year 2000. However, these were few in number, and also tended to focus exclusively upon the small independent sector. By 2008, when this research project began, the notion that academic studies of Hong Kong documentary film should mainly or even entirely focus on this sector, and its small number of auteurs, had become generally accepted. But, in my mind, this raised a number of questions. Why only consider these few very recent films and film-makers? What about previous films and film-makers? What about the official film? What about television documentary film? As I continued my pilot research I began to realise both that these questions opened up important new directions for research and that the notion that Hong Kong did not possess a substantive and long-standing tradition of documentary film was fallacious. In fact, I discovered that documentary film-making in Hong Kong had begun as far back as the 1890s, and had, since then, led to the appearance of thousands of films. My sense of dissatisfaction gradually faded away and I began work on what would eventually become a six-year-long – and ongoing – programme of research. This book is a major outcome of that programme and explores this long history of under-researched and often forgotten film-making.

It could be argued, albeit contentiously, that Hong Kong popular feature-film cinema might be studied without the imperative need to pay too much regard to the overarching historical context surrounding that cinema, one that encompassed the existence of Hong Kong as British colony, and, later, semi-detached component entity of the People's Republic of China. Of course, such a thesis on this sort of bracketing-out is open to challenge, but there is at least some credibility in the proposition, given that the Cantonese popular cinema was rarely affected *directly* by nationwide historico-political problematics, of one sort or another. Indeed, and as some scholars have argued, that cinema in part developed so as to avoid over-encounter with its uncomfortable authoritarian settings. However, it would be impossible to defend an argument as to such circumvention in relation to the Hong Kong documentary film, which has, in contrast, virtually always sought to address the historico-political dimension directly. Whether one is referring to a film from the 1930s, such as Lai Man-wai's *The Battle of Shanghai* (1937), a television documentary from the 1980s, such as the RTHK *The Hong Kong Case* (1989), or an independent film from more recent times, such as Tammie Cheung's *July* (2003), the documentary film in Hong Kong has invariably attempted to address the imperative history and condition of the city. Given this, it would be an error of judgment for this book to consider the documentary film in Hong Kong in isolation, and outside of historical context, and, consequently, this study will attempt to place the development of such film within that context.

As a consequence of adopting this historical approach, this book is structured more or less chronologically. Chapter 1 covers the history of the development of Hong Kong up to the outbreak of the Second World War, and the history of the documentary film in Hong Kong from 1898 to 1941, when Japanese occupation put an end to documentary film-making in the colony. Chapter 2 then explores the period from 1945 to the end of the 1960s, and the beginning of the era of television. Chapter 2 explores films made by the Chinese community, and outside of the State. However, Chapter 3 investigates films and film-makers – some expatriate, some Chinese – associated with the British colonial establishment. This particular history of the Hong Kong official film has been completely un-researched until now, and no academic publication on this subject had appeared before the publication of my 'The Development of the Official Film in Hong Kong', in December 2012.[2] The general model followed in each of the chapters of this book is also to combine general accounts with in-depth case studies of particular films. Initially, this was also the model intended for Chapter 4, in which a study of the Hong Kong public television broadcaster, Radio Television Hong Kong (RTHK), was to be followed by such case studies. However, so much material emerged concerning the relationship between RTHK, the colonial government, and the Hong Kong Special Administrative Region (SAR) and Chinese governments, that Chapter 4 was forced to depart from this approach in order to investigate that relationship in greater depth. Initiated in similar spirit – though not institutional structure – to the iconic British Broadcasting Corporation (BBC), RTHK developed as a putative public-service broadcaster within an authoritarian setting, and many contradictions flowed from this. Chapter 4 covers this, and Chapter 5 then looks more closely at the films of RTHK, focusing on series of films dealing with controversial issues such as the Tiananmen massacre of 4 June 1989.[3] A similar division to this is also adopted in Chapters 6 and 7, which explore the independent sector of documentary film-making in Hong Kong from the 1970s onwards. Chapter 6 carries through a general survey of the sector, whilst Chapter 7 looks more closely at a number of important independent documentary films.

This has been a long and complex research project, which I could not have brought to fruition without support from others, and I would like to acknowledge that assistance. First, I would like to thank the Research Grants Council of Hong Kong for funding my four consecutive General Research Fund awards.[4] I would also like to thank the University Research Committee, Research Committee of the School of Communication, and Specialist Sub-Committee, Business and Communication, all of Hong Kong Baptist University (HKBU), for generous additional financial support over the years. For all matters related to research application and administration I remain indebted to the ever-helpful Iris Kam, and, for financial matters related to research, to Shirley Yeung.

I also wish to acknowledge the help given to me by the various research assistants who have worked with me over the course of this research programme: Seth Henderson, Venus Lam, Natalie Wong, Hety Wong, Kelly Li, Xu Yaping, Karina Yim, Yvonne Young and Norman Bird. It has been a pleasure to work with them, and to also play some role in the advancement of their respective careers. In addition, I also wish to thank staff at the following institutions for their support: National Archives of Singapore, Shell Oil Company, British National Archives, Hong Kong Film Archive, RTHK, Hong Kong Government Information Services, and the Hong Kong Government Records Service. I also wish to acknowledge the following colleagues who have shown me collegial support over the course of this programme of research: Deane Williams, at Monash University; Gina Marchetti, at Hong Kong University; Brian Winston, at Lincoln University; Chris Berry, at Kings College London; Camille Deprez and Lo Wai Luk at HKBU; and others. I also wish to thank Mike Ingham, of Lingnan University, who contributed Chapters 6 and 7 of this book, for his support over a lengthy period of time. Finally, I would like to thank those colleagues who have presented papers at the three conferences associated with this research project, and also those who have granted interviews over this period of time. Amongst the latter are Dominica Siu, Peter Moss, Ed Kong, Raymond Wong, Anson Mak and Law Kar.

There are many findings to emerge from this research project, but one which can be set out briefly here relates to those important documentary films to have emerged in Hong Kong. Mike Ingham remarks on the more recent of these, and also earlier films emanating from the independent sector, both in Chapters 6 and 7, and in the Conclusions section of this book, and, given this, I will restrict myself here to mention only those films which appeared prior to 1990. All of these films will also be discussed in depth later in this book. The most significant early film to appear in Hong Kong was Lai Man-wai's *The Battle of Shanghai* (1937). With its gritty, activist account of the Japanese attack on Shanghai, this film deserves to be set alongside better-known later 'battle' films such as, for example, Patricio Guzman's *The Battle of Chile* (1973-9). *This is Hong Kong* (1961), made by the Hong Kong Film Unit, is not a 'great film' in itself, but it was important at the time, and deserves to be better known than it is. Two other films made by the Hong Kong Film Unit – Charles Wang's *A Race against People* (1965) and Albert Young's *The Sea and the Sky* (1972) – must also be singled out here for attention. Following this, the next most significant film to appear is the strange, fascinating, and historically significant *Water Comes over the Hills from the East* (1965). Ed Kong's *Rising Sun* (1980), with its saturnine portrayal of the Japanese advance into China and South-East Asia during the Sino-Japanese War and Second World War, also deserves special reference. Then there are two television documentaries from 1989 about the Tiananmen protest: *Spring of Discontent* (TVB *Pearl Report*), and *The Hong Kong Case* (RTHK). These two searing films, which depict the prolegomenon to and aftershock of capital tragedy, should be much better known than they are.

This then, in my view, represents a considerable part of the pantheon. However, it is a pantheon in great need of considerable maintenance. This book has brought the Hong Kong documentary film back into view, but the films themselves remain in difficulty. It is hard to locate and view many of them and available prints are also often of poor condition. Some – indeed many, from the television sector – will soon deteriorate beyond repair. Some are held in private institutions, some in government depositories. In either case the conditions of access can be inadequate and restrictive. Some films have no subtitles. In addition, many films have already been lost. Much work has to be done here on preserving this neglected heritage of the Hong Kong documentary film. Remastering, reconstruction and subtitling have to take place, and searches for lost films also have to be initiated. I hope this book will help to hasten this process.

Ian Aitken, Hong Kong, May 2013

NOTES

1. Conference: 'The Documentary Film in South and South-East Asia (including Hong Kong/Macau)' (HKBU, September 2013). Website: 'Documentary Film Research Programme, South and South-East Asia': (Documentary-film.af.hkbu.edu.hk).
2. Aitken, Ian, 'The Development of Official Film-making in Hong Kong', *Historical Journal of Film Radio and Television*, Vol. 32, No. 4 (December 2012), pp. 531–51.
3. On the morning of 4 June 1989 the Chinese military dispersed a student protest taking place in Tiananmen Square, in central Beijing, using live ammunition and tanks. Many students were killed and injured. The massacre, which official media in Hong Kong and China still refer to only as an 'incident', or, more adventurously, a 'crackdown', sparked international outrage, and is remembered each year in Hong Kong by candlelight vigil.
4. Cited Hong Kong Government grants:

   HK RGC GRF (240007): 'Documentary Film in Hong Kong 1974–2006' (2007).
   HK RGC GRF (240109): 'Hong Kong Documentary Film 1959–2006: The Documentary Film Series' (2009).
   HK RGC GRF (240111): 'The Colonial Film Units of Hong Kong Singapore and Malaya, and the Influence of British Official Film-making, 1946–1969' (2011).
   HK RGC GRF (240112): 'Documentary Film in HK (1957–2006): The Documentary Films and Film Series of Television Broadcasts Ltd. and Asia Television' (2012).

CHAPTER I

Hong Kong, Britain, China: The Documentary Film, 1896–1941, *A Page of History* (1941) and *The Battle of Shanghai* (1937)

HISTORICAL SUMMARY

Hong Kong entered the orbit of British imperial power when that power was almost at its zenith in the middle of the nineteenth century. The manner of entry was also a particularly violent, and in some ways also atypical, one. At that point in time the British Empire was expanding across the world out of the older eighteenth-century mercantile imperium, in search of new trading opportunities elsewhere. At the same time, imperial strategy was moving away from the formal annexation of new territories to the establishment of trading settlements, some of which also doubled as strategic military outposts. The older, more ruthless mercantilist approach, in which a conquered country's markets would be deployed to the advantage of the metropole, and that country then be forced to import goods from said metropole, generated inevitable hostility amongst subject populations, and, in addition, and most importantly from the point of view of the British Treasury, finally proved to be overly expensive to maintain.

By the mid-nineteenth century British imperialist officials and traders had largely moved on from this subjugation-mercantilist model to one based on adherence to the principles of 'free trade', and the establishment of trading settlements and arrangements based – usually quite loosely – on such principles. Now, the primary concern was to ensure that trade could take place 'fairly', according to the 'laws' of supply and demand, and unhindered by local protectionist obstructions. 'Free trade' inevitably came to favour the biggest and most developed players in a supposedly free market, and Britain was the biggest of them all in the mid-nineteenth century. That favouratism was augmented by the fact that free trade rarely if ever existed in the pure form that its ideological proponents, such as Smith and Ricardo, envisaged; and, in fact, a mercantalist insistence on trade-balance calculation also ensured that, where that balance went against British interests, action would be taken to remedy the situation.[1] Hence, from the mid-nineteenth century, Britain took on a role of imperial arbitrator, enforcing a *Pax Britannica* based overtly on adherence to the rules and practices associated with free trade, and covertly on mercantalist trade-balance calculation. Within this new stratagem the gunboats were no longer sent in directly, and it was only when the balance of trade went seriously askew, or when impediments to British trading interests emerged, through local internal political struggle, supply restrictions, or the imposition of tariffs, that military force would be proposed. Before such force was employed attempts would be made to persuade recalcitrant rulers to trade 'fairly'. However, when such persuasion failed, and sufficient interest was at stake, overwhelming force might be, and was, used quickly and decisively, in order to force a prompt return to the apposite ante.[2] When matters had reached this stage, the British also showed scant regard for the sensitivities of humbled rulers or states, as became apparent when the British and Chinese empires came into conflict with each other in the 1840s.

By the mid-nineteenth century, British (and other western) officials, politi-cians, businessmen and others generally regarded the international exchange of trade based on free-trade principles as inseparable from the notion of benevolent 'modernisation'. Modernisation, as far as British and other imperi-alists were concerned, implied taking underdeveloped countries into the inter-national economic order, establishing the rule of law in those countries, and also abolishing disagreeable local customs such as torture, slavery or radical nationalism. The apologia was that, when a country became engaged within the international economic order, and modernised in this manner, it would be enhanced. However such modernisation also provided an *a priori* rationale for the use of force, and such engagement always took place on terms dictated by the metropole. Since the sixteenth century, it had supposedly been illegal under 'international law' for any country to stand outside of fair international exchange in trade. However, one country that had always done so was China. Consequently, by the mid-nineteenth century, 'modernising' China through the opening up of the huge Chinese market, and the establishment of European business, legal, political and other practices there, became a key objective for free-trade imperialists. It was also inevitable that, by the mid-nineteenth century, those imperialists should form the vocal pro-interventionist advance guard of the then leading industrial and military power: Britain.[3] Prior to the mid-nineteenth century, Britain had sought to conduct diplomatic negotia-tions with China in the standard western manner. However, this had proved to be a difficult undertaking given the very large differences in legal and diplomatic practice which existed between the two empires, and also given a proclivity for Chinese officials to treat visiting British diplomats as inferior foreign 'barbarians'.[4] This lack of respect for the British servants of Queen and country caused sizeable and long-lasting umbrage in London. Beyond all this, what was also occurring in this series of early-to-mid-nineteenth-century spats between Britain and China was that two antinomic empires were jostling for position, with the more powerful of the two entities intent on achieving trade parity, at least. Conflict between Britain and China was, therefore, virtually inevitable, and it was a conflict that could only ever have one outcome.

The feudal Qing dynasty had always been insular, hostile to foreign influence, intrusion and trade; and, by the mid-nineteenth century, to the seditious idea that its own laws could be superseded by international imperatives related to the so-called fair exchange of trade. During the 1830s, and counter to such imperatives, the dynastic government repeatedly acted to limit the ingress of foreign trade into China through, amongst other means, allowing such trade to occur in only one port: Canton (Guangzhou); and applying a sizeable 20 per cent tariff to imported goods. Such protectionism was regarded by Britain as insupportable in itself, but, more to the immediate point, it also led to the emergence of a serious trade imbalance between Britain and China, with British traders suffering significant losses. These traders, spurred on by the mercantalist trade-balance imperative, responded by exporting opium to China, thus restoring the balance of trade in their favour. Opium sales to China then grew from 300 tons in 1810 to 2,600 tons in 1839.[5] Opium was legal in Britain, where it was used as a medicinal drug, but had been banned in China from as early as 1729 because it was being consumed there as a debilitating intoxicating one. The British traders knew full well that they were exporting a harmful proscribed drug into China, but they viewed this as the only way to stop Chinese manipulation of the market, and stem their mounting losses. The Chinese response was then to stop the flow of opium coming into China through confiscating and destroying supplies of considerable monetary value to the British, and also incarcerating British merchants and their ships under threat. This was a violation of the free-trade desiderata, and also threatened the commercial future of British traders. Beyond that it could also be construed as an assault upon British subjects that might require a military response. The Chinese officials who initiated and carried out these acts seemed unaware that they were providing the British – or at least the opium traders and their political allies – with a pretext for war.

After attempts at negotiating a way out of the predicament failed, British traders, headed by the Jardine Matheson Company, lobbied hard for the British Government to take military action.[6] That lobbying was also sweetened by a provision of £20,000 which the traders made available to help finance any such action.[7] Eventually the traders managed to convince the British Government to proceed. However, the Government did not act on behalf of the opium trade, which was criticised at the time in Britain, but in order to defend and advance British trade generally. Indeed, from the beginning, a considerable gulf existed between British high officials and the opium traders, with both sides antagonistic to each other. Despite such antipathy, though, a powerful naval expeditionary flotilla was eventually sent into China, and that fleet then proceeded to bombard Chinese military forces into submission. In this confrontation between feudalism and modernity the Qing government had underestimated the power of the largest and most advanced navy on Earth.

The first stage of the 'First Opium War' of 1839–42 resulted in the Chuenpi Convention, which ensured continued British trade into Canton, the provision of reparations to Britain, and the cession of the small, undeveloped island of Hong Kong to Britain. However, the decision to annex Hong Kong was not made by London but by British military officers engaged in the China expedition egged on by China traders such as Jardine Matheson. London had never wanted anything to do with Hong Kong in the first place. The objective of the British expedition was to punish China for transgression, obtain reparations, and open up trade. To this end, the expedition commanders were instructed to seize control of another island of the Chinese coast, Zhoushan, far to the north of Hong Kong, and close to Shanghai. In addition, this island was to be captured, not formally annexed. However, the commander in charge of the British expedition, Captain Charles Elliot, came to the stand that Hong Kong offered greater security, and then also came under pressure from the traders to take the island on a permanent basis. The traders' primary concern here was that Hong Kong be used to protect the nearby trading base in Canton. However, in seizing Hong Kong, Elliot exceeded his powers, and disobeyed the instructions of his superior, the Foreign Secretary Lord Palmerston.[8] Elliot, who had no authority to insist upon such a forced cession from China, was reprimanded for forcing this through, and eventually replaced.[9] Nevertheless, and before London could do anything about the matter, Elliot took formal possession of the island, and British rule of Hong Kong began on 26 January 1841.

The treaty which Elliot concluded satisfied neither the British Government's intent to open up the China market, nor the opium traders' desire that further islands off the Chinese coast be seized in addition to Hong Kong.[10] Largely ignoring the opium traders over the issue of further sequestration, though, the Government now continued to pursue its own objectives through the further and more determined exercise of force; and the second stage of the 'First Opium War' commenced. The chastened Elliot was replaced by Sir Henry Pottinger and the British expeditionary squadron, now increased in size and strength, proceeded to pound the forces of the Chinese dynastic government into submission once more. The final outcome was the Treaty of Nanking (1842), which opened up a number of new trading posts along the Chinese coast and led to the formal ratification of Hong Kong as a Crown

Colony on 26 June 1843. After the unanticipated annexation of the island, London's initial intent had been to eventually hand Hong Kong back to China, even though Elliot had taken formal possession of the island on behalf of the Crown. However, the holding had now proved its clear worth as the base from which a victorious British fleet had sailed to force the Treaty of Nanking. In addition, before Hong Kong could be given up, it had already been quickly settled by a significant number of British and Chinese adventurers, including the opium traders. London was therefore forced to accept the *fait accompli*, although Pottinger, who would become the first Governor of Hong Kong, was instructed – in an ordinance which would also anticipate the future development of the colony – to ensure that the new colonial administration would not become a burden on the British Treasury, and would cover its limited costs as best it could.

Britain's 'informal' commercial empire in its far-flung tropical places began to experience a number of problems during the last third of the nineteenth century, caused largely by an inevitable and predictable contradiction between a British desire to ensure, and often control, the flow of trade, and local resentment of such control, and of the colonial presence itself. These problems also continued to emerge in China as, following the Treaty of Nanking, Chinese obstruction of foreign trade continued in violation of the terms of the treaty: a treaty which the Chinese authorities regarded as forced, prejudicial, and rightly to be opposed. Eventually, such opposition, and the British response, led to the 'Second Opium War' of 1857–60, which further opened up the Chinese market for British commerce, and also annexed the adjoining area of the Chinese mainland to Hong Kong – Kowloon – to the colony. The Second Opium War was a major defeat for China, and the Anglo-French expeditionary force which successfully prosecuted the war, and could have taken Peking if its commanders had so wished, had, like the fleet of 1841, sailed from Hong Kong. After this, Hong Kong's position within the British Empire was established for the foreseeable future. It would, in the first place, be a military imperial outpost whose primary purpose was to secure and protect British trading posts along the Chinese coast; and only in the second place would it be a sustainable trading settlement in its own right. However, this also meant that Hong Kong had little *general* strategic value for the Empire outside of the China coast, and this lack of imperative strategic consequence would come to influence the progress of the colony from then on.

It was partly because of this martial mandate that Hong Kong was established as a Crown Colony in 1843, though this was also a common form of constitutional structure for British overseas territories at the time.[11] The Crown Colony model did, in theory, allow for some degree of local representation, even though all formal power was vested in the Governor, who, in turn, answered directly to London. However, the model adopted in Hong Kong did not allow for any representational element, and even the Executive Council was granted an advisory role only.[12] This *was* unusual. During the late nineteenth century highly autocratic forms of Crown Colony were gradually modified as local and expatriate inhabitants demanded a degree of representation, and as London and colonial administrations saw no good reason to deny this. So, for example, during the latter half of the nineteenth century, some elected members were permitted in Jamaica, Trinidad and Mauritius. However, in 1895 the Colonial Office warned against extending such reform to Hong Kong, and, whilst other colonies proceeded towards the inclusion of elected members of government, no such members were permitted in principle in Hong Kong until as startlingly late as 1985.[13]

However, the autocratic form of the Crown Colony should not necessarily, or automatically, be considered a form of despotisim, and, at one level, was founded on a faith in the incorruptibility of high officials: men (rarely women) who had been trained always to put duty and responsibility to the Empire above personal and sectarian interests at all times. These were the individuals who would rule the Crown Colony. Amongst other things this meant that, in practice as well as theory, these senior officials would not allow the dominant colonial expatriate class in a colony to run the colony in *their* interests, and at the expense of the local population. This was particularly important and necessary in the case of Hong Kong because, from the very founding of the colony, senior officials in London and the Crown Colony did not trust the expatriate community in the territory to treat the extensive Chinese community humanely or fairly. Thus the Crown Colony model was adopted partly in order to keep this dubious expatriate minority from establishing itself as a race-based oligarchy; although it was, of course, also adopted in order to keep the majority colonised Chinese population out of power. Finally, the autocratic form of the Crown Colony was adopted for Hong Kong because London felt that almost any issue that arose in the colony would inevitably involve or relate to China in some way, and would, therefore, have a bearing on general Anglo-Chinese relations. This was important, and it was because London insisted upon exercising oversight of these relations that it also insisted upon taking direct control of the colony's affairs through the Governor.[14]

What happened in Hong Kong during 1841–61 was characteristic of British imperial strategy at the time. A limited but decisive military intervention was employed to defend or advance economic interests. When the desired result was achieved, action was halted and the business of trading resumed.[15] In order to continue defending such interests, though, something relatively *untypical* happened: the island of Hong Kong was formally annexed, and not as a settlement colony run primarily on the basis of trade, but as an imperial outpost with a remit to defend and advance trade elsewhere.[16] This distinguished Hong Kong from the newly established British trading settlements on the Chinese coast, and also from others nearby. For example, in Malaya Britain established coastal trading settlements in Penang, Malacca and Singapore, and only resorted to political and military intervention when those settlements were threatened by native power struggles occurring within the hinterland. In Malaya the local population was still largely governed by local rulers, with the British playing an 'advisory' but covertly executive role through various forms of treaty and contract. As in China, in Malaya the British were primarily interested in developing trade and commerce, and not in expensive and risky annexation on the eighteenth-century model. However, Hong Kong was different. The colony was formally annexed, and completely controlled by the British. At the beginning, its native population of around 7,000 fishermen and farmers was only slightly double that of the substantial colonial presence, and could have easily been subjugated, had that proved necessary. This degree of colonial domination was also to have important consequences for the future development of culture and society within the colony.[17]

After 1861 the situation in imperial China deteriorated sharply as internal political divisions led to the deaths of millions, and to the great Chinese diaspora of the late nineteenth and early twentieth centuries. A significant part of that diaspora also came to Hong Kong. By 1901 census figures indicate a population of 301,000; by 1921 it was 625,000; and by 1939 over 1 million. By 1939 around 95 per cent of the population in Hong Kong was Chinese, with the colonial class and other ethnic minorities (such as Sikh soldiers and policemen brought in from India) amounting to no more than 5 per cent of the total population. Against this background of native population explosion Hong Kong also began to modernise and develop industrially. Traders such as Jardine Matheson eventually gave up the controversial opium trade (though it was not formally abolished until 1911) and invested in a variety of less injurious industries and services. The port of Hong Kong expanded, and important new capital industries such as shipbuilding and electricity generation grew rapidly.[18] The newly expanded Chinese population also worked in these industries, developing technical, engineering and other modern skills in the process. In addition, many new, small-scale production units and factories sprang up which were owned and staffed by this local population. As this occurred, this previously rural immigrant population became increasingly integrated into a modern, knowledge and skills-based western way of life.[19] However, despite this process of grass-roots economic augmentation and incorporation, the major companies in Hong Kong remained firmly under colonial control, and this was also especially true of the big trading companies, given that, although industrial production had expanded significantly by 1939, trade, and particularly trade with China, remained the most important sector of the Hong Kong economy.

Such control also stemmed from the persistence of what has been described as a 'colonial' culture in Hong Kong, within which a significant separation existed between a dominant expatriate minority and a subordinate Chinese majority.[20] The expatriate class in Hong Kong was not required to, and did not want to mix with the Chinese population. Most of the members of that class came from the middle class or lower middle class, rather than upper-class, well educated or aristocratic backgrounds. However, their privileged racial position within the colony bred arrogance and worse, leading them to behave as though they were the 'merchant princes' and 'senior mandarins' that they were most definitely not.[21] Such conduct on the part of the expatriates may have played a role in causing the Chinese community similarly to want to stay at arm's length from these status-conscious elitists, but, in truth, that community generally shared a similarly racial-segregationist predilection anyway. Up to the 1880s, and beyond, a more or less completely parallel society existed in Hong Kong, as racial exclusion became accepted as the preferred resolution by both communities.[22] It would have been near impossible for liberal-minded expatriates to traverse this divide as such an act would bring attendant upon it significant loss of status and social position. However, some Chinese could, and did, aspire to do so, as when some amassed sufficient wealth to build or buy houses in expatriate areas. Up to that point segregation had not required legislation, but that was now introduced in 1888, 1904 and 1919, in order to create exclusive 'European districts' from which the Chinese were excluded. This legal basis for racial discrimination was not annulled until as late as 1946.[23]

Nevertheless, this cultural and racial divide was not absolute. Hong Kong may have been founded as a 'colony of rule', in which expatriate settlement was not even particularly encouraged at the beginning, and in which a tiny minority of colonial officials, and other expatriates, held sway over a substantial population of locals;[24] but, in practice, it was impossible for the colonial minority to control such a colony alone, and, therefore, the emergence of a – compliant – local elite was encouraged almost from the founding years of the colony.[25] Although this elite group did not have a place within the system of government, its members were consulted by high officials, and played a role in helping to manage the fast-growing local population. From the earliest days, individual members of these elites also distinguished themselves from their counterparts in mainland China, and contrasted the administration of nearby 'chaotic Canton' with the stability brought to Hong Kong by the British.[26] This cut both ways, though, as mainland elites, in turn, regarded Chinese in Hong Kong as less than fully Chinese because they lived within a compromised colonised jurisdiction.[27] These contrasting affiliations and differences marked the source, rise and internal paradoxes inherent to the development of an initial sense of 'Hong Kong Chinese' identity within the colony of Hong Kong, though that sense remained the preserve of select Chinese groups, and was not shared by the general Chinese population, who remained psychologically and emotionally affiliated to the mainland.

From the late nineteenth century onwards the racial gulf between the expatriate and overall Chinese community in Hong Kong also took on a more pronounced political dimension as anti-imperialist, anti-foreigner Chinese nationalism began to flourish in China. The situation then deteriorated further following the overthrow of the Chinese Imperial Government in 1911 by the nationalist and republican Kuomintang (KMT). British officials in Hong Kong had earlier reached a disdainful accommodation with the declining and dissolute Qing dynasty, which had more pressing problems to deal with than the question of Hong Kong's retrocession. However, the KMT had always been stridently critical of British imperialism and the annexation of Hong Kong, and, after the events of 1911, helped provoke an upsurge of nationalist sentiment and activity within the colony, leading the British to believe that they had more to fear from the new government than its predecessor.[28] However, the British position over the KMT was to change during the late 1920s as the KMT Chinese Nationalist Government took up arms against Chinese communist authorities, who were by then more actively trying to destabilise Hong Kong than were the KMT; and who were also abhorred more by the British precisely because they were communist. During the 1930s, and particularly after the Japanese invasion of China in 1937, the Nationalist Government also became a political and military ally of Britain in the build-up to the Second World War; whilst, during the war, the KMT commander, Chiang Kai-shek, was granted overall military command of China-theatre operations, including those affecting Hong Kong. Even so, and despite such co-operation, as Chinese nationalists, the KMT retained an unyielding conviction that Hong Kong must be returned to China as soon as was practicable.

By 1930 Hong Kong remained the same culturally 'colonial' society that it had been in the 1840s and a substantial division still persisted between the bulk of the population and the small dominant expatriate class. That division had, to a large extent, also been both sustained and augmented by a policy of minimum government intervention in the affairs of the Chinese community. The British preference was to allow informal native committees led by members of the local elite to run most Chinese affairs, whilst the colonial administration retained a firm, arm's-length hand and watch over proceedings.[29] This policy of limited intervention also, of course, stretched to limited fiscal intervention, and, under direction from both the British Treasury and its own intrinsic predilections, the colonial administration tried to spend as little money as possible on the Chinese community.[30] During the 1930s gradual but persistent social and economic enlargement and concomitant problems did, however, force a reluctant administration to become more involved in Chinese civil society, and, amongst other matters, this eventually led to the enactment of legislation concerning areas such as child labour, employment rights and the protection of domestic helpers. Educational provision for the local population was also improved (though compulsory primary education was not introduced until the 1960s). However, in virtually all these, albeit still limited, reforms, the pressure to force through change came mainly from concerned groups in London, rather than from colonial philanthropists in Hong Kong. The Hong Kong Government did not yet particularly see that it had a responsibility to aid the Chinese population overmuch, whilst pressure for reform was resisted by the highly conservative expatriate (and Chinese) elites within the colony.[31]

In this sense, the model of the Crown Colony actually worked relatively benevolently. The model was premised on the idea that colonial officials and governments would ultimately be subject to the British Parliament, and what happened in the 1930s was that a democratically elected House of Commons forced through social-welfare legislation in Hong Kong against the wishes of much of the city's official, Chinese and expatriate elites. However, this also meant that these elites had no real power and authority within the colony other than that granted to them by London, and, whilst London-empowered high officials might have few problems with this, given that they remained in control of local power structures, it was a different matter for the disenfranchised expatriate community and Chinese elite. From the 1860s onwards expatriate and Chinese groups in Hong Kong had – mainly separately, it has to be said – called for additional democracy to be introduced, as was occurring elsewhere in the British Empire. However, the Colonial Office in London continued to believe that such democratisation would have been impossible in Hong Kong, and for three principal reasons related to the three main parties involved. First, the Colonial Office recognised that any attempt to create a franchise for a whites-only electorate would have been rejected by Parliament. Second, it was believed that extending any franchise to a privileged sector of the Chinese community would have led to civil resentment and unrest within the Chinese population overall. Finally, it was believed that extending the franchise to a substantial sector of the largely antagonistic Chinese population might hasten the return of the territory to China.[32] This is why, by 1939, no elective, representational reform had taken place in Hong Kong.[33] However, this is also partly why, by the time war broke out, the vast majority of the Chinese population there had developed little or no allegiance to the British Empire or colonial Hong Kong.[34]

DOCUMENTARY FILM IN HONG KONG, 1898–1941

The first films shot in Hong Kong portrayed the colony from a western perspective and for western spectators. This was inevitable given that film was a western invention, and it was not until the early 1920s that the first locally made documentary films, directed at local audiences, began to appear. Film first reached China in 1896. That year an unidentified operative screened films as part of a vaudeville programme in Shanghai, though it is not known if he also shot films there. It is also not known for certain who this person was, though it appears that he was not associated with the French Lumière brothers, whose *cinématographe* camera-projector appeared in 1895, as it has been claimed that Lumière operatives did not go to China that year, but only to 'Indochina and Cambodia'.[35] In July 1897 the American Edison Company sent its showman and photographer James Ricalton to China, where he shot and screened films in Shanghai and several other large cities (though it is not known which). Edison was quickly off the mark here, as the first screenings using the company's Vitascope machine only took place in April 1896.[36] These relatively few film-based activities in China do also have to be put in perspective, because, by 1897, hundreds of projectors were then in use in America, screening films regularly in a wide variety of exhibition venues to an extensive audience. By 1897 China remained an insular and inward-looking imperial dynasty which habitually tried to limit foreign intrusion, and this made it difficult for western films to enter.

The years 1895–7 were those in which the main attraction of film lay in its ability to reproduce temporal perceptual reality and show foreign or unusual sights, or celebrities. During this period, and for some years to come, the camera was static, and films consisted of only a single shot. Usually, an event was filmed from beginning to end or as that event passed off in front of the camera. Sometimes referred to as the 'animated photograph' at the time, this was the first format of the film.[37] Although it remains unclear what films were actually shown in China in 1896–7, they would necessarily have been of this type, and, in 1897, would have been part of an Edison travelling stock of films, supplemented by films shot on the road. This also means, of course, that many of these films were shot in America, not China, and that the Chinese audiences who saw them would, therefore, have been treated to a glimpse of the 'exotic' occident.

In 1898 the Edison Company sent another studio photographer, James H. White, to China. White filmed, and possibly also projected, in Shanghai, before travelling on to Japan, where he shot footage, and may also have projected films, in Osaka. He then embarked for Hong Kong by ship from Yokohama, near Tokyo, in February 1898, and, in Hong Kong, shot what may well have been the first Hong Kong films (White also shot film in Canton, though it is not known whether this occurred on a trip from Hong Kong, or before he went to Shanghai). There is no evidence to suggest that White screened any Edison films in Hong Kong. Nor, in addition, is there any evidence to suggest that the footage he shot in Hong Kong was screened there; and it seems that it may have been sent back to America, where the exotic orientalism and colonial imagery it had captured was displayed before American audiences. Fourteen of White's Edison films can be found in the Hong Kong Film Archive, and, of these, six were shot in Hong Kong. They are: *The Sikh Artillery, Hong Kong*; *Street Scene in Hong Kong; Hong Kong Wharf Scene; Hong Kong Regiment No. 1*; *Hong Kong Regiment No. 2*; and *Government House at Hong Kong*. All are 50 feet (one reel) in length.

What is foregrounded in these films, perhaps unsurprisingly, is both the 'orientalism' (or 'Chinese-ness') of Hong Kong, and the British colonial presence. For example, *The Sikh Artillery, Hong Kong* shows members of the Sikh force practising in their battery. The Indian community in Hong Kong was originally derived from soldiers and policemen brought in by the colonial authorities from the 1860s onwards.[38] They were a relatively isolated, lower-class community in Hong Kong around the turn of the century, and this simple film appears to bring out such seclusion to some extent by showing the soldiers as an autonomous, sequestered group. Perhaps White thought American audiences might find it of interest to see turbaned Indian soldiers in a colonised Chinese place: an aggregation which throws up paradoxes related to differentiated racial hierarchy, and colonial power and subjection. *Street Scene in Hong Kong*, on the other hand, accentuates the oriental/Chinese setting. Like all these films, this one consists of a single fixed shot, this time of a traditional Chinese local street, probably in the China Town of Sheung Wan, adjacent to the colonial city of Victoria. The film shows rickshaws, single-wheel and double-wheel vehicles, and Chinese people bustling along the road against a background of traditional two-storey Chinese residences. *Hong Kong Wharf Scene* occupies a thematic and pictorial point between these two films. Shot on the harbour side of the port area, this film shows a variety of police-men, coolies and rickshaw passengers walking along the wharf, thus mingling the colonial and Chinese elements together. *Hong Kong Regiment* returns to the colonial theme fully, and is divided into two parts. The first reel is a static shot of the regiment marching in full colonial uniform past the camera, the second a long-shot of a section of infantry equipped with rifles and bayonets, and engaged in drill practice. What is also of note here is that the 'regiment' seems to consist entirely of turbanned Sikhs, without any white soldiers or officers being evident. The final film, *Government House at Hong Kong* shows the Governor's residence with hawkers seen in the foreground. What is chiefly of interest about this film, though, is that the shooting angle employed hardly shows Government House at all. Only a small section of the doorway of the official residence is shown, and nothing is seen which indicates that this is an important or imposing colonial headquarters. There is no attempt to portray colonial grandeur here, and, instead, the emphasis is on the everyday business and imagery of people walking past the camera.

Despite their limited capacity, these simple short films provide an important record of mores, places, dress codes and behaviour. What they also demonstrate, through their imagery, is the deep divide which existed between the colonial and Chinese communities at the time, and, also, the overriding position of the colonists. The colonists and Chinese are shown mingling together in these films because the chief intent is to show a visual panoply of people in movement against an oriental-colonial background. However, the two groups appear as very different from each other in terms of appearance, status, wealth and race. The fact that these films do not, in addition, overly emphasise or celebrate colonial stateliness may also be due to the American background of White and the Edison Company, and also to their understanding of the ultimate audience for these films: a largely lower-class American audience unlikely to be overly impressed by scenes of British colonial stateliness. These films also display the prevailing western conception at the time of Hong Kong as a far-flung colonial outpost, peopled locally by an obviously underprivileged native population (some of the Chinese coolies shown appear decidedly undernourished). Nevertheless the films do not intentionally show poverty, squalor or hardship, and neither do the very poor living conditions endured by the vast majority of Hong Kong Chinese at the time enter their sphere of representation. These films are essentially *scenic*, in the sense of providing and relating to views of things, and they are mainly concerned to display an ordinary, everyday context of lived experience.

In 1899 the first known screening of films is believed to have taken place in Hong Kong, organised by an American named 'Binton', whose affiliation still remains unknown. He first screened his films in an exterior location in an empty plot of land on the colony's harbour front, and then in a restaurant somewhere. All the details about this remain vague and open to conjecture, including even the designation 'Binton'. Other sources, for example, name him as 'MacDunn'.[39] The films consisted of a number of reels on different subjects, shot in different countries, and it is unlikely, though not impossible, that some were also shot in Hong Kong (unfortunately these films have been lost, and so the latter cannot be verified). Again these films were single-reel, or 50 feet, in length. What these particular screenings also indicate is that, by 1899, there was still no dedicated place to screen films in Hong Kong, and, from 1899 until around 1914, the most common venues for such screenings were buildings or lots used for the performance of Cantonese opera. After the opera had ceased, films would be shown.[40] There is some debate as to when the first dedicated cinema appeared in Hong Kong, with sources dating this variously as 1907,[41] and as late as 1910 (the latter date is, of course, long after numerous small cinemas had appeared in most of the major North American and European cities).[42]

In addition to the Edison films already referred to, it appears that approximately fourteen other films were shot in Hong Kong up to 1910 by British French and American companies. The companies involved here were the American Mutoscope and Biograph Company, Lubin (USA), Urban-Eclipse (France), Warwick Trading Company (UK), Hepworth (UK), Harrison (UK) and the Charles Urban Trading Company (UK). The predominance of the British companies here presumably reflects the overall British governance of the colony. As in the other Crown Colonies, whilst the rhetoric of free trade might be bandied about, British trade interests were often privileged, and these early British film may have benefitted from this. Whether that was so or not, it remains the case that all four films shot and produced in 1900 were made by British companies, with Warwick Trading Company predominating. From the beginning, in 1900, these films also often went beyond a single reel in length. For example, *Review of the Fourth Gurkhas at Hong Kong* (Joseph Rosenthal, Warwick Trading Company, 1900) is 125 feet in length, whilst *Circular Panorama Hong Kong* (Rosenthal, Warwick Trading Company, 1900) is 100 feet in length. Later, length increased significantly, as, for example, in *Through Hong Kong* (Urban-Eclipse, 627 feet, 1907), *Hong Kong From Peak To Shwsika* (Charles Urban Trading Company, 575 feet, 1907), and *Up The Mountain From Hong Kong* (Urban-Eclipse, 287 feet, 1909). Again, it is unlikely, though not impossible, that these films were shown in Hong Kong, and they were probably shipped back to Britain, the USA or France, instead.

The titles of these films also reveal that their main concern was to show the scenic – and usually urban – landscape of Hong Kong, as in *Panorama of Hong Kong* (Hepworth, 1904), *Chinatown Bazaar* (Warwick, 1900), *Chinese Junks in Hong Kong Harbour* (Warwick, 1900), *Queens Road Hong Kong* (Warwick, 1901), and *In Old Hong Kong* (American Mutoscope and Biograph Company, 1901). Interestingly, the colonial context does not feature strongly in these films in a direct sense, as it did to a greater extent in the earlier Edison films; and a film such as *Review of Fourth Gurkhas* (Warwick, 1900) is, in this respect, an exception. Whilst the Edison films did not exactly celebrate colonialism, they did *show* it. However, in these later films there is more of a shift away from this to the presentation of daily life, and none of the British companies involved appears to be particularly interested in the British colonial context. Because of their scenic orientation, these films are rich in detail, and full of objects, places, people and events. Compositionally, the content of the films is fairly disorganised, as the intent is to fit in as much as possible for the visual enjoyment of the spectator. The films also mainly retain the standard convention of the time of showing movement occurring across a fixed camera point

Over the period between 1910 and 1939 only a further ten of these films can be identified through the available record, a considerable decline if the record is correct, though one corroborated by the fact that most of the pioneering American, British and French companies just referred to disappeared from the scene over the same period. In fact, most of these small companies failed to survive the First World War. The Charles Urban Trading Company, Warwick Trading Company and Urban-Eclipse all ceased production during the First World War, whilst Hepworth went over to making entertainment films. The American Mutoscope and Biograph Company actually moved away from documentary film-making from as early as 1903, as the early fascination with the tableaux-style 'animated photographs' gave way to a preference for narrative-based fiction-film entertainment. One new, late arrival on the scene, however, in terms of Hong Kong scenic film-making, was Pathé Frères, who made *La Chine moderne* in 1914. At the time, French film companies were shooting films in the nearby French colonies of Indochine (Laos, Cambodia and Vietnam), and this may have led to the additional filming of footage for *La Chine moderne* in Hong Kong. Whether that was the case or not is unclear, but what is clear is that, as with the British companies, this type of French colonial scenic film-making tailed off during the First World War, and sadly, like so many other early scenic-documentary films, *La Chine moderne* has also disappeared.

These films shot in Hong Kong were destined for the international market, rather than Hong Kong. However, the companies which shot them also made films in and for their own home markets which were distributed to and screened in Hong Kong from as early as 1900. Between 1900 and 1914 screenings of such western films took place frequently. For example, a screening of 'Exotic Western Pictures' was held in the Chung King Theatre, Hong Kong Island, in February 1900;[43] whilst, in 1902, the Kok Sun Garden Theatre in Kowloon staged a programme which included recordings of Chinese and western music and song, and a screening of the British film *The Coronation of King Edward VII* (1902).[44] By the time that the first film actually made in Hong Kong appeared, in 1909, the city already had a 'bustling' film market consisting of the distribution and exhibition of western films, and, up to the rise of the fictional silent feature film, around 1915, western documentary films dominated the film industry in Hong Kong.[45] After the First World War, as the early pioneering documentary film-making companies disappeared, the flow of western actuality films into Hong Kong largely dried up, and, in place of such films, western – mainly American – feature films then continued to dominate the local cinema up to and long after the Second World War. The divided society created by both the colonial British establishment and the local Chinese population was, therefore, at least to some extent, recoupled through the experience of watching film; and, through this meeting of east and west, a nascent and tentatively composite Chinese-Hong Kong culture began to crystallise; or, at the least, the local population in Hong Kong became more familiar with the west not only as colonial autocracy in Hong Kong but also as more extensive place of interest, entertainment and, possibly, identification.

From 1918 to 1945 documentary film-making activity in Hong Kong developed in a number of new and different ways, one of which was through the establishment of local production companies. For example, Guangya Film Company made five films between 1925 and 1928, one of which was the documentary film *The Hong Kong Grand Hotel Fire* (1925). Another company to emerge in the 1920s, China Sun, was of particular importance and will be discussed in more depth shortly. In the 1930s another major company to emerge was Grandview Film Company Ltd, which produced, amongst other films, *The King's Coronation Parade* (1937), *Commander in-Chief Yu Han-Mou Reviews the Troops on His Hong Kong Visit* (1937), and *Provincial Government Chairman Wu Tiecheng on Transit via Hong Kong* (1937). As their titles indicate, the latter two of these films were also made against a backdrop of the run-up to the Sino-Japanese war. As with China Sun, Grandview is important, and so will also be discussed in more depth later. Yet another direction which documentary film-making took in relation to Hong Kong during this period related to the expansion of the Hollywood film industry into South-East Asia. During the 1920s, as the Hollywood studio system consolidated and expanded, capital was channelled into the production of bigger-budget feature films, and, against this context, the early 'scenic' documentaries ceased to be made, and American companies also ceased to come to shoot film in Hong Kong. However, this was to change in the late 1930s, albeit on a small scale, when films such as *Hong Kong: The Hub of the Orient* (Metro Goldwyn Mayer, 1937) and *From Singapore to Hong Kong* (Columbia Pictures Corporation, 1940) were produced. These films were, of course, sound documentaries, as were the Grandview films just referred to. They were made by the American documentary film-maker James Fitzpatrick. Fitzpatrick made feel-good, undemanding, scenic travel documentaries. For example, in 1937 he made both *China: Land of Charm* and *Floral Japan*. 1937 is, of course, the year that Japan invaded China, though that seems to have passed this particular film-maker by. Fitzpatrick continued to make such films, which only showed affirmative aspects of the places he filmed, up until the mid-1950s. Like the early western films of 1898–1914, these films were also destined for an international audience, but unlike those early films, the Fitzpatrick films were also shown in Hong Kong.

LAI MAN-WAI

The first locally produced documentary film to be made in Hong Kong was *Chinese Competitors at the Sixth Far East Sports Games in Japan* (1923). As the title indicates, this film was not shot in Hong Kong. However, it was produced by the Hong Kong China Sun Film Company, which opened in 1923, and was shot by the owner of the company, photographer and director Lai Man-wai. Lai, who would go on to become one of the most influential figures in the early Hong Kong and Chinese film industries, initially came from a theatrical background, and also had a strong interest in photography, and both of these factors may have helped direct him towards the cinema. In 1913 Lai met the American financier and businessman Benjamin Brodsky, who had earlier produced the first commercial film in Hong Kong, a melodrama entitled *Stealing a Roast Duck* (1909). In 1913 Brodsky also established the first film studio in Hong Kong, Chinese American Film. However, the studio made only one film: *Zhuangzi Tests His Wife* (1913), scripted and acted by Lai, and adapted from Cantonese opera, before closing the same year that it was founded. *Zhuangzi Tests His Wife* was never shown in Hong Kong, as Brodsky took the only print back to the United States with him when Chinese American Film closed. It then became the earliest Hong Kong-produced fiction film to be screened in the United States.[46] One year after Lai made *Zhuangzi* came the outbreak of the First World War, and the film industry in Hong Kong came to a complete standstill, as not only were the rare metals used to produce nitrate film stock in short supply, but the enemy power, Germany, was then also the main provider of such stock to Hong Kong.[47]

After forming China Sun in 1923, and making *Chinese Competitors at the Sixth Far East Sports Games in Japan*, Lai went on to shoot a number of short films of local scenes and cultural events, somewhat on the model of the pre-First World War western films. In 1923 these included *Hong Kong Scenery*, *Hong Kong Soccer Match*, *Hong Kong Dragon Boat Race*, and *Hong Kong Police Force Parade*. In these films we see the same combination of colonial and local subject-matter as in the early scenic western films. However, the tone is rather different now, and the Chinese people who appear in the films are no longer either the impoverished pre-modern figures from the nineteenth-century films, or the indistinct ones from the early twentieth-century films. As in these earlier films, colonialism is displayed but not celebrated. After 1923, China Sun also became the most important newsreel producer in the crown colony, and, in most of these newsreels, Lai Man-wai, or his associate, Law Wing-cheung, was the cinematographer.

In addition to being a film-maker Lai was a committed political activist and revolutionary. In 1909, at the age of only sixteen, he joined the Hong Kong branch of the anti-feudal Revolutionary Alliance of Sun Yat-sen, and, after the founding of the KMT (the successor to the Revolutionary Alliance) in 1912, he engaged in pro-KMT activities up to and beyond the outbreak of the Second World War.[48] As a committed Chinese nationalist Lai believed, and openly advocated, that Hong Kong should be returned to China. However, as a consequence of such advocacy, when, in 1924, he asked the British colonial government for permission to build a permanent stage set for China Film, his request was refused. Lai then moved the company to Guangzhou, close by Hong Kong, where he made the melodrama *Rouge* (1924), often considered to be Hong Kong's first feature-length film (though it was not produced in Hong Kong).[49] Then, in 1925–6, labour unrest and an outbreak of Chinese nationalist sentiment led to the declaration of a general strike in both Guangzhou and Hong Kong. This, once more, effectively closed down the developing Hong Kong film industry, and led Lai and China Sun to relocate again, this time to Shanghai, then the centre of the Chinese film industry. Lai continued to make both feature films and documentaries in Shanghai. However, his documentaries now became more politically oriented, and centred on the KMT, and, later, Sino-Japanese War.[50] Thus, from making minor scenic documentaries such as *Hong Kong Scenery* in 1923, and against the background of the KMT attempt to establish a unified republican China, Lai moved on to the type of committed documentary film-making which found expression in his most imperative, though nevertheless flawed work, *A Page of History*. In order to make proper sense of *A Page of History*, though, it will first be necessary to outline the complex historical events and developments which the film attempted to depict.

A PAGE OF HISTORY (LAI MAN-WAI, 1921–8, 1941)

In 1911 the declining Qing dynasty in China was finally overthrown. Sun Yat-sen, leader of the republican Revolutionary Alliance which had helped to bring down the dynasty, was then proclaimed Provisional President of the new Republic of China on 1 January 1912. However, Sun quickly handed over the post of President to Yuan Shikai, the most powerful figure in the service of the previous regime, in order to strike a deal which would ensure the final abdication of the Emperor.[51] Later, though, Yuan attempted to overthrow the republic and restore the empire, with himself as emperor. In 1916 the Yuan regime collapsed and China fragmented into a number of dictatorships ruled by regional warlords, who also dominated what was left of the Peking administration. In response, in 1917 Sun moved the central base of the KMT to the relative safety of the southern city of Guangzhou. In 1919 Sun was forced out of Guangzhou by the then Governor of Guangdong Province. In 1920, though, he returned to re-establish his base in the city, and, in 1921, was elected 'Grand Marshall' of the KMT Military Government, which he founded that year. In 1923 Sun was forced to leave Guangzhou once more, but again returned, quickly, to take overall control of the city in 1924.

By as early as 1919–20 Sun had already come to the conclusion that the only way to reunify China was through building an army which would march northwards to engage and defeat the various cliques, and the clique-controlled Beijing government, which then ruled a divided China. To this end, in 1924, and with the help of the Soviet Union, he established the Whampoa Military Academy in order to train such an army for what would become known as the 'Northern Expedition'. At the same time, Chiang Kai-shek, whom Sun had known since 1918, was designated Commander-in-Chief-in-Waiting of the nascent army, which was in turn given the honorific of National Revolutionary Army (NRA). The NRA was then formally instated the following year, in 1925. Prior to that, in September 1924, Sun and various KMT dignitaries, including Chiang, had left Guangzhou to address a KMT rally in the city of Shaoguan, just north of Guangzhou. At that point in time the intention was to begin the Northern Expedition more or less immediately. However, before that could occur Sun received an invitation to come to Beijing in order to enter into discussions which might dispel the need for any military action. The context of this was the 'Beijing Coup' of October 1924, in which the existing government in Beijing was overthrown, and a new Provisional Government established which sought national unification through negotiation and reform. Believing that an important new development had occurred, Sun suspended the Northern Expedition, and travelled to Beijing by ship in November 1924. However, he died in Beijing in March 1925, and KMT negotiations with the Provisional Government were first deferred, and then annulled.

Following this, in July 1926, Chiang Kai-shek addressed a gathering of KMT troops in Guangdong which had met in order to begin the First Northern Expedition. Along with the KMT, the other major power group to have emerged from the 1911 revolution was the Chinese Communist Party (CCP). The two groups were politically apart: the KMT under Sun committed to western-style democracy, the CCP to Soviet-style communism. Both also had their own standing armies. Despite these differences, though, both KMT and CCP had a shared and vested interest in ending the political fragmentation widespread in China, and, in 1926, their combined forces marched north, under the overall leadership of Chiang. However, Chiang was a more politically conservative figure than Sun had been, and, as part of this, was also anti-communist in disposition. Consequently, and unlike Sun, Chiang chose to form an allegiance with anti-communist Nazi Germany, rather than the Soviet Union and Chinese communism. Chiang would come to rely on military and tactical support from Germany throughout the late 1920s, and into the 1930s. However, the first major manifestation of his new ideological alignment came in 1927, when he violently expelled communists from the Northern Expedition; a contentious move which also created serious divisions within the KMT. Despite these difficulties, though, the Northern Expedition continued onwards, gradually overpowering the forces arraigned against it, and finally achieving a victory which led to the eventual consolidation of large sections of the country under one regime, based in the new capital of Nanjing, south of Beijing. This, in brief, is the complicated story of Sun, Chiang and the Northern Expedition which Lai Man-wei attempted to tell in *A Page of History*.

Between 1921 and 1928 Lai Man-wai and his cinematographers travelled across China shooting footage of the surrounding scenery. However, Lai and his group also produced fifteen separate but loosely structured and unfinished 'films' on Sun, Chiang and the Northern Expedition which were then gradually edited together by Lai over the period between 1937 and 1941. The result was *A Page of History*.[52] *A Page of History* had – or was victim to – an extremely complex history itself, and, because of this, it will be necessary to reconstruct that history here before proceeding further. This will also have to be attempted in some detail, as much of what happened to *A Page of History* is difficult to grasp clearly. The final 34-minute master-negative of *A Page of History* was completed in October or November 1941. It appears that three prints were then made from this negative, and that these were released on 12 November 1941 by Lai's China Sun Motion Picture Company, and shown in cinemas in Hong Kong, and possibly also in the southern Guangdong area, during November–December 1941. However, the details of these screenings remain unclear.[53] During the Japanese attack on Hong Kong the China Sun film studio suffered bomb damage and most of the films made by Lai during the 1920s and 1930s were destroyed. Apparently, the only ones to survive were *A Page of History* and *The Battle of Shanghai*. Following this substantial loss the occupying Japanese authorities 'asked' Lai to oversee film production in Hong Kong. The patriotic Lai of course refused to comply, a response which then forced him to flee Hong Kong with his extensive family of nine.[54]

Whilst preparing to leave Hong Kong, Lai attempted to smuggle the master-negative of *A Page of History* out of the territory on board a ship bound for Zhanjiang, on the southern coast of China near Hainan Island. However, the ship was sunk by the Japanese and the master-negative lost. This meant that only the three prints of the film remained, all of which were, at that point, in Lai's possession. Before leaving Hong Kong, Lai decided to bury one of these in a sealed container in the garden of his house. After this the Lai family left Hong Kong for the city of Guilin, in Guangxi Province, to the west of Guangzhou, and then outside the Japanese area of occupation in southern China. From here Lai sent the second of the three prints of *A Page of History* to the Chinese Government in Chongqing to be used for propaganda purposes.

Utility for such purpose had, of course, been the reason that Lai had made the film in the first place. This print was then later taken to Taiwan in 1949 when the retreating KMT government was forced into exile there. However, in 1961 the print was destroyed by fire.[55] Upon returning to Hong Kong following the defeat of Japan in 1945 Lai dug up the buried print of *A Page of History* but ill-advisedly kept it in its container without seeking to preserve it further. At that point Lai, therefore, had two prints of *A Page of History* in his possession. Shortly before his death in 1953, and apparently virtually destitute, Lai requested that one of these prints (not the one in the container) be bequeathed to the 'authorities [in] . . . Beijing'.[56] Lai wished the film to be given to the nation as a mark of his legacy. The print was then taken to Beijing in 1954 by Lai's widow, along with a print of Lai's other major war-time documentary *The Battle of Shanghai* (1937), which will be discussed in further depth later in this chapter. By 1954, therefore, two prints of *A Page of History* remained: one in a box kept in unknown condition in the Hong Kong home of the Lai family, the other in the Central Film Bureau in Beijing.[57]

In the late 1970s and early 1980s the Lai family was visited by the film critic and historian Yu Mo-wan, and, during this period Yu persuaded the family to open the boxed print of *A Page of History*.[58] Yu discovered that the film had been badly damaged by humidity, and, with the Lai family's permission, he organised its restoration by a curator referred to as Luo Jinghao. However, in the process much of the print had to be disposed of, and the original 34-minute print was eventually reduced to a final copy of only 16 minutes duration. [59] Then, in 1985, Lai's wife and others went to Beijing in order to have a copy made of the print which Lai had bequeathed to the Central Government in 1954. They paid for the film to be copied themselves, and then brought the copied print back to Hong Kong. Unfortunately, they found the 34-minute film to be in poor condition, with many sections virtually unviewable. In contrast, the 16-minute version which had been restored in the early 1980s was in much better condition. In 1995 the Lai family then donated the 34-minute version of *A Page of History* to the Hong Kong Film Archive and followed this up by bequeathing the 16-minute version in 2002.[60] Finally, in 2003 curatorial staff at the Archive, assisted by Lai's son, Lai Shek, produced an edited amalgamation of the two prints in an attempt to create a definitive version. It is this copy which is currently available for viewing at the Hong Kong Film Archive. This 26-minute version covers a period from the appointment of Sun as Grand Marshall of the Military Government in 1921 to the final success of the Northern Expedition under Chiang in 1928. This, then, is the highly complicated and troubled history – one that covered a period of approximately eighty-two years – of one of the most important documentary films to be made in Hong Kong.

When the Sino-Japanese War broke out in 1937, Lai found himself in a position to film the Japanese attack on Shanghai. He then used this footage to make *The Battle of Shanghai*. It was also while carrying out the shooting and editing of this film that Lai decided to re-edit the extensive amount of material on the KMT he had shot during the 1920s. In particular, Lai believed that this was the ideal time to foreground Sun's nationalist idealism as a boost for the war effort against Japan. Consequently, when, after the fall of Shanghai, Lai returned to Hong Kong, he commenced work on what would eventually become *A Page of History*. This context of the events of the late 1930s shapes the overall point of reference of *A Page of History*, and, although the film's imagery portrays events which took place in the 1920s, the late-1930s commentary which accompanies this is mainly directed towards the struggle then taking place against Japan. So, for example, at the beginning of *A Page of History* we are informed that the film is 'a great revolutionary historical film' which shows the New Revolutionary Army under Chiang 'reuniting China'; whilst, near the end of the film, we are told that such reunification was not won without the 'sacrifices of soldiers', and that 'now we are facing new problems' which will entail further sacrifice. Here, the idealistic nationalist spirit of Sun and Chiang's attempt to overcome hostile forces and re-establish national sovereignty is appropriated in order to boost the morale of those engaged in the contemporary struggle against Japan. In this sense, therefore, it could be argued that the ideological project of *A Page of History* is presented in the form of a lesson based on prior, hard-won experience; and that what we see and hear in the film is meant to function both as exemplar and inspirational instructional treatise.

Japan also features elsewhere in *A Page of History* more directly. For example, as we see the expeditionary force moving northwards to engage warlords, we are told that 'Japanese forces are intervening' to help the warlords. This is a reference to Japanese troops stationed in Shandong province at that time, and allied to one of the northern warlords the KMT were marching against. More specifically, the reference is to the 'Jinan Incident' of 3 May 1928, and subsequent related events which eventually led to the Japanese execution of a senior KMT negotiator, and the defeat and expulsion of KMT forces from around the city of Jinan. However, although *A Page of History* refers to the execution of the KMT mediator, it makes no mention of the Chinese military defeat. Instead, and in contrast to such reference, towards the end of this section of the film we see KMT troops entering Jinan on horseback, apparently 'liberating' the city, and receiving the enthusiastic welcome of its residents.

The portrayal of the Jinan Incident in *A Page of History* is indicative of both the propagandist imperatives of Lai's film and how those imperatives also created limitations for and within the film. As mentioned, the fact of the defeat by the Japanese is not referred to, and neither is the role played by KMT troops in bringing about the Incident in the first place. Japanese soldiers had been placed in Jinan for some time with the collusion of local warlords. However, in 1927 their numbers were increased incrementally, an act which KMT and Beijing government commanders deemed to be intentional provocation. Nonetheless, when this supplementation took place, a Beijing government army which was also based in the city withdrew in order to avoid possible confrontation. However, and against Chiang's explicit orders to the contrary, KMT militias then moved into the city. The inevitable conflict – the 'Jinan Incident' – erupted on 3 May when a confrontation between KMT and Japanese troops left twelve Japanese soldiers dead (and castrated). An uneasy truce was then declared, and both KMT and Japanese forces regrouped outside the perimeter of the city. The truce ended when the Japanese general in command, also disobeying orders, engaged and defeated the KMT forces (this is the battle which *A Page of History* fails to make reference to). Whilst *A Page of History* gives the impression that the KMT somehow liberated Jinan from the Japanese, the record shows that the Japanese simply left the city of their own volition some ten months later, in 1929. Moreover, given that no footage from *A Page of History* dates from as late as 1929, the sequences in the film showing KMT troops entering Jinan, if at all authentic, must have been of the detachment which entered the city against Chiang's orders prior to the 3 May Incident. If this is the case, then Lai, or one of his cameramen, must also have been with that detachment. As far as the Jinan Incident itself is concerned, what we have, in reality, is a shambolic situation in which KMT troops disobey their commander, Japanese troops disobey theirs, KMT and Japanese leaderships try but fail to avoid an escalation of conflict, a city which was not, and could not have been, 'liberated' by the KMT, and a significant KMT defeat. However, this confused and muddled scenario could not be accommodated within the partisan and schematic ideological trajectory propounded by *A Page of History*.

A Page of History is structured as a straightforward narrative which covers the outset, progress and conclusion of the Northern Expedition. However, in addition to this linear, chronological structure, the film also contains a series of tableaux in which the narrative largely stops, and in which people and events are displayed in a more exhaustive manner. This is also particularly the case with the opening sequences of the film, which are made up of footage shot during the 1921-6 period, and before the march of the Northern Expedition. And the film actually begins with one of these sequences, in which the leadership of the KMT is portrayed. The backdrop for these shots is a number of imposing buildings, and it is reasonable to conclude that the shots were taken in the city of Guangzhou. Unsurprisingly, the first person we see is Sun. After that, we are shown the various other KMT leaders, including Chiang. The photography here is classical, and, in its way, impressive, possibly revealing Lai's talents and previous training as a photographer, although, as will be argued shortly, there is considerable doubt as to whether Lai actually shot this footage. However, whoever did shoot these sequences knew how to construct the background and prepare the sitter. One by one the KMT leadership faces the camera formally and directly, looking as though carved out of stone, as the film seeks to emphasise the gravity and earnestness of their commitment. After these opening sequences introducing the leadership we see Sun, Chiang and the others board a train headed for a KMT rally. In one significant shot we see Sun and Chiang sitting opposite each other in one of the compartments of the train as the commentary informs us that we are witnessing the auspicious propinquity of the 'President' and 'new commander'. Sun and Chiang are very clearly singled out from the rest of the KMT leadership here, and joined emblematically as one. Following this we arrive at the rally. At this point the 1930s commentary gives us some of the background to the need for the KMT to expand its influence and initiate the Northern Expedition. We are told that the northern warlord-controlled government in Peking is 'corrupt', that the warlords are 'evil', and that it is the duty of the KMT New Revolutionary Army to 'unite the four-hundred million' Chinese. Throughout these sequences we also cut frequently to images of the KMT flag. It appears that the rally shown at this point in *A Page of History* was the 1921 inauguration of Sun as 'Grand Marshall' of the KMT and Military Government, and that the train journey we see was the relatively short journey from Guangzhou to Shaoguan, where the inauguration ceremony was held. The key part of this section of the film is also one in which Sun takes his oath as Grand Marshall and delivers a long speech outlining the aims of the KMT, and future Northern Expedition.

As previously mentioned, this first section of *A Page of History*, covering events in Guangzhou and Shaoguan, was shot in 1921. However, there are doubts as to whether or not Lai and his team actually shot them, and it has been suggested that the footage was actually shot by a visiting French team.[61] This suggestion is also backed up by a number of factors. First, the photography in this section of the film differs from that found in later sections in the sense that, and as stated earlier, this prefatory photography is quite formally set and framed. Later photography in *A Page of History* is less arranged and relatively more disordered, and the same is also the case with Lai's other major film, *The Battle of Shanghai*. Second, in his diary, Lai himself mentions that the first time he filmed Sun was in February 1923, when Sun visited Hong Kong.[62] The picture here in terms of authorship remains unclear. However, the weight of evidence seems to suggest that this section of *A Page of History* may not have been shot by Lai and his team. But whether Lai shot these sequences, he certainly edited them into *A Page of History*.

After this *A Page of History* moves on unexpectedly to 1924 as we see Sun journeying by ship to Beijing, an event which occurred in November 1924. It seems, therefore, that there is no footage in the film from 1922 or 1923. We then see Sun in Beijing, and see some of the landmarks of Beijing. Then *A Page of History* takes a curious historical lacuna. The next sequences we see consist of shots showing NRA troops marching north, out of Guangzhou (or Shaoguan, it is unclear which); and the commentary informs us that they are already in Jiangxi Province, the adjacent province to the north and east of Guangdong. This means that these sequences must be of the Northern Expedition, and that they must date from July 1926. However, after this, the sequences which follow first show Sun in Beijing, still very much alive, and then his coffin, lying in state – Sun died of cancer of the liver in March 1925. We therefore appear to have journeyed from November 1924 to July 1926, then back to March 1925. How can the insertion of sequences showing NRA troops moving into Jiangxi Province at this point in the film be explained? How can 1926 occur before 1925? If this is supposed to be a subjective sequence – a vision of the future *imagining* the progress of a future Northern Expedition – it has to be said that there are no other sequences of such a kind in *A Page of History*, and the more likely explanation is that this is an error of editing, caused by the various vicissitudes that *A Page of History* underwent during its difficult production and post-production history. In particular, this apparent error in the editing may have occurred either during the Beijing restoration of the film in 1978, or the Hong Kong restoration of 2003.

After this, *A Page of History* does take us to 1926: to be precise, July 1926, when Chiang gave a key address to 100,000 NRA troops who had assembled for the ceremony that was to launch the Northern Expedition, which began later that month. As Chiang gives his address, the commentary informs us that he is cautioning his troops to keep their morale firm, despite the fact that the Grand Marshall, Sun, had passed away. Like the speech given by Sun in 1921, this is also a long one, and the camera focuses insistently on the uniformed Chiang, who is on horseback, whilst the commentary paraphrases his speech, and also stresses the nationalist-idealist sentiment of the address. After this we see more shots of troops marching on parade in front of a raised platform on which Chiang, other KMT leaders and some foreign dignitaries sit. Particular attention is given to the American representative here (which may reflect the Chinese Government's attempt to attract US aid and assistance during the Sino-Japanese War). This section of *A Page of History* then ends with a full-screen copy of the written version of the oath taken by Chiang and the troops of the NRA.

A Page of History then proceeds to follow the chronological narrative of the progress of the Northern Expedition beginning with the first engagement at Wuhan, south-west of Shanghai. After this we see a succession of troop movements and what look like re-enactments of battle scenes. The composition of the shots is relatively unsystematic here, displaying a mass of soldiers scurrying across the countryside. We also see shots of enemy planes bombing the NRA troops, and then some obviously staged explosions. At one point there is also a sequence of photography taken from on board an aircraft, though it remains unclear who the cameraman was, or why there is only one sequence of such photography. The general purport of the narrative mission is very clearly stated by both the imagery and commentary here: continuous and unremitting NRA victory, without setback. Then we come to the previously mentioned sequences dealing with the Jinan Incident, and 'Japanese interference' with the onwards march of the Northern Expedition. Around this point we also have an extensive sequence in which the narrative of the Northern Expedition's progress is set aside. Suddenly, and confusingly, we see KMT ships and aircraft. There is no indication of where we are here, and, indeed, that does not particularly matter, because the purpose of this section of the film is not to advance the narrative or contribute to narrative coherence, but to display the substantial military might of the KMT and NRA. This is, in effect, an extensive tableau sequence within the film, similar in form to those sequences of the KMT leadership which open *A Page of History*, and is not linked to the film's otherwise persistent linear, chronological narrative. Finally, *A Page of History* comes to its finale in Beijing, as Chiang and the KMT celebrate the final success of the Northern Expedition. The KMT flag fills the screen as the commentary pleads that the spectator should 'remember the sacrifices of the soldiers'; and *A Page of History* finally concludes with a reference to the previously mentioned 'new problems' that China was facing in the late 1930s. The film then cuts out unexpectedly, without any concluding fade-out or closing citations, and it appears that the final sequences may be missing.

As a work of history, *A Page of History* must be found wanting. The narrative it presents of continuous military success leading to inevitable victory flies in the face of the historical reality. Many things are left out of *A Page of History*. To name but a few, the film does not mention events in the chaotic year of 1927, in which the KMT split following Chiang's decision to turn against the communists. The Shanghai Massacre of 12 April 1927 led to the execution of thousands of communists and their sympathisers, and Chiang was directly responsible for this. However, *A Page of History* could not accommodate such a diminishing reference within its unalloyed story of triumph and unity. Neither does the film mention the serious military defeats which occurred in 1927, or Chiang's resignation in August 1927 as a result of those defeats. Finally, *A Page of History* does not mention the fact that, following the end of the Northern Expedition, China was *not* fully united. The reality was that warlordism was not vanquished, but actually became stronger during the 1930s. In addition, by 1928, when Lai was still filming the sequences which he later inserted within *A Page of History*, virtually the entire north, west and centre of China remained outside KMT control. Even by as late as 1941, when Lai completed the final edit of *A Page of History*, large parts of the country were still under the control of warlords and other parties. However, *A Page of History* was never intended to be a critical study of its subject, but a highly partial valorisation of Sun, Chiang, the KMT and Chinese nationalism. Whilst the film's account of its subject provides us with images which are important, the lack of detail and balance evident here, when combined with the crowing, over-strident commentary, leads, in the end, to a film which holds intrinsic weakness. In particular, *A Page of History* is characterised by a substantial disparity between the essentially *descriptive* nature of its images from the 1920s, which *show* us things, and the fundamentally *propagandist* nature of its 1930s commentary, which *instructs* us on how to think. These content-related weaknesses, plus the various vicissitudes suffered by *A Page of History* during its tortuous pre- and post-production history, have resulted in a film which cannot be regarded as any kind of masterpiece. The discontinuities which marked the film's origins, despoilments and editorial development are clearly evident, to the detriment of narrative coherence, and the film as a whole. Essentially, it is a rather fragmented compilation film: a film, precisely, composed of *segments*, shot over a wide span of time, which do not, in the end, add up to an overall totality. In fact, without the commentary, the sense of a linear structure present in the film would be seriously weakened. However, the film remains important at the level of its documentary film footage of historical record, which contains sequences showing major historical figures and events.

DOCUMENTARY FILM AND THE SINO-JAPANESE WAR, 1937-41

In 1933 the first Cantonese-language sound film, *White Golden Dragon*, was made in Shanghai by the Tianyi Film Company, then one of the three major producers in the city.[63] Tianyi had frequently incurred the displeasure of KMT authorities in Nanking for not adhering closely enough to the government policy of making anti-feudal anti-imperialist films which embodied Chinese-nationalist rhetoric. In other words, Tianyi did not play the role expected of it in helping the KMT to develop an officially endorsed model of Chinese national cinema. Instead, the company made generic martial arts and horror films, and costumed melodramas set in the Imperial past which KMT associated critics and others condemned as 'feudalist'.[64] Tianyi incurred even more official wrath in 1934 when, following the success of *White Golden Dragon*, the company opened operations in Hong Kong through a company called Nanyang with the intention of specialising in the production of Cantonese sound films, thus directly contravening the official policy of establishing Mandarin as both the national language and basis of a new Chinese sound-cinema.[65] In 1934 'Tianyi-Nanyang' (as the company will be referred to here) also produced its first sound documentary in Hong Kong, entitled *The Soccer Clash between South China and the Infantry*. As the title suggests, the film records the highlights of a football match between the British army team and one of the best known teams in Hong Kong: 'South China'. Tianyi-Nanyang continued to make documentaries after 1934, though none was of any great merit or significance. That, however, was to change after 1937, when the company made more committed documentary films against the background of the Sino-Japanese War.

In addition to Tianyi-Nanyang, another important company to emerge in the 1930s was the Grandview Film Company, which was established in 1933. The two founders of the company, Joe Chiu Shu-sun and Moon Kwan Man-ching, had been educated in California, and, when they returned to Hong Kong, they attempted to set up Grandview along down-scaled Hollywood studio lines, raising technical standards of film-making in the process. Grandview eventually became a fairly large-scale enterprise, and, like Tianyi-Nanyang, largely concentrated on the production of martial arts films, horror films, melodramas and filmed versions of operas. However, Grandview also made documentaries, and, after the outbreak of the Sino-Japanese War, would go on to become the most important producer of documentary film in Hong Kong up to 1941, when the territory fell to the Japanese. From 1936 the company also produced the first magazine-type sound documentary film series to appear in Hong Kong entitled *The Grandview Review*. The Review covered a mixture of nationalist and colonial news. For example, the December 1936 edition contained items on 'The Funeral of Chairman Hu' (a KMT leader) and 'Appointments to the Hong Kong Government'. [66] In addition to the *Review*, between 1936 and 1937 Grandview also produced eleven or so individual documentary films on a variety of topics, including the local scenery, local and national festivals, the activities of celebrities, and the visits of important figures from the Chinese government. These latter films included the previously mentioned 1937 *Commander in-Chief Yu Han-Mou Reviews the Troops on His Hong Kong Visit*, and *Provincial Government Chairman Wu Tiecheng on Transit via Hong Kong*. Prior to 1936 neither Grandview nor Tianyi had produced overtly political films. However, from 1936 both companies began to produce feature films and documentaries which addressed the evolving political-military situation.

The population of Hong Kong almost doubled between 1937 and 1939 as mainland refugees flooded into the colony in order to escape the Sino-Japanese War. The huge influx involuntarily created an unregulated industrial and commercial boom, and, as part of that, also led to significant growth within the film industry, to the extent that, by 1939, up to forty film studios were in operation. A significant number of these were also Mandarin-language studios staffed by recently arrived incomers from Shanghai.[67] Many of these northern Mandarin-speaking film-makers were committed nationalists, keen to observe the KMT stratagem of creating a cinema based on nationalist, anti-feudal and anti-western lines. Others were communist sympathisers with a similarly strong, though communist-oriented, commitment to make films which would advance their cause. However, when they reached Hong Kong just prior to the outbreak of war these upright film-makers encountered a Cantonese genre cinema that appeared to uphold few of their ideals; a cinema characterised by the sort of horror, fantasy and 'feudal' films which Chiang Kai-shek had sought to have removed from mainland screens. Given the urgent context of a seemingly inevitable war with Japan, these film-makers then began to lobby for reform of what appeared to them to be a dissolute cinema, and for the production of more purposive films; and pressure was also applied to achieve these ends by KMT officials in both China and Hong Kong.[68] By late 1937, and shortly after the outbreak of war, the Chinese government had become so concerned about the situation within the Hong Kong film industry that it proposed a ban on the entry of Hong Kong-made Cantonese films into China. However, faced with opposition over this from the Hong Kong film industry, and sectors of the film industry in China which relied upon the importation of these films, the Nationalist government eventually decided to postpone any such action for a period of three years, after which the issue of 'whether the ideological content of Cantonese film was suitable to the Chinese nation' would be re-evaluated definitively.[69] Faced with the prospect of such a re-evaluation, and possible interdiction, and also given the fact that the China market was of fundamental importance for the film industry in Hong Kong, Cantonese film studios in the colony began to make a number of patriotic and anti-Japanese films. However, such production soon declined as it was not commercially successful.[70] This decline was, in addition, also hastened by the policy of neutrality which the British and Hong Kong governments adopted towards the Sino-Japanese War during the late 1930s; a policy which led the colonial Hong Kong Government to proscribe the more blatantly anti-Japanese films produced within the colony. This, in conjunction with a lack of box-office appeal, led to a reduction in 'patriotic' film-making in Hong Kong which only served to increase nationalist protestations further.

One consequence of these various pressures was that a considerable gulf opened up between the two main communities of film-makers in Hong Kong: the newly-arrived northern Mandarin-speakers and the longer-established Cantonese-speakers. That division was, though, also blurred and complicated by the fact that some of the recent incomers had previously made Cantonese films in Shanghai, and had come to Hong Kong in order to continue making them, and also escape the sort of 'ethical' KMT film policies now being advocated for Hong Kong by other Shanghai film-makers who had come into the colony. The film-making community within Hong Kong was, therefore, riven by factional disagreement. Under pressure, and as the Sino-Japanese War advanced, some uneasy and hesitant collaboration did eventually take place within the Mandarin and Cantonese groups over the production of the patriotic films referred to previously, films such as, for example, *Little Cantonese* (1940), directed by the mainland director Tan Xiaodan but made in the Cantonese language. However, *Little Cantonese* was also seen in some quarters as a somewhat conceited northern Chinese portrayal of Cantonese society, whilst the idea of the Cantonese being 'little' was also perceived to be a possibly condescending reference to their typically shorter stature.[71]

Setting such real or imagined condescension aside, the nationalist film-makers and their supporters also failed to appreciate something that the colonial Hong Kong government understood well. In a way, the development of a Cantonese sound cinema during the 1930s was in line with the Hong Kong government's preferred policy of establishing a local culture and society in Hong Kong which would be apart from but also framed by the colonial order of things. Essentially, and as argued previously, the colonial approach was to persuade local society that the government would provide a framework (of law, order, stability and other alleviating factors) which would enable a local culture and society to consolidate, prosper and develop its own means of intra-civic expression and communication. The development of the Cantonese sound film in the 1930s fell squarely in line with this strategy, as it enabled a local culture to express itself relatively unfettered through the familiar myths and stories of southern China. In encouraging – or even merely sanctioning – the use of the film to reinforce Cantonese culture within Hong Kong, the colonial authorities played a role in inculcating a sense of Hong Kong Chinese identity within the local population, because, precisely that identity, culture and cinema, was developing *within* the colonial context and environment of Hong Kong, a setting and milieu quite unlike that to be encountered in nearby southern China. To the chagrin of KMT adherents the rise of the Cantonese sound film augmented a developing sense of Chinese Hong Kong rather than (or as well as) mainland China identity within the local population, and, rather than attack the Cantonese cinema as they had, it might have been more productive for such adherents to attempt to accommodate that cinema within their own ideological project, as the colonial government had theirs. Here, northern haughtiness and refutation had not borne fruit, whilst it could be argued that the colonial stratagem had done so.

In July 1937 Japan launched full-scale war against China, eventually taking over most of northern and eastern China, and establishing a puppet government in the capital, Nanking, in December 1938. In addition to northern and eastern China, the Japanese also eventually took Canton and Hong Kong, the latter falling on 25 December 1941. However, Japan failed to complete the conquest of China. The Soviet Union halted Japanese expansion to the north in 1938 and 1939, and also supported the Chinese resistance, which was then head-quartered in the Nationalist Government's war-time capital of Chongqing, to the far south-west of Nanking. In the north and south of the country Chinese-communist forces – now working loosely with the KMT – also resisted the Japanese advance. As KMT and communist forces became better supported, organised and armed, a stalemate was reached which continued up until the surrender of Japan in 1945. It is also against this context of conflict and war that important documentary films were produced in Hong Kong, and shot by Hong Kong-based film-makers.

Over the period from the appearance of the first sound documentaries in 1933 to the Japanese invasion of 1941, documentary film-making in Hong Kong expanded exponentially, and also fell into a number of distinct genres. The largest of these, the 'political-military', will be dealt with here last, and in depth, as it was also the most important. In total, around nine distinct genres of production can be identified over this period. Of these, the 'colonial' film group was relatively small in number, accommodating only four (or so) films. They are: *Scenes of the King's Silver Jubilee Celebration in Hong Kong* (Tianyi, 1935); *Dragon Dance in the Government House* (Quanqiu, 1935); *Views of Hong Kong* (Hong Kong Tourist Association, 1936); and *The Hong Kong Parade/The King's Coronation Parade* (Grandview, 1937). It is also notable that when the Sino-Japanese war broke out, this particular genre of film-making virtually ceased, as though a victim of the rise of Chinese nationalist and anti-imperialist sentiment. In addition to these 'colonial' films, another minor genre evident over this period was the 'sport and leisure' genre. Films falling into this category include *The Athletic Meet: Day One to Day Seven* (1935); *Cooking Competition at the Meifang School* (Grandview, 1939); *Soccer Match Between Opera and Movie Stars* (Grandview, 1939); *The Grand Soccer Match* (Nanyue, 1939); and *The Opening Ceremony of the Fourth Chinese Goods Exhibition* (Hong Kong Newsreel Agency, 1941) (this latter film could also be classed as 'colonial', as it featured the then acting governor of Hong Kong).[72] Related to these genres were also two others: the 'celebrity-song' and 'scenic' genres. Both of these apparently consisted of only two films each during the period in question: *Cantonese Song Review* (1933) and *The Private Lives of Movie People* (Grandview, 1937) in the first genre; and *Scenery of the West Lake* (Grandview, 1937) and *Scenery of Suzhou* (Grandview, 1937) in the second. Apart from these genres, one film which can perhaps be classed as a 'scenic-disaster' film was *Calamity in Sichuan* (Nanyue, 1937). However, this film, on the effect of an earthquake on the landscape of Sichuan, appears to have been singular. Virtually all of these films were made in Cantonese rather than Mandarin, and, with the exception of the two 'scenic' films, their locale is Hong Kong, rather than China. It is also apparent that Grandview was involved in making the majority of them.

As mentioned, by far the most important genre of documentary film-making to appear in Hong Kong over the period from 1934 to 1941 was the 'political-military'. It seems that three of these films also predated the Sino-Japanese War by some distance. They are: *Eliminating the Communists at Qiong Cliff* (1933), which depicts military conflict between nationalists and communists; *Life in the Military Academy* (1935), which may have been set in the KMT Academy in Guangdong; and *The Death of Chairman Hu Hanmin* (1936). All of these films were in Cantonese. In addition to these earlier films a flurry of 'political-military' films also appeared in 1937, just prior to the outbreak of war. They are: *Commander in Chief Yu Hanmou Visits Hong Kong* (Grandview, 1937); *Provincial Government Chairman Wu Tiecheng on Transit via Hong Kong* (Grandview, 1937); *Tour of Nationalist Government Chairman Lin Sen to Guangdong and His Tribute to the Revolutionary Martyrs* (Grandview, 1937); *The Naming Ceremony of Military Aircraft in Guangdong* (Grandview, 1937); *The Southern Trip of Nationalist Government Chairman Lin Sen* (Nanyang, 1937); and *Convocation of the Guangzhou Government School* (Nanyang, 1937). All of these, with the exception of the latter two, are in Cantonese. As is evident, all of these films support the Chinese Nationalist Government cause in the coming struggle with Japan, and, once more, Grandview is the major production company involved. What is also evident is that the locale for these films has now switched from Hong Kong to China; a harbinger of things soon to come.

The year 1937 also saw the appearance of the earliest major war-time films. *The War Effort in Guangzhou* (Grandview, 1937) was a large-scale production directed by Lee Man-kwong and Tong Kim-ting. The film shows how:

> The people of Guangzhou are mobilized towards the war effort, including the organization of machine gun forces, the security force, the fire-fighting brigade, the ambulance brigade, and the general work force. The film also shows Guangzhou during a Japanese air attack. War hero Fang Zhenwu and flying ace Huang Guangqing also appear in the film.[73]

In addition to *The War Effort in Guangzhou* 1937 saw the appearance of at least two films shot during the Japanese assault on Shanghai in 1937: *Massacre in the Shanghai Region* (China War Front News Agency); and The *Battle of Shanghai* (Lai Man-wai, Minxin, 1937), which will be discussed in depth later in this chapter. The year 1938 marks a high point of Hong Kong documentary film production, and virtually all the films made that year were concerned with the Sino-Japanese War. That year, eight films appear on the record, though more may have been made. They are: *Protect Southern China and Guangdong: Special Edition* (Dazhonghua); *The War in Xiamen* (Jianhua); *The Anniversary in Memory of the 13 August Episode* (North China News Agency; *The Achievements of the Guangdong-Guangxi Troops* (Hualian Newsreel Company); *The Eighth Route Army Recovers Pingxing Pass* (International Photography Group); *The Bombing of Sanzoo Island* (unknown producer); *Xiamen on Alert* (unknown producer); and *Protect Guangdong* (Dapeng).

Over 1939–41, and as the Japanese advanced into the southern China region, the number of these political-military films declined sharply. In 1939 there are only *Flame of Southern China* (China Newsreel Agency) and *Battle at the West and the North Rivers* (Aiqun Photography Group). Nothing appears on the record for 1940, and, in the final year of Hong Kong documentary film production, 1941, there are only four films, one of which merits particular attention. In June 1938, with the support of the China War Time Film Research Association, Hong Kong director Lam Tsang went to Yan'an, in the north-west of China, and lived there for nine months shooting the documentary film *On the Northwest Frontline*. The film, which eventually appeared in 1941 as a silent film, is significant because it has a certain degree of communist focus, unlike virtually all the other films made over the 1937–41 period. The film shows various scenes of life in Yan'an, which was, as the title of the film suggests, on the frontline of the Japanese advance into China; and also a centre for communist forces under Mao Zedong. The film is divided into eight sections, entitled: (1) 'The activities of Mao Zedong, Lin Biao, and writer Ding Ling'; (2) 'The Anti-Japanese Military University'; (3) 'The Lu Xun Art Academy'; (4) 'The battle strategy of the Eighteenth Corps'; (5) 'The youth of Yan'an'; (6) 'Labour Day festive activities'; (7) 'The New Fourth Army'; and (8) 'The Life of people in the 'Red' Territories. As these titles suggest, the film was essentially a compilation effort rather than a fully structured film, and, like all the films referred to in these last few pages, was intended to drum up support for the anti-Japanese struggle. In addition to *On the Northwest Front Line*, the final films to appear are *The Guangdong Front* (China War-Time Film Research Association); Lai Man-wai's *A Page of History*; and *A Bowl of Rice Movement in America* (Grandview). The latter film shows Chinese-American support for the struggle in China. Originally organised by the American Bureau for Medical Aid to China, the Bowl of Rice Movement collected donations from Americans and Chinese-Americans in order to send medical and food supplies to China. The film records a series of charity events organised by the Chinese-American community in San Francisco, and also includes footage of anti-war demonstrations and the unveiling of a bronze statue of Sun Yat-sen.[74]

THE BATTLE OF SHANGHAI (1937)

Probably the most important film to emerge from the context of Hong Kong associated film-making during the Sino-Japanese War was Lai Man-wai's *The Battle of Shanghai* (1937). *The Battle of Shanghai* is a very different film to *A Page of History*. Whilst *A Page of History* consists of footage shot over an expansive period of time, *The Battle of Shanghai* was shot entirely during the Japanese assault on the city between August and November 1937. This gives *The Battle of Shanghai* a heightened focus which is further accentuated by the film's driven, instrumental objectives. *The Battle of Shanghai* is an activist film, shot for a purpose: that of gaining national and, above all, international support, for the China war effort. *The Battle of Shanghai* was also filmed amidst actual hostilities, a factor which further intensifies the trenchant quality of the film; and, in place of the re-enactments evident within *A Page of History*, we see tangible conflict here. In addition, despite the fact that the subject-matter of *A Page of History* is military engagement, we do not see a single body in that film, whilst, in *The Battle of Shanghai*, we see many bodies, and also many body parts. In one particularly poignant scene, for example, we see a father grieving over the prostrate bodies of his wife and children. These are *actual* corpses that we see here, and the film does not flinch from showing them. If *A Page of History* was meant to inculcate a refined sense of idealist nationalism, *The Battle of Shanghai* was designed to inculcate much stronger and darker emotional reactions, and to shock.

Because *The Battle of Shanghai* was to a large extent directed at winning international sympathy and support for the China war effort, it was made with some English titles, and this in itself makes the film unusual for its period. The film's internationalist strategic orientation also led it to address the issue of foreign connection almost from the outset. For example, although *The Battle of Shanghai* begins with the now more-or-less obligatory image of Chiang Kai-shek it quickly turns to the notion of a coming together between China and the west, and to a contention that foreign nationals were being directly and adversely affected by the events in Shanghai, as we are told that 'several hundred Chinese and Foreigners had been killed'. Later, we are informed, more particularly, in terms of the target nations involved here, that 'British and German property also suffered heavy losses'. Pairing Britain and Germany together here may in retrospect seem paradoxical given that the two countries were at war with each other two years later. However, by 1937 it was not yet clear that this would definitely occur and, from the Chinese point of view, what mainly mattered in 1937 was that Germany had been helping the KMT militarily since 1927, when Chiang Kai-shek broke with the communists; and that Britain was a potential future ally in the fight against Japan. By 1937, therefore, as far as the KMT were concerned, these two countries were amongst the most important for China, and so it is no surprise that they are especially invoked in *The Battle of Shanghai*, which, in one sequence, provides that invocation with a forceful, though uncommon symbolism. The sequence in question shows two bombed-out buildings adjacent to each other, one with a British flag obtruding from it, the other a German flag. In an obviously staged shot both flags hang forlornly downwards at the same angle, and also point towards each other, as though coupled together in their respective fortunes. Although, as with the overall bonding of Britain and Germany, this intentionally poignant pennantic juxtaposition may appear paradoxical today, that was again not the way the KMT saw things at the time. Beyond Britain and Germany it was also important for the Chinese authorities to maintain and augment as much international support as possible during this period and that imperative is also foregrounded in *The Battle of Shanghai*. Elsewhere in the film, for example, we see shots of westerners of various nationalities caught up in the crowds of Chinese fleeing the conflict, and, at the conclusion of one of these sequences, we are told that China was not just fighting for itself but also for 'international justice'.

The Battle of Shanghai utilises three distinct stylistic approaches in order to carry through its ideological project. One of these is realism, and, in line with this, the film contains a number of sequences in which the disordered city is shown under attack, with smoke billowing from battered buildings. Much of the camera-work in these sequences is unsteady and hand-held. Editing is also not as important here as simply *showing* the devastated cityscape, and, as a consequence of this need, and through constant camera movement, a disorganised, but highly affective, form of film-making emerges. What is required here is to show *as much as possible*, and, this requirement leads the camera to behave as though it were a continuously shifting observing eye, repeatedly changing focus and direction of gaze. These sequences are also, as just suggested, highly effective, and that effectiveness is accentuated by the fact that we know the cameraman was very close to the action here, and putting himself at some risk. It is, perhaps, above all else, these actuality shots of the conflict that give *The Battle of Shanghai* its lasting power as a hard-hitting work of cinematic activism.

In addition to such granular realism, *The Battle of Shanghai* contains sequences in which a more emblematic 'performative-tableaux' approach is adopted. In these sequences the narrative about the progress of the battle virtually stops, and, instead, the opportunity is taken to ratchet up the level of patriotic expression. The principal means through which this is achieved in these sequences is via the presentation of patriotic songs, though this is backed up by shots of KMT troops on the march, the KMT flag, and so on. There are two principal examples of such sequences in *The Battle of Shanghai*. In the first of these we see a group of children, refugees from the conflict who have presumably become separated from their families. The children begin to sing a partisan song, their high-pitched voices lending a sense of innocent fervour to the performance, and we then see extra-diegetic footage of KMT troops marching past. This is also the sequence previously mentioned which ends with the refrain that 'we are fighting for international justice'. In some respects, this sequence, which is intended to intensify patriotism and raise morale, is similar to sequences in *A Page of History* in which first Sun, and then Chiang, address their audiences. The difference here though, is that, in *The Battle of Shanghai*, patriotism does not emerge from a position of growing strength, but from trampled-on, beaten-down defiance. As just mentioned, there is also one other sequence like this, later in the film, in which children are again used to invoke determined resistance through the enactment and singing of patriotic songs; and, in this sequence, we again see extra-diegetic shots of marching troops and the Nationalist flag.

The third main type of stylistic device used in *The Battle of Shanghai* is different again from both the realist and tableaux approaches. Despite being shot on the battlefield, *The Battle of Shanghai* is a comparatively large-scale work and some sequences in the film reveal the presence of concomitantly high production values, as well as sophisticated, well-organised pictorial composition. These sequences, which are considerably dissimilar in style to the grittily realistic ones found elsewhere in *The Battle of Shanghai*, occur towards the end of the film, and are often shot at night. Here, the contrasts of darkened night and illuminating flashes from gunfire establish a more pictorially dramatic atmosphere than can be found elsewhere in the film, as *The Battle of Shanghai* employs forceful and dramatic filmic technique in order to drive home its message. *The Battle of Shanghai* does not end with this, but returns to a more realist mode near the conclusion of the film. Surprisingly, though, and as with *A Page of History*, the print of *The Battle of Shanghai* which is available for viewing does not really have any clear ending as such, but just fades away. Again, and as with *A Page of History*, it seems that the final sequences of the film may be missing. Nevertheless, *The Battle of Shanghai* remains a major achievement, and, arguably, the most important documentary film with a strong Hong Kong association to emerge during the period from the outbreak of the Sino-Japanese War in 1937 to the fall of Hong Kong, in 1941.

CONCLUSIONS

If the documentary film production of Hong Kong between 1898 and 1941 is taken as a whole, a number of points become evident. Up till 1914 documentary film-making was entirely the province of western film-makers and most of the films shot in Hong Kong were destined for western, rather than Hong Kong audiences. During this period Hong Kong functioned as a scenic, exotic location to which film companies in Britain, the US and France sent film-makers. And Hong Kong was also a film market, within which western films were distributed and screened. However, this period of film-making more or less came to an end with the outbreak of the First World War in 1914, although, even prior to that, the genre of the 'scenic documentary' had been diminishing, at least as a substantive, industry-backed genre. These films also followed the general development of the actuality film up to 1914. At the beginning, the Edison 'short', 'animated photograph', or 'living picture' *Hong Kong Wharf Scene* (1898) was one reel (50 feet) in length, and one minute in duration. Like all the earliest films it is concerned only with capturing movement through space and time, and evoking 'awe and admiration for their faithfulness to true-life action'.[75] There is no organisation within the shot here, and, instead, the objective is to capture the random and chance events of the everyday. The added dimension here is, of course, the combination of exotic oriental and colonial. However, this exists as a sub-text only, and it is the realist imperative of *Hong Kong Wharf Scene*, and the other Hong Kong Edison shorts, which is the predominating factor. These films *show* a far-off place. As such, these 'animated photographs' take on the role and legacy of the nineteenth-century photograph, their subjects selected on the basis of visuality and 'expressing no idea or feeling . . . their frame of reference limited'.[76] As with all the early actuality films shot around the world, by 1900 films shot in Hong Kong were already becoming longer. For example, *Circular Panorama of Hong Kong* (Rosenthal, Warwick, UK, 1900) is already two reels, and two minutes long. Such films still did not employ editing, however, and it appears that it was not until 1907, four years after editing was introduced in America, that the first edited films shot in Hong Kong appear. So, for example, *Through Hong Kong* (Urban-Eclipse, France, 1907), is 627 feet in length, twelve minutes long, and employs basic cuts. As its title suggests, a film such as *Through Hong Kong* is also a film about the *city*, and it is the city of Hong Kong, rather than its landscape, that predominates in these films. In fact it appears that it was not until 1909 that the first film to explore the Hong Kong landscape in a substantive manner appeared: Urban-Eclipse's *Up the Mountain from Hong Kong* (1909), which, however, still begins with the city.

The First World War put an end to the genre of the simple scenic documentary film shot in Hong Kong, and also brought the emerging Hong Kong film industry to a halt. It was not until 1923 that one of the first documentary films to be made in Hong Kong appeared: Lai Man-wai's *Chinese Competitors at the Sixth Far East Sports Games in Japan*. After that, documentary film production continued in a very limited manner, adversely affected by, first, the growth of the silent feature film, and, second, the growth of the sound film; and it was not until 1936, and the run-up to the Sino-Japanese war, that important documentary films, and also newsreels, began to be made. From 1936 to 1941, apart from a few scenic documentaries made by Hollywood companies, and Grandview's newsreel, *Grandview Review*, the documentary film in Hong Kong was increasingly dominated by a China focus, and, amongst other factors, this reflected the fact that, by the late 1930s, the Chinese documentary film-making community in Hong Kong had yet to develop much of a sense of identity with the territory as either Chinese 'home' or British-maintained colony. As argued earlier in this chapter, colonial Hong Kong entered the Second World War without any substantive degree of committed support from its local population, and it seems that this lack was reflected in the documentary films which emerged from the colony during the late 1930s, and up to the Japanese invasion of December 1941.

NOTES

1. Reinhard, Wolfgang, *A Short History of Colonialism* (Manchester: Manchester University Press, 2011), p. 162.
2. Porter, Bernard, *The Lion's Share: A Short History of British Imperialism, 1850–1995* (London and New York: Longman, 1996), p. 10.
3. Reinhard, *A Short History*, p. 166.
4. Tsang, Steve, *A Modern History of Hong Kong* (Hong Kong: Hong Kong University Press, 2009), p. 7.
5. Reinhard, *A Short History*, p. 167.
6. Pepper, Suzanne, *Keeping Democracy at Bay: Hong Kong and the Challenge of Chinese Political Reform* (New York: Rowman and Littlefield Publishers, 2008), p. 26.
7. Reinhard, *A Short History*, p. 167.
8. Tsang, *A Modern History*, p. 11.
9. Pepper, *Keeping Democracy at Bay*, p. 25.
10. Ingham, Michael, *Hong Kong: A Cultural and Literary History* (Oxford: Signal Books, 2007), p. 15.
11. Tsang, *A Modern History*, p. 18.
12. Pepper, *Keeping Democracy at Bay*, p. 40
13. Ibid. p. 41.
14. Tsang, *A Modern History*, pp. 27–8.
15. Porter, *The Lion's Share*, p. 62.
16. Tsang, *A Modern History*, p. 62.
17. Porter, *The Lion's Share*, p. 10.
18. Tsang, *A Modern History*, p. 107.
19. Ibid. pp. 107–8.
20. Ibid. p. 62.
21. Ibid. p. 63.
22. Ibid. p. 66.
23. Ibid.
24. Reinhard, *A Short History*, p. 4.
25. Carroll, John M., *Edge of Empires: Chinese Elites and British Colonials in Hong Kong* (Hong Kong: Hong Kong University Press, 2007), p. 18.

26. Ibid. p. 12.
27. Ibid. p. 11.
28. Pepper, *Keeping Democracy at Bay*, p. 73.
29. Ibid.
30. Carroll, John M., *A Concise History of Hong Kong* (Hong Kong: Hong Kong University Press, 2007), p. 160.
31. Tsang, *A Modern History*, p. 112.
32. Pepper, *Keeping Democracy at Bay*, p. 76.
33. Ibid.
34. Tsang, *A Modern History*, p. 110
35. Law, Wai-ming, 'Hong Kong's Cinematic Beginnings 1896–1908', in *The 19th Hong Kong International Film Festival: Early Images of Hong Kong and China* (Hong Kong: Hong Kong Government Printer, 1995), p. 23.
36. Bordwell, David, and Thompson, Kristin, *Film History: An Introduction* (New York: McGraw-Hill, Inc., 1994), p. 20.
37. Christie, Ian, 'The Captains and the Kings Depart: Imperial Departure and Arrival in Early Cinema', in MacCabe, Colin and Grieveson, Lee (eds) *Empire and Film* (London: British Film Institute and Palgrave Macmillan, 2011), p. 23.
38. Tsang, *A Modern History*, p. 65.
39. Law, Wai-ming, 'Hong Kong's Cinematic Beginnings', p. 23.
40. Ibid. p. 24.
41. Ibid.
42. Stokes, Lisa Odham and Hoover, Michael, *City on Fire: Hong Kong Cinema* (London: Verso, 1999), p. 18.
43. Law, Wai-ming, 'Hong Kong's Cinematic Beginnings', p. 24.
44. Ibid.
45. Lai, Linda, 'Hong Kong Cinema in the 1930s: Docility, Social Hygiene, Pleasure-seeking and the Consolidation of the Film Industry', http://www.latrobe.edu.au/www/screeningthepast/firstrelease/fr1100/Ilfr11h.htm, p. 21.
46. Stokes and Hoover, *City on Fire*, p. 18.
47. Yang, Jeff, *Once Upon a Time in China: A Guide to Hong Kong, Taiwanese and Mainland Chinese Cinema* (New York: Atria Books, 2003), p. 7.
48. Lam, Agnes (ed.), 'Oral History: Lai Man-wai', in *The Hong Kong-Guangdong Film Connection* (Hong Kong: Hong Kong Film Archive, 2005), p. 132.
49. Stokes and Hoover, *City on Fire*, p. 19.
50. Ibid. p. 18.
51. Tsang, *A Modern History*, p. 84.
52. Yu, Mo-wan, 'History of the Development of Hong Kong Newsreel Documentary Film', in *Changes in Hong Kong Society through Cinema* (Hong Kong: Urban Council, 1988), p. 97.
53. 'Lai Man-wai's Struggle to Make Documentary on Sun Yat-sen', *Beijing Youth Daily*, 12 August 2011.
54. Ibid.
55. Ibid.
56. Lam, 'Oral History', p. 139.
57. *Beijing Youth Daily*, op. cit.
58. It is not entirely clear if this person was Yu Mo-wan, as the *Beijing Youth Daily* gives the name of a person by the name of Yu Mu-yung.
59. *Beijing Youth Daily*, op. cit.

60. Ibid.
61. Law, Wai-ming, 'Hong Kong's Cinematic Beginnings', p. 23.
62. Lai, Shek, *The Diary of Lai Man-wai* (Hong Kong: Hong Kong Film Archive, 2003), p. 8.
63. Chu, Tinchi, *Hong Kong Cinema: Coloniser, Motherland and Self* (New York: Routledge Curzon, 2003), p. 7.
64. Ibid.
65. Ibid.
66. Wong, Mary (ed.), *Hong Kong Filmography, Vol. 1, 1913–1941* (Hong Kong: Hong Kong Film Archive, 1997), p. 597.
67. Fu, Poshek and Desser, David, *The Cinema of Hong Kong: History, Arts, Identity* (Cambridge and New York: Cambridge University Press, 2000), p. 201.
68. Ibid. p. 208.
69. Chu, *Hong Kong Cinema*, p. 8.
70. Ibid. p. 9.
71. Fu and Desser, *The Cinema*, p. 213.
72. Wong, *Hong Kong Filmography*, p. 605.
73. Ibid. p. 600.
74. Ibid. p. 606.
75. Jacobs, Lewis, 'Precursors and Prototypes (1894–1922)', in Jacobs (ed.) *The Documentary Tradition* (New York; London: W. W. Norton and Company, 1979), p. 3.
76. Ibid.

CHAPTER 2

Hong Kong, Britain, China: The Documentary Film, 1947–69, the 'Picturesque' Committed Film and *Water Comes over the Hills from the East* (1965)

These guys who advocate for Hong Kong independence are sheer morons. Deprived of support from the mainland, Hong Kong will be a dead city. Where do they think the water comes from?[1]

By the time of the outbreak of the Second World War in September 1939 the British Government had already come to the conclusion that Hong Kong could not be defended against expected attack by Japan. The most that could be hoped for, given the then improved relationship with China, one that is also signalled in *The Battle of Shanghai*, was that, if such an attack were to occur, China might help to delay the inevitable collapse of the colony by providing temporary military support. The object here was not, therefore, to save Hong Kong at all but to make the eventual fall of the colony appear less precipitous and chastening. To this end, in the summer of 1941 the British and Chinese governments reached an agreement whereby Chinese forces would engage any Japanese militias attacking Hong Kong. On 7 December 1941 Japanese aircraft attacked the American air base at Pearl Harbour, bringing the United States into the Second World War. Four hours after that assault began Japanese bombers struck Hong Kong and Japanese ground troops also began an advance on the territory from the southern Guangdong area. Under the terms of the agreement reached with Britain Chiang Kai-shek then ordered Chinese forces south to engage the Japanese in and around Guangzhou in order to open up a new front, and slow down the assault on the colony. However, the speed of the Japanese advance was such that Hong Kong fell before the Chinese army ever reached Guangzhou.[2]

Hong Kong fell to the invading Japanese Imperial Army on 25 December 1941. The resulting occupation was to last three years and eight months. Following the Japanese surrender in August 1945 a British fleet entered Hong Kong waters on 30 August, and the Crown Colony was re-established under military administration on 1 September. However, the British recovery of Hong Kong in 1945 was controversial. Throughout the course of the war discussions had taken place within the British Government on whether to retake the colony on the cessation of hostilities, or hand it back to China. American pressure to do the latter was considerable, and, in both Washington and London, senior officials felt it more imperative to build an alliance with a post-war China than to hold on to the small imperial outpost of Hong Kong. A clear division of opinion also emerged here between the British Foreign Office, which thought in terms of the wider geo-political picture, and the Colonial Office, which was determined not to give up a British colony. In 1944, however, intra-departmental irresolution over the future of Hong Kong finally came to an end when the Government decided that the colony would be retaken as soon as practicable, and returned to the Crown. The problem was, however, that Chiang Kai-shek was then overall commander of the China theatre, including Hong Kong, and it was in him, rather than Britain, that military authority for liberating the colony was formally vested. Fearing that Chinese troops might attempt to take the colony British authorities hastily made ready a fleet of ships with a remit to sail for Hong Kong and reach the city before any Chinese army might do so. However, the British still had to wait for a formal Japanese surrender, and, when that occurred on 14 August 1945, the fleet immediately set sail, reaching Hong Kong on 29 August. For the British Government retaking Hong Kong had been a matter of restoring British prestige in the east, as a political briefing paper prepared in July 1945 made clear. Britain sought to recover Hong Kong because 'having lost the colony to the Japanese, it was a point of national honour . . . to recover it, and restore it to its normal state of order and prosperity'.[3] However, and leaving points of honour aside, such hopes as to continuity and 'restoration to a normal state' of affairs would prove difficult to achieve, as the situation on the ground in post-war Hong Kong had changed considerably.

Between 1945 and 1949 new waves of immigrants entered Hong Kong fleeing the Chinese Civil War and the final communist victory in 1949. To these post-war immigrants, as with those who had arrived in the late 1930s, colonial Hong Kong provided a haven, and the possibility of rebuilding lives. However, and as with earlier incomers, the immigrants who arrived in the 1940s had no particular liking for the British colonial state itself, and did not generally consider themselves to be prospective 'Hongkongers'. Instead, their psycho-emotional affiliation remained China-oriented.[4] These fraught and often destitute newcomers were largely preoccupied with the vicissitudes of daily life, and, initially, made few demands of the colonial government. However, as those vicissitudes grew, the claims increased. After the war, longer-established elements of the local population in Hong Kong also began to petition for greater social reform and enfranchisement; requests which colonial officials saw as constituting a '1946 outlook'. However, during the 1940s, those officials had no intention of meeting such an outlook in any substantive, step-change way.[5]

But if the colonial attitude in Hong Kong did not change overmuch during the immediate post-war period, British government policy towards the colonial sphere in general did. Prior to the war it had already been accepted within the British establishment that most if not all colonies would eventually be granted independence. Initially though, and even immediately prior to the war, an extensive time-line of some sixty or so years had been envisaged for that process. However, the post-war Labour government, and then succeeding Conservative governments, proceeded to truncate this schedule considerably, and, by the late 1940s, official policy was that most colonies would be granted independence within the ensuing twenty years. During the 1950s this policy was ushered in and many colonies progressed along a path towards independence which would culminate in the wave of decolonisation that occurred during the 1960s.[6] Even so, a distinction can be drawn between those colonies moving towards independence in the 1960s and those not, and during the 1950s Hong Kong can be linked to other colonies within which nation-building through localisation and preparation for independence was put on hold: the Bahamas, which did not achieve independence until the 1970s; Antigua and Belize, which became independent in the 1980s; and the fourteen Overseas Territories, including Bermuda, which still remain under British authority today. Hong Kong was never part of the post-war contract of decolonialisation, and successive British governments had no intention of handing governance of Hong Kong to the local population, largely because it was believed that, if a deterioration of relations were to occur between Britain and China, that population would ally itself with the latter. In addition, one new reason for retaining Hong Kong under British control had also emerged. Hong Kong had not been thought strategically important in the late 1930s, but during the Cold War and the international 'struggle against communism' the Crown Colony became viewed as a strategic anti-communist outpost in the east.[7] Thus, and for all these reasons, from 1945 onwards, as colony after colony gained independence, Hong Kong remained a bastion of colonial conservatism, and what was required from colonial officials there was not post-colonial nation-building but the preservation of the colonial status quo.

Such continuation was begrudgingly tolerated by much of the local population during the 1950s. It has been argued that the 'fundamental justification' for the British Empire from an imperialist perspective was the promise of harmony, peace, and social stability.[8] During the 1950s the East and South-East Asia region was highly volatile, and doubts proliferated in the Hong Kong populace as to whether the colony would in the end be able to survive in such an unhinged environment.[9] Such presentiments generated feelings of considerable insecurity, against which the capacity of the colonial government to ensure stability was seen as imperative. The priority for the Chinese migrants who flooded into Hong Kong after 1945 was to establish a viable economic foundation for themselves and their families, and the quid pro quo here was that if the government provided the conditions for such a foundation, colonial rule would be at least tolerated. Such a covenant was also particularly underpinned by traumatic events occurring in communist China during the period 1949–69. Collectivisation of agriculture policies introduced in 1950 drove further waves of dispossessed immigrants into Hong Kong, causing the colonial government to temporarily close the border. Between 1958 and 1961 the Maoist 'Great Leap Forward' also resulted in a famine in China which killed over 20 million and drove yet more immigrants into the colony. From 1945 to the mid-1950s alone, well over 1 million mainlanders came into Hong Kong.[10] Initially, the colonial government's response to this massive influx was to stand back from it, as government policy was that the destitute arriving from China should not be fed and watered in case such donation encouraged even more to come. In addition, and as mentioned previously, from almost the foundation of the colony, British policy had been to interfere as little as possible in the lives of its Chinese inhabitants. Whatever altruism may have been involved in this, based on the notion that local populations should be allowed to maintain their cultural mores untainted by the colonial presence, this stance also provided a rationale for limiting expenditure on social provision.[11] As a consequence, and up till as late as the early 1970s, the colonial government took the view that as little as practicable should be spent on social amenity and allocation for the Chinese commonality.[12]

However, as the years went by this policy became increasingly unsustainable, not to say reproachable, and, as both the population and demand for change increased, the colonial government could not avoid aggregating its degree of involvement in the social affairs of its disenfranchised Chinese citizens. In fact, though, the untenability of the old arm's-length colonial position had already begun to be felt a long time prior to this, and as early as the late nineteenth centuriy, when increasing pressure on welfare delivery forced the colonial administration to enact small-scale measures of social and educational reform. However, the mass-immigrant incursion of the 1950s ratcheted up the need for such measures, and, when a series of deadly fires broke out in makeshift shanty towns during the early 1950s, the government was forced to embark on a major and expensive programme of house building and resettlement.[13] However although this constituted a major step-change, colonial Hong

Kong still remained as ideologically wedded as it could to a small-government model of 'positive non-intervention'. Here, intervention to ensure social stability and create a favourable climate for business was permissible, but, beyond that, as much 'non-intervention' as was practicable was the desired norm.[14] As a consequence of this, the gap between the colonial authorities and the bulk of the local population remained a considerable one throughout the 1950s, and, as in the nineteenth century, two parallel and largely disconnected societies continued to persist alongside each other.[15] However, this situation began to change during the 1960s, as the process of decolonisation taking place within the Empire finally began to affect Hong Kong in a consequential manner. In 1959 the re-election of a Conservative government in Britain under Harold Macmillan led to an acceleration of decolonisation,[16] and, one consequence of this was that, between 1960 and 1965, virtually all of Britain's tropical colonies were granted independence.[17] Against this context the British Government came under increasing pressure from various sources to reform the autocratic model of the Crown Colony in Hong Kong,[18] and talks on constitutional reform for the colony were eventually initiated in London in 1963-4; talks which, for the first time, entertained the real possibility that a local, elected legislative element might be inaugurated.[19] However, circumstances and events then intervened, and, for a variety of reasons, some more acceptable than others, the British failed to carry through their proposed reforms.

The principal event to intrude here, and one which effectively stopped this embryonic process of reform in its tracks, was the Chinese Cultural Revolution of 1966-76. There is no doubt that the British Government intended to enact major political reform in Hong Kong in 1965-6. However, the atrocities and disruption caused by the Cultural Revolution produced the greatest turmoil in China seen since the founding of the People's Republic of China, and also forced yet another wave of dispossessed and desperate immigrants into Hong Kong.[20] As the Revolution gathered pace in China, pro-communist organisations and infiltrators in Hong Kong also attempted to build on that momentum. Large-scale disturbances then broke out in 1966-7. The Cultural Revolution was to a large extent the outcome of political struggle taking place within the ruling communist elite in China and did not have consequences of fundamental magnitude for Hong Kong. The colonial government understood this, and, accordingly, adopted a measured response to the 1966-7 riots. This restrained approach, when set against the communist-inspired violence taking place on the streets then led many local people to tacitly support a government which appeared to be mainly concerned with keeping the peace. Ultimately, by the end of the crisis, it seems that the bulk of the Chinese population in Hong Kong had sided with the colonial government in this particular challenge, and not the communist forces and powers many of them had fled from in the 1940s, 1950s, and now 1960s.

However, that did not mean that resentment over the colonial incursion, and the discriminatory and inequitable condition of the colony, had disappeared. The disturbances which took place in 1966–7 were, in fact, only in part caused by communist insurrection and sympathy, and were, to a much larger extent, the product of a general dissatisfaction with the poor state of social and economic conditions within Hong Kong. Having supported the colonial government against the communist insurgency, the local population now expected change, and the expectation was for better living conditions, and for a fairer, more inclusive society, in which the mass of the population could feel that they had a stake. This demand, in turn, led to the appearance of something relatively new: the development amongst an extensive section of the local population of a sense of Chinese Hong Kong identity. Of course, the colonial regime was aware that support for colonial rule within the local population remained largely based on the perceived mantra that the only existing alternative to such rule was far worse, but that support still provided a basis for reform to be implemented, and, propelled into such reform by London, the colonial government began to transform the old-fashioned Crown Colony into a society more responsive to public opinion and need.[21] Social services were expanded, compulsory free primary education eventually introduced, and action taken to deal with endemic corruption. Hong Kong remained a divided society ruled by a distant colonial class, but the extension of civil society, and development of a sense of local identity, had begun to occur on a larger developing scale.

And yet, a great opportunity was also lost, because democratic representative reform did not take place. Ultimately, the events of 1966–7 and larger context of 1966–76 led successive British governments to suspend the process of democratic reform which had been scheduled for Hong Kong, and the plans which had been mooted in 1963–4 were shelved indefinitely.[22] In 1966–7 South-East Asia was at the centre of the Cold War, with conflicts occurring in Malaysia, Thailand, Burma, Vietnam, Laos, Cambodia, the Philippines and Korea. In 1968 the Cultural Revolution also reached its peak in China, threatening to plunge the country into even greater chaos. And one consequence of this hazardous regional situation was that Hong Kong now took on a new strategic importance for western powers. In America the election of a Republican government in 1964 led by Lyndon Baines Johnson played a crucial part in the eventual British decision to halt the process of political reform in Hong Kong. At the time the US was actively and militarily supporting the 'anti-communist struggle' throughout South-East Asia, and was fully stretched as a consequence of such intervention. When a Labour government under Prime Minister Harold Wilson was elected in Britain in 1964, that government came under immediate and strong pressure from the Johnson administration to maintain and further develop Hong Kong as a strategic base and intelligence centre.[23] Given the Cold War context, and involvement of China in supporting communist insurgency, the Johnson administration did not want any transferral of jurisdiction to the local Chinese population to take place in Hong Kong, and, given this and other factors, London eventually decided to abandon plans for constitutional democratic reform of the colony. Wilson may have been a modernising Labour Party prime minister, but, when taking office, he was briefed, as were his post-war predecessors, on the crucial importance of the strategic military 'special relationship' with the US. It may have been that had American pressure to the contrary not been brought to bear, Britain would have introduced political reform in Hong Kong in the late 1960s. However, that pressure was brought, and influenced the decision that was finally made. Nevertheless, and despite accommodating American requirements, Britain still failed to obtain a formal agreement from the US that the latter would support Britain militarily in the case of a Chinese attack on Hong Kong; something that had been a British policy objective since 1945. Many circumstances conspired against the institution of democratic reform in Hong Kong in the mid to late 1960s. Nevertheless, such reform was both desired in the colony and merited, and a crucial opportunity was lost which was never to recur.

HONG KONG DOCUMENTARY FILM, 1947–69

As in the late 1930s, the mainland immigrants who flooded into Hong Kong between 1945 and the late 1960s included film-makers, and, after 1945, many of these attempted to play an active role in the ongoing political and military struggle taking place between mainland communist and KMT nationalist forces, the latter of whom were based in Taiwan after 1949. For these film-makers that struggle did not only consist of general political contribution but also direct intervention within the Hong Kong film industry, and, as before the war, film companies in the colony continued to ally themselves to one or other of these two parties. These alliances also became more consolidated during the 1950s and 1960s, and, during this period, against a background of political and social turmoil in China, 'leftist' companies such as Union Film Enterprises and Great Wall associated themselves with the pro-Beijing camp,[24] whilst 'rightist' outfits such as the Asia Film Company, which was established with the help of American funding as part of the US post-war struggle against communism in South-East Asia, associated themselves with pro-KMT and anti-communist positions.[25] It also appears that, generally speaking, the leftists were more forceful and committed in their tactics than were the rightists. One of their more aggressive tactics was, for example, to covertly infiltrate and then eventually take over existing commercially oriented companies. This even happened to what would become one of the most important leftist companies of the period: Great Wall, which was originally established as an ordinary

commercial enterprise but was then penetrated by communist film personnel following the founding of the PRC in 1949. Great Wall mainly produced
feature films during the 1950s and 1960s, but also made some documentary
films, including the one that will be discussed in depth later in this chapter:
Water Comes over the Hills from the East (1965).[26]

The Japanese occupation of 1941–5 closed down documentary film-making
in Hong Kong and the first post-war film did not appear until 1947. Significantly,
that film, *Gala Performance of Opera and Movie Stars*, also fell into the most
pervasive genre of documentary film production to develop over the 1947–69
period: that of the 'celebrity' film. Between 1947 and 1949 the production of
documentary film remained at a low level, with only six films made. Four of
these concerned celebrities, whilst two – *The Boxing Championship Title* (1948)
and *Sweden Hong Kong Soccer Match* (1949) – covered sporting events. All six
films were in Cantonese. During the 1950s production of documentary films
increased further, and, as in the 1930s, a wide range of genres can be identified. As mentioned, the largest of these concerned celebrities: film stars, opera
stars, beauty queens, and so on. Around eighteen out of an approximate total
of thirty-five films produced during the 1950s fall into this genre, including
films such as *The Wedding of Law Yim-hing and Ho Fei-fan* (1953), and *Three
Opera Stars* (Yunsheng, 1959). In addition to this dominant genre a number
of minor genres continued on from pre-war days. Only one colonial – or semi-
colonial – film appears to have been made in the 1950s: *Hong Kong Coronation
Parade* (Li'er, 1953), although, here, the 'parade' in question mainly consists
of Chinese cultural events such as a dragon dance. Three films were also made
celebrating film companies during the 1950s. They are *The First Anniversary
of the Union Film Enterprise Ltd* (Union, 1954); *The Fifth Anniversary of the
Union Film Enterprise Ltd* (Union, 1958); and *Stand Up and Cheer* (Hsin Hwa,
1958). Of note also are two films tackling social issues: *The Great Fire in Shek
Kip Mei* (Union, 1954), and *Newsreel on the Restricted Areas of Twelve Hong
Kong Reservoirs* (1954). These are, in all probability, the only documentary
films dealing with social issues produced during the 1950s. In addition to these
a number of films were made which fall into the 'scenic' category mentioned
in the previous chapter. These films will be discussed later, when *Water Comes
over the Hills from the East* is considered. Of the thirty-five or so documentary
films on the record for this period around fourteen or fifteen appear to have
been Mandarin productions, indicating the gradual growth in influence of
the Mandarin cinema in Hong Kong; a growth which would become near-
hegemonic during the 1960s. The main production companies evident here
are Great Wall and Union, with Shaw coming in more towards the end of the
1950s.

During the 1960s commercial production of documentary film in Hong
Kong doubled from approximately thirty-five or so in the 1950s to around

sixty. As in the 1950s, the same genres tended to prevail, with films on opera and film celebrities remaining predominant and accounting for over thirty of the films produced. Possibly also reflecting growing affluence in Hong Kong, the number of films made depicting various leisure pursuits also increased, with around seven films, including *Wonderful Youth Gala Special* (1968), falling into this category. Again, and as in the 1950s, only two films were made which could be described as 'social' films, and both were made in the year of the most severe drought. They are *Praying for Rain* (1963) and *Drought in Hong Kong* (1963). Amongst other matters, what much of the documentary film production of the 1960s reveals is the gradual growth of a local, popular leisure culture centred on film and opera and the activities of celebrities associated with these activities; but also spreading beyond that to encompass areas such as sport and beauty contests. However, the most significant development over this period, as also in the late 1950s, was the emergence of what will be referred to here as the 'scenic' or 'picturesque', committed pro-China documentary film.

THE COMMITTED 'PICTURESQUE' FILM

During the 1950s and 1960s documentary films were made in Hong Kong which centred on the Chinese landscape and traditional culture of mainland China, and which also sought to evoke affiliation with that landscape and culture. This is what is referred to here as the genre of the committed 'picturesque' or 'scenic' documentary film, a genre which was to expand exponentially during the 1960s. As indicated earlier, during the 1950s and 1960s film companies in Hong Kong affiliated with pro or anti-communist positions sometimes made feature films that embodied their respective ideological stances. For example, leftist companies such as Southern Film, Union Film Enterprises and Great Wall made a number of idealistic 'social-realist' films that focused on issues of class struggle and capitalist exploitation, whilst rightist companies such as Southern Film produced films which focused on notions of forced exile, the decline of the Chinese middle class, and communist repression.[27] Both types of films tended to have a relatively contemporary focus, and were often situated diegetically within the period of KMT–communist rivalry, from 1911 onwards; unless the primary concern was to portray the corruption of the previous feudal Chinese empire – a form of portrayal attractive to both camps. These films also attempted to appropriate Chinese tradition, culture and landscape to their respective projects and it is also within the parameters of this attempt at scenic-cultural appropriation that the documentary film entered the scene in an important way.

In addition to making feature films, leftist companies in particular (perhaps exclusively so – the picture remains unclear) also made committed documentary films during this period. However, because the documentary film cannot generally employ the forms of cinematic pleasure which the feature film can – characterisation, drama, melodrama, elaborately constructed psychological motivation, and so on – other means had to be employed in order to convey the requisite political message, and the strategy eventually adopted in these films was one of promoting a general idea of China and Chinese culture through showing the visual and aural landscape and cityscape, and aspects of folk tradition. Since the production companies involved here were also quite large, these films often had relatively high production values, and this contributed to their commercial and popular success. As with the feature films produced by the leftist companies, these documentary films were rarely crudely propagandistic, as such an approach, when adopted in the late 1930s and early 1940s, had proved to be commercially unsuccessful. In addition, a more subtle and indirect strategy of ideological address within the committed documentary film was required in order to circumvent the colonial censorship system in Hong Kong. Documentary film is arguably more open to intervention by censors than the feature film because its ideological content is more evidently foregrounded. A clearly pro–communist documentary film might, therefore, be banned, whilst a film about Chinese folk traditions and scenery, which also included considerate coverage of contemporary Chinese – that is, communist – society, might not be. For all these reasons, the committed leftist documentary films produced in the 1950s and 1960s conveyed their values in a generally understated manner, and their objective was to engender a similarly inexplicit, but still and also wide-ranging, sense of sympathy and affiliation for the motherland. However, and as we will see in relation to *Water Comes over the Hills from the East*, these semi-concealed underlying values and inexplicit depictions were sometimes also propounded and portrayed more explicitly, just to make sure the message was driven home.

The appearance of these documentary films from the late 1950s onwards must also be seen against the context of changes then taking place in Hong Kong society. This was a period of rapid economic development in Hong Kong in which the local population was becoming more accustomed to modern, western work practices, procedures and protocols. Despite a continuing general psycho-emotional affiliation with Chinese identity, and also despite a general lack of interest in and promotion of the matter of Chinese Hong Kong identity on the part of the colonial authorities, a sense of the latter was beginning to form through this encounter with a modernising economy and its attendant social structures, and this was of concern to leftist film-makers in Hong Kong committed to the communist regime in China. Those film-makers believed that the ongoing battle for hearts and minds now had to be intensified, and the documentary films produced by these film-makers in the 1950s and

1960s were intended to play a role in that, by turning the local population away from western colonialism and towards eastern Chinese communism. However, that battle was eventually lost for these films as a result of the fallout from the Cultural Revolution.

The first post-war documentary film to fall into this category of those attempting to create ideological picturesque affiliations with the motherland was Great Wall's *The Arts of Chinese Folk Arts* (Hu Xiaofeng Su Chengshou, 1956).[28] At thirteen reels in length this was the first feature-length documentary produced by Great Wall, and it was also one of the few long documentary films produced in Hong Kong during the 1950s. Like later such films, this film had relatively high production values, and this was a factor in its commercial success. *The Arts of Chinese Folk Arts* features highlights from performances given by the Chinese Folk Arts Troupe, and includes a lion dance and excerpts from Chinese opera. This was to become the sort of populist, variety-format model followed by later films in this genre. For example, the following year, Great Wall produced an eleven-reel film of the same title, but this time as a full recording of a single Chinese Folk Arts Troupe performance.[29]

In addition to these documentaries on traditional Chinese culture, other films that celebrated the Chinese heritage also featured the Chinese scenery and landscape. The first of these films to appear was the Huawen Film Company's inaugural production, *Home Thoughts from Abroad* (1958), which presents the scenery of southern China, and includes views of cities such as Guangzhou, Shantou, Chaozhou, Meixian, Zhanjiang and Hainan Island. In addition to such scenic tourism, *Home Thoughts from Abroad* attempts a kind of southern Chinese musical synthesis by featuring excerpts from the Cantonese opera *A Forced Match*, the Chaozhou opera *Chen San and Fifth Madam*, and an ethnic Li tribe dance from Hainan: *The Third Day of the Third Month*. The lyrical, nostalgic treatment of southern China in *Home Thoughts from Abroad* proved to be highly popular with an audience still pining for the absent motherland, and paved the way for other documentary films that were similarly high in production values. According to the *Hong Kong Filmography*, after *Home Thoughts from Abroad*, three years elapsed before three more scenic films were produced, in 1962. They were: *The West Lake* (Motion Picture and General Investment); *Beautiful Zhejiang, Jiangsu and Shenjiang* (Media Chinese International); and *A Tour around Beijing* (Media Chinese International. In 1963 Media Chinese International made *The Great Wall is 10,000 Li Long*, and, in 1965, both *Around Tai Mountain* and *The Shandong Acrobats*.[30] However, the most important of these scenic films to emerge in 1965, and also the most important film to emerge within this genre of the committed, picturesque, leftist documentary film, was *Water Comes over the Hills from the East*.

WATER COMES OVER THE HILLS FROM THE EAST (LO KWAN-HUNG, 1965)

From the 1950s onwards Hong Kong was affected by serious droughts which made life extremely difficult for the poor in particular, and these droughts, and their eventual alleviation through the building of a water supply from southern China into Hong Kong, is the subject of *Water Comes over the Hills from the East*. In 1963 Hong Kong was struck by an exceptionally severe drought, and, in response, the colonial government was forced to introduce a drastic water-rationing policy in which water supply to the community was restricted to only four hours every four days. The same year Lo Kwan-hung, the director of *Water Comes over the Hills from the East*, made *Drought in Hong Kong* for the leftist Feng Huang Motion Picture Company. The colonial government in Hong Kong had been negotiating with mainland authorities in Guangdong over water supply since 1960, and with no small amount of difficulty. However, the seriousness of the 1963 drought forced the government's hand and an agreement was eventually reached with the Guangdong authorities – one which suited the latter more than the former – to build and implement a water supply system from China into Hong Kong, moving water from the Chinese East River, a tributary of the Pearl River. This eventually helped to resolve Hong Kong's water-shortage problem to a significant extent, though it did not end the droughts entirely.

The period dating from the decline of the Great Leap Forward in 1961–3 to the outbreak of the Cultural Revolution in 1966 was one of relatively calm political coexistence between colonial Hong Kong and China. Following the resignation of Mao Zedong as Chairman of the PRC in 1959 a succeeding, revisionist leadership in China was chiefly preoccupied with recovery from the failure of the Great Leap Forward, and the economic and industrial developments required for such recovery were facilitated in large part through expedient existing and newly commissioned financial and trade links with Hong Kong. After 1961 the waves of refugees coming into the colony also diminished and a limited, negotiated annual refugee quota was administered. A colonial Hong Kong film of 1961, *This is Hong Kong*, which will be discussed in depth in the next chapter of this book, shows the border crossing into Hong Kong as relatively porous and informal at this time, with considerable trade and personnel coming and going randomly through the checkpoint. Internationally, China also became a less contentious entity and player over 1960–5. In 1960, for example, the PRC distanced itself from the escalating Cold War confrontation between the west and the Soviet Bloc by rejecting closer collaboration with the USSR. Of course the Vietnam War did escalate in 1963, when American forces became fully committed, and China then supported the North Vietnamese Viet Kong in various ways. However, American intervention here to prop up a non-democratic South Vietnamese regime was – to say the least – not universally supported in the west, and, hence, China's involvement on the part of the North Vietnamese was, similarly, not universally condemned either. In general, therefore, China enjoyed more relaxed diplomatic relations with both the west and Hong Kong during this period, and this moment of relative calm also establishes the contextual framework for *Water Comes over the Hills from the East.* .

Water Comes over the Hills from the East portrays the building and completion of a water supply from southern China into Hong Kong, showing all the areas in Guangdong which were involved in the process, and the construction of the 83-kilometre artificial channel and eight pumping stations which eventually delivered water to the Hong Kong border. The centre-piece of this construction process was the fabrication of a water-raising system which elevated the water level in eight stages to a height of 46 metres above sea level (thus the film's designation of water coming 'over the hills' into Hong Kong). This was, clearly, a very large project, involving huge amounts of manpower and machinery, all of which, as is proudly proclaimed in *Water Comes over the Hills from the East*, was provided by China. The film itself was also an extensive undertaking and took two years to complete by a five-man team which included Lo Kwan-hung as writer, director and cinematographer. *Water Comes over the Hills from the East* was, as the account of the film just given suggests, shot largely in southern China. However, it also contains some footage shot in Hong Kong taken from Lo's earlier documentaries on the Hong Kong drought. The first sections of the film are in black and white. However, as the water project nears completion the film switches to colour in order to additionally commemorate the degree and scale of Chinese achievement.

During its ten days of theatrical release in Hong Kong *Water Comes over the Hills from the East* played to full houses at every screening. It was not only the first documentary film in Hong Kong to achieve box-office revenues of HK$1 million but was also one of the most popular local films to be produced in the colony up to that point in time. Clearly, the film's story of how the motherland, with its vast resources, came to the assistance of an ailing Hong Kong touched a substantial patriotic and nostalgic cord within a large section of the local population; and this was, after all, the intention of the film-makers. However, the success of the film was also testimony to the extent to which the Hong Kong population had suffered during the droughts, and the extent to which that population was so relieved by their passing. What was not mentioned in the film, however, as this would have contradicted the positive-celebratory tone adopted, were then contemporary fears in Hong Kong that the colony had in fact handed the regime in communist China a 'water weapon', which might be – and, during the Cultural Revolution, was – used to intimidate the colony.[31]

Water Comes over the Hills from the East is intended to generate sympathy and identity for China. It is, therefore, an ideological film, though one in which, as in other films within this genre, ideology is often embedded, and thus concealed, within an overall evocative celebration of the Chinese land and landscape. This tone is signalled from the very beginning of the film as we see lyrical images of a lake which was one of the sources of the water supply, and hear similarly effusive-expressive traditional Chinese music. Southern China, from which many of the inhabitants of Hong Kong had fled only a few years before during the Great Leap Forward, is invoked here as a place of wistful natural melodious beauty. Immediately after this redolent opening, and in stark contrast, we see a series of sequences depicting the effect of the drought in Hong Kong: long lines of people waiting to receive their quota of water, and people digging forlornly in the hope of finding elusive underground water. There is no natural beauty here, only human privation, and these sequences, which are taken from Lo's previous documentaries on the drought, are grittily realistic in their depictions of life in the squatter camps and urban streets of the city. One striking sequence, for example, shows a group of women fighting over water rations, and tearing out clumps of each other's hair in the process. Here, a granular realism is appropriate to the film's political project, as that project requires colonial Hong Kong to be shown in a compromised light. The narration also takes a clear reinforcing stance here, declaring that the British colonial authorities 'are not doing enough' to help with the drought, and that, as a consequence, the people were suffering unnecessarily. Of course, the film makes no mention of *why* there were so many people in Hong Kong living in shanty towns, and in such need of increased amounts of drinking water. The real reason for this, that millions had fled from communist China into Hong Kong putting enormous strain on existing resources, would not have fitted the ideological mission of the film particularly well, to say the least. There is, therefore, a clear denial of the imperative political reality here in this attempt to promote Chinese patriotism and allegiance to the communist state in China. But, then again, this is a propaganda film

Following this criticism of British slackness and lack of interest in the well-being of what the narration refers to loosely as 'the people of Hong Kong', the film cuts to China, to show a number of mainland officials, including the then Governor of Guangdong Province, Chen Yu, discussing ways in which to 'help Hong Kong'. The idea here is that it is philanthropic mainland leaders who are taking the initiative whilst the colonial government in Hong Kong is not. In fact, the colonial government of Hong Kong is hardly ever seen or mentioned in *Water Comes over the Hills from the East*, and, even when a reference does occur, it is usually an unfavourable one. We are then given a brief potted history of the water-shortage problem. The film describes how, at first, ships carried water into Hong Kong from China but that, in the end, this proved to be an inadequate response to the problem. As this brief, weighted history lesson comes to an end, we are also informed that 'China', seemingly evoked here as a unitary entity encompassing Chinese people in the Crown Colony, then 'decided to help Hong Kong' by developing a water-relief system. Details concerning how the agreement to build the system was reached, and the challenging negotiations that went into that, are left out here, and masked under the rubric of a benevolent disinterested China 'deciding to act' selflessly in the interests of Chinese people. In fact, the reality was more complicated.

After the Second World War the colonial government in Hong Kong attempted to solve the water-shortage problems of the colony through means such as the building of reservoirs. Although such projects took a long time to bring to fruition, by the early 1950s planners in Hong Kong were confident that, by the end of the decade, Hong Kong would be sufficient in terms of water supply. Such confidence was, however, soon undermined by the waves of immigrants who arrived in Hong Kong during the late 1950s. The new arrivals increased demand for water exponentially, to the point where it became apparent to the colonial government that existing plans for water storage and supply would have to be augmented further.[32] The government then instituted a number of new infrastructural schemes, including the damming and dredging of a huge reservoir out of the sea. The problem was, though, that these developments would not bear fruit until the late 1960s, and, until then, Hong Kong would experience water shortages. Taking strategic advantage of this quandary, the PRC built a reservoir near the border with Hong Kong in 1959 with the intention of making water available for transport into the colony. The incentive for this project was not economic, but political, and, initially, PRC officials even offered to provide water to Hong Kong for free. Essentially, the PRC wished to bestow water to the territory in order to raise the profile of communist China in Hong Kong through making it appear that the motherland was coming to the aid of suffering Chinese compatriots. However, the Hong Kong government, fully alert to the political price to be paid for accepting such a bequest, refused the offer of free water, and insisted instead that Hong Kong's involvement in the arrangement be placed on normal commercial terms. Even so, the PRC still levied unusually low rates for the water, as, to repeat, profit was not the key consideration.[33] A first water-supply agreement was then signed as early as November 1960, and water began to be channelled into Hong Kong from the Shenzhen Reservoir in 1961.[34] The water-shortage problems of Hong Kong had been alleviated, though, as it turned out, not for long.

From late 1962 to early 1964 the southern China region, including Hong Kong, was struck by a serious drought. In Hong Kong the situation became so serious that the government was forced to take the highly expensive emergency measure of shipping water from the Pearl River in China, until, by October 1963, HK$55 million had been spent on this.[35] Faced with this extreme and unsustainable situation the colonial government then approached the PRC with a proposal to extend the 1960 water-supply agreement. It was, therefore, the colonial government, and not the PRC – as *Water Comes over the Hills from the East* claims – which instigated discussion on, and eventual construction of, the water-relief system that the film portrays.[36] Furthermore, the PRC did not exactly rush to support the scheme once it had been presented, but instead procrastinated for up to six months – the colonial government presented the proposals to the PRC in May 1963, but, by October, had still not received a response – whilst the water shortage in Hong Kong worsened. The delay here was almost certainly caused by a felt need within suspicious upper echelons of the PRC to discuss the British proposals cautiously, and evidence suggests that the proposals were, indeed, considered at the very 'highest levels of the State'.[37] Be that as it may, the lateness here clearly gainsays the claim of PRC proactivity made in *Water Comes over the Hills from the East*. Eventually, though, a second supply agreement was finally arrived at in April 1964 to bring water from the Chinese East River to the Shenzhen Reservoir, and, from there, into Hong Kong. The project was finally completed in January 1965, and water began to flow into the colony from March of that year onwards.[38]

As with the first settlement of 1960, the PRC entered into the 1964 supply agreement for political rather than economic reasons. The main purpose, as with *Water Comes over the Hills from the East*, was to 'win hearts and minds' in Hong Kong. Today, as the quotation from Li Ping set out at the beginning of this chapter suggests, Hong Kong is virtually dependent upon water supply from China. Estimates vary, but it is possible that, if the supply were to be turned off, Hong Kong's reservoirs would empty in three to six months. Underlying Li Ping's words here is the covert warning that the 'water weapon' could – if the PRC felt the matter to be unavoidable – be used; and this then raises the question as to why, during the 1960s, the British and Hong Kong governments agreed to participate in a venture which had as its outcome that a British colony became dependent in terms of a primary resource upon a foreign power, and one which, moreover, sought to eventually appropriate that colony to itself? The decision to enter into negotiations over purchasing a large and recurrent flow of water from China was certainly controversial at the time. Neither Britain nor the colonial government wanted Hong Kong to become overly dependent upon China for water as such reliance threatened the autonomy and future of the colony well in advance of any putative retrocession in 1997. In addition, at this time, and as previously mentioned, American foreign policy was based in part upon the premise that Hong Kong would act as an intelligence centre for the American 'war against communism' in East and South-East Asia; and so, like Britain, the US was highly concerned that the colony might be undermined by any over-dependence upon China for water. According to one source, as a consequence of such concern, some American interests – it is not clear who – even offered to fund a desalinisation operation in the colony as an alternative to the taking of China water. At the time desalinisation would have been an extremely expensive means of acquiring fresh water. Nevertheless, it appears that such a means may have been offered.[39] However, no US-backed desalinisation scheme materialised, almost certainly because such a scheme would have been impracticable, both then and for the foreseeable future. For example, although the colonial authorities in Hong Kong began building what would eventually become the largest desalinisation plant in the world in 1973, the costs proved so prohibitive that it was forced to close down only nine years later.[40]

In retrospect, therefore, it becomes clear that the 1964 water-supply agreement provided the PRC government with the basis and means to exercise eventual control over Hong Kong, and it also appears – surprisingly – that Britain and the colonial government were alacritous parties to the covenant which led ultimately to that future consequence (though the Americans, it seems, remained opposed to it). However, evidence suggests that this is not how things looked at the time to Britain, the colonial government or, for that matter, the PRC; and, in fact, all three parties seem to have considered the water-supply issue to be of second-level importance because all three believed that Hong Kong would become self-sufficient in water by the end of the 1960s, when new and very large reservoirs would come on stream.[41] This conviction led Britain and the colonial government to view the 1964 agreement with China as only a short-to-medium term expedient, and the Chinese side also shared this conviction. The depth of British and Hong Kong sanguinity over all this is also borne out by the extent to which China was allowed to build the water-relief scheme in the way that it wanted. As mentioned earlier, the scheme was planned in such a way as to take water from the East River and deposit that water in a recipient reservoir in Shenzhen, the city on the border with Hong Kong. All that came into Hong Kong would be a pipeline, which could easily be shut down. Initially, though, the British had suggested that the water could go to either the Shenzhen Reservoir or the Indus River, which was actually inside Hong Kong. Given that the issue of a 'water weapon' was being raised at the time, it surely would have been better from the British perspective if the relief water were to flow into a holding facility within Hong Kong, rather than China. However, it appears that British officials were not particularly discomforted by the eventual decision – and probable Chinese insistence – that the water went to Shenzhen.

Colonial officials in Hong Kong planning water infrastructure development in the early 1950s could not have predicted the flood of immigration engendered by the Great Leap Forward of 1958–61, and neither could officials in 1963-4 have predicted the further waves which would arrive during the Chinese Cultural Revolution of 1966–76. The idea that Hong Kong could become self-sufficient in water by the late 1960s would soon prove to be a chimera, and, in contrast, the colony became increasingly dependent upon water from its huge neighbour. However, that was not at all clear at the time of the making of *Water Comes over the Hills from the East*. There is no doubt that, amongst other things, the 1964 water-supply scheme was a major propaganda effort and triumph for the PRC, and a sizeable propaganda defeat for Britain and the colonial government. *Water Comes over the Hills from the East* was part of that effort, and associated with that triumph. However, none of the Chinese political calculation and British and colonial demission (and, as just mentioned, sang froid) that led to the 1964 agreement is evident in this chauvinistic film.

After the introductory section, *Water Comes over the Hills from the East* goes on to portray the preparatory stages of the water-supply construction project. There is extensive use of basic, crudely drawn animated maps here which often fill the whole screen, and show the proposed direction that the canal will take and sites of the pumping stations. The film as a whole uses such maps extensively as a simple though inexpensive way of structuring information within the overall narrative. We then see sequences showing the preliminary phases of the scheme, including research into its viability. The emphasis here is on the modern scientific and technical knowledge available to China, as we are shown water and soil samples analysed by white-coated laboratory technicians. Then, we see the ceremony at which the agreement to formally commission the project is finally signed. Here, at last and for the first time, we see a colonial official. However, we only see him briefly, and he remains un-named by the commentary. Throughout these sequences strident and cacophonous Chinese orchestral music evokes a sense of Chinese aptitude and determination for the task in hand, and this highly animated musical tenor leads on to, and establishes continuity, with the next section of the film. In many ways these sequences, and in fact all the sequences which went before them, can be said to end the first section of the film, as, in the next section, which shows the actual construction of the project, the mood becomes both more generally vociferous and explicitly patriotic.

What might be termed 'Part 2' of the film begins with a proclamation that a number of different Chinese cities participated enthusiastically and generously in the building of the water-supply system. We then see footage of large-scale digging machinery, including cranes which 'can save the energy of 700 people'. The emphasis here, as in the earlier sequences, is on Chinese technological prowess, but this time it is combined with evocations of scale: the *massive* amount of industrial material available and necessary for the project, and the *mammoth* labour force involved, which the film shows through long-shots, and sometimes also through photography taken from an aircraft. Some of the images of workers shown here are framed in an intentionally socialist-realist heroic style, whilst the musical accompaniment is concomitantly triumphalist. From the music now also emerges an emotional patriotic song from the period. From time to time these sequences sometimes erupt suddenly and unexpectedly into crescendos of patriotic nationalist discourse in which the communist party is explicitly referred to. However, these impulsive eruptions fit somewhat incongruously with the tone of the rest of the sequences here, which, although implicitly patriotic, do not have the same fervent tone of these exclamatory passages. Alongside all of this, and in considerable contrast, are more quiet lyrical sequences showing the landscape and – according to the commentary – 'beautiful lakes' of the area. This more gently evocative imagery provides a degree of relief from the realistic sequences of the construction activity, the didactic commentary accompanying these, and the extreme communist patriotism which is periodically propelled at the spectator. In addition, these sequences serve to reinforce others in the first part of the film which attempt to establish a sense of nostalgia for and identity with the Chinese terrain. These lightly expressive sequences end this second section of the film, and a third and decidedly peculiar final section then begins.

This third section of *Water Comes over the Hills from the East* is peculiar, and also striking, first, because it is in colour, and, second, because it brings the narrative of the film to an almost complete stop. As the section begins, the musical accompaniment seems to have become more traditionally Chinese, and this is also in tune with the sequences to come, which are concerned with aspects of habitual Chinese popular culture. What, in effect, is conjured to happen in this section of the film is that the workers employed on the project are entertained by a visit from a well-known circus troupe of the time: the Qiqihar National Circus of China. The narrative of building the waterway is discontinued now, and we are shown, instead, a series of tableaux-based entertainment events, including acrobatic displays and performing bear and dog routines. The diegetic notion here is that the workers are watching these events, and, from time to time, we do indeed see shots of said workers responding enthusiastically to the performances. The workers appear to be all male at this point, although, earlier, some shots of female workers employed in the construction project were evident. In addition to these sequences, which appear to show events being staged in front of a live audience, this section of the film contains more formally staged re-enactments which seem to be performed in a closed studio environment. It is not always entirely clear which of these is live event and which studio-based.

This section of *Water Comes over the Hills from the East* fulfills a number of different filmic and ideological functions. As argued previously, this was one of a genre of films that attempted to promote communist China through the presentation of Chinese classical and popular culture, and, also, the Chinese rural – and sometimes urban – landscape. The sort of interruption to the narrative which we see in this section of the film was, therefore, typical of the genre, and would have been expected by much of the film's audience (though this film also had a particularly *large* eventual audience on account of its politically topical subject-matter). However, the reason that the generic interruption is so extensive in this film is that the film's overall narrative structure was, to a degree, *atypical* of the genre. Most other picturesque committed films did not have the sort of strong linear narrative of *Water Comes over the Hills from the East*, which must, precisely, *tell a story from beginning to end* about one process and event: the building of the water-supply system. It is perhaps because of this atypically strong story-line that *Water Comes over the Hills from the East* is obliged to have recourse to an equally atypically extensive 'popular–cultural interruption' to that story-line: it is, in other words, an over-compensatory move back towards the more expected conventions of the genre. However, this attempt to conform to the expectations of the given audience so blatantly also imparts to the film what has been described in this chapter as a degree of peculiarity. Nevertheless, and despite this degree of idiosyncrasy, this section of *Water Comes over the Hills from the East* helps the film fulfill both its generic responsibilities and 'picturesque' ideological mission.

The second function which this section of the film fulfills is related to the first, but also to the type of audience that the film was seeking to address. A large part of that audience, in both Hong Kong and China, would have been poorly educated and probably illiterate. What this section of the film provides here, therefore, as a break from the portrayal of prosaic construction processes, occasional outbursts of pro-communist jingoistic rhetoric, and *language* – lots of it – is, precisely, visual and aural non-linguistic *entertainment*, and the sort that the audience would have been both familiar with, and easily able to accommodate. The documentary film has never been a truly popular genre, and, in order to maximise audience pleasure, what this particular film does here is actually stop being a documentary film, in the usually understood sense of that phrase, in order to *record* a series of amusements. Finally, this section of the film fulfills the film's overall ideological assignment by encouraging us to identify with the on-screen workers watching (some of) the events. Just as they watch the performances, so do we, and from the same perspectival direction, as the camera cuts between shots of the workers watching, and a central viewpoint directed towards the eye-line view of the off-screen spectator. We, the spectators, are, therefore, placed in consort with the worker-audience, and this tends to reinforce both identification with these workers, and the infrastructural and ideological mainland mission they are charged with fulfilling.

After this strange interlude, we again return to the narrative of the construction project as the film comes gradually to a close. The two themes of 'China' and the project become more intertwined now, as images of landscape intermingle with sequences concerning the project. Alongside the beautifully photographed shots of the landscape – some, again, taken from an aircraft – we are told that the project took 'less than one year to be completed', and that 'everything was done by Chinese people'. So we have China as both 'old' land and modern, technological accomplishment. There is also a sense of stillness about much of these sequences: a quietness which marks the film's gradual climb-down from its earlier peaks of high emotion. The musical sound-track has now also become more lyrical. After this we see a large inauguration ceremony held to start up the water flow into Hong Kong, and are told that the project has also provided irrigation water for Guangdong, perhaps in an attempt to inform those refugees in Hong Kong who had fled from the region that the land they yearn for is also a place they might now safely return to. The final sequences of the film take us back to Hong Kong, and also bring the film full circle. However, instead of the images of colonial deprivation and scarcity with which the film began, we now see a China-delivered water-laden arcadia, with water flowing freely through fields in which Chinese rural workers plant abundant crops. The music then builds to a final crescendo as the film comes to an end.

Leaving aside the colonial film-making, which will be discussed in the following chapter, for the moment, it could be argued that, along with *The Battle of Shanghai*, *Water Comes over the Hills from the East* is the most significant, or important, documentary film to be made in Hong Kong prior to the emergence of television-released documentary film in the early 1970s. Parts of the film are overtly ideological, and these are also the least successful: far too strident, and unlikely to have attracted many new converts to the communist cause at the time. However, the film is particularly successful in its mission of conjuring up the longed-for southern China landscape, and the quality of the landscape photography, with its subtle palate of browns and greens, is, at times, high. The documentary footage of urban and rural Hong Kong at the time, and of the Chinese workforce in Guangdong, is also both realistic and informative, and serves as important archival footage. The film is also, and as previously argued, illuminating of a certain moment in the history of colonial Hong Kong and mainland China: a hiatus between the Great Leap Forward and both the 1967 Hong Kong riots and Chinese Cultural Revolution. However, that interregnum was to end only a year later, as the Cultural Revolution broke out. *Water Comes over the Hills from the East* was made at the very end of this intermission, and this proximity to chaos lends its picturesque qualities a certain degree of naivety and guilelessness. Nevertheless, the film does speak of this brief moment of relative calm and stasis, and this sense of tranquility does come through, in much of the fabric of the film, where it is rendered as an effective lyricism.

Following the highly successful release of *Water Comes over the Hills from the East* only two further committed 'scenic' films were made during the

1960s: *Scenes of the Northern Land* (1966), and *Spring in Kunming* (1966). Both were produced by Media Chinese International. After the 1960s left-wing companies such as Feng Huang, Sun Leung and Great Wall continued to make this type of theatre-released documentary film. However, after the excesses of the Chinese Cultural Revolution, and the manifestation of those excesses within Hong Kong in 1966–7, support for communism waned in Hong Kong, and, as one consequence of this, the audience for these leftist documentary films also declined, as, despite their attempted appearance to the contrary, they became more widely perceived to be ideological and manipulative.[42] Other factors also had a role to play in this decline, though, most notably the continued rise and downward spread of consumer capitalism in Hong Kong, and the emergence of the openly anti-communist Shaw Brothers and Cathay Studios as dominant producers within the Hong Kong film industry. In response to all this, many of the left-wing companies were forced to moderate the political content of their films, and this affected the tone and style of the documentaries which appeared in the late 1960s and 1970s. These still consisted of the usual mixture of depictions of scenic spots, acrobatic troupes, or exotic ethnic tribes in China. However, the ideological edge of such films had become diluted, as the audience turned away, and the producers chased an audience becoming less politicised in terms of leftist sympathy. Nevertheless, even in this less ideological form, or perhaps also because of it, the tradition of promoting China through this sort of scenic documentary retained a degree of popularity with the Hong Kong audience until as late as the mid-1980s. In 1982 four of the left-wing companies which made these documentaries – Great Wall, Feng Huang, Sun Luen, and Chung Yuen – merged to form Sil-Metropole. Today, though a Hong Kong-registered company, Sil-Metropole is essentially managed by the mainland Chinese Government, and is just one of the mainland's many propaganda outlets in Hong Kong. Currently, *Water Comes over the Hills from the East*, a film greatly in need of restoration and greater access, languishes as a washed-out, un-subtitled print, only available for viewing in the private premises of Sil-Metrople, and at a hefty price. However, and irrespective of viewing fees, *Water Comes over the Hills from the East* is also regarded as a 'sensitive' film by Sil-Metropole, and viewings are, accordingly, further restricted on account of this.

CONCLUSIONS

It can be argued that the documentary film production discussed in this chapter was influenced by two major factors and contexts. The first of these was an ongoing struggle between pro- and anti-communist groups. However, it seems that the documentary films made as part of that struggle were all pro-communist. In addition, these films carried out their ideological projects obliquely, within scenic 'picturesque' formats intended to promote generalised notions of China, rather than extoll the ruling communist regime. This was very different from the militant stance adopted by a late 1930s film such as *The Battle of Shanghai*, which was discussed in the previous chapter of this book. Of course, the contexts here were unalike in that, in the late 1930s, committed documentary films such as *The Battle of Shanghai* were promoting the cause of China as a whole in a perilous war–crisis context, whilst, in the post-war period, the leftist films discussed here were promoting the cause of the *communist* PRC in a less immediately life-threatening peace-time and Cold-War context, and one also riven by divisions between Chinese leftists and rightists, undecided Hongkongers and the KMT. This latter context required a difference in tone from the pre-war, and anything approaching the strident tenor of a film such as *The Battle of Shanghai* would have proved counter-productive in winning hearts and minds for the communist cause in the 1950s and 1960s – and, in any case, such a film would have been banned in colonial Hong Kong. Instead, what was required was the more covertly manipulative ideological pictorialism of a film such as *Water Comes over the Hills from the East*.

The second factor to influence the development of the documentary film in Hong Kong after the Second World War was the continuing growth and consolidation of a local Hong Kong Chinese culture. The popularity of documentary films on local film stars, opera stars and other celebrities is testament to that. As argued in the previous chapter, a local Hong Kong Chinese culture began to form on a more substantial scale during the 1930s, and one of the main vehicles for this was the Cantonese sound feature-film. Such films continued to be made in numbers during the post-war period, but, by the late 1960s, had been virtually eliminated from the screen by the dominant Mandarin cinemas of the Shaw Brothers, Cathay and others. There were many reasons for this but two of the most important were that the larger size of the Mandarin market, and power of the Mandarin corporations, made it almost inevitable that Mandarin film-making would eventually come to dominate. However, if a local Hong Kong Chinese cultural identity was removed from representation in the feature film it found a home in the documentary film production of the period. Consequently, whilst, in 1969, the local audience in Hong Kong might watch a Mandarin Shaw costume-feature film set in a northern location, they could also watch *Connie Chan Po-chu Returns from Her Southern Tour*, and the *Miss Cinderella and Miss Songbirds Contests*.[43] No masterpiece arose here, of course, but that is not to gainsay the importance of these films for their audience. In addition to these and other films, however, a different sort of film altogether had entered the scene by 1960: the British colonial documentary film; and this will be the subject of the following chapter.

NOTES

1. Lu, Ping, former Head of the State Council's Hong Kong and Macau Affairs Office, *South China Morning Post*, 12 October 2012.
2. Tsang, Steve, *A Modern History of Hong Kong* (Hong Kong: Hong Kong University Press, 2009), p. 125.
3. Ibid. p. 132.
4. Fu, Poshek and Desser, David, *The Cinema of Hong Kong: History, Arts, Identity* (Cambridge: Cambridge University Press, 2000), p. 215.
5. Tsang, *A Modern History*, p. 141.
6. Porter, Bernard, *The Lion's Share: A Short History of British Imperialism, 1850–1995* (London and New York: Longman, 1996), p. 331.
7. Hyam, Ronald, *Britain's Declining Empire: The Road to Decolonialisation, 1918–1968* (Cambridge and New York: Cambridge University Press, 2006), p. 139.
8. MacCabe, Colin, 'To Take Ship to India and See a Naked Man Spearing Fish in Blue Water: Watching Films to Mourn the End of Empire', in Grieveson, Lee and MacCabe, Colin (eds), *Empire and Film* (London and New York: BFI and Palgrave Macmillan, 2011), p. 13.
9. Tsang, *A Modern History*, p. 168.
10. Chu, Tinchi, *Hong Kong Cinema: Coloniser, Motherland and Self* (New York: Routledge Curzon, 2003), pp. 4–5.
11. Havinden, Michael and Meredith, David, *Colonialism and Development: Britain and its Tropical Colonies* (New York: Routledge, 1993), p. 312.
12. Carroll, John, M., *A Concise History of Hong Kong* (Hong Kong: Hong Kong University Press, 2011), p. 160.
13. Tsang, *A Modern History*, p. 204.
14. Carroll, *A Concise History*, p. 160.
15. Tsang, *A Modern History*, p. 199.
16. Hyam, Ronald, *Britain's Declining Empire*, p. 244.
17. Havinden and Meredith, *Colonialism*, p. 317.
18. Tsang, *A Modern History*, p. 182.
19. Carroll, *A Concise History*, p. 159.
20. Tsang, *A Modern History*, p. 184.
21. Ibid. p. 190.
22. Carroll, *A Concise History*, p. 159.
23. Childs, David, *Britain since 1945* (London: Routledge, 1986), p. 170.
24. Stokes, Lisa Odham and Hoover, Michael, *City on Fire: Hong Kong Cinema* (London: Verso, 1999), p. 21.
25. Teo, Stephen, *Hong Kong Cinema: The Extra Dimensions* (London: British Film Institute, 1997), p. 24.
26. Ibid. p. 16.
27. Stokes and Hoover, *City on Fire*, p. 21.
28. This is the English translation of the title found in the *Filmography* of the Hong Kong Film Archive, and, although awkward, will be employed here.
29. Kwok, Ching-ling (ed.), *Hong Kong Filmography, vol. IV, 1953–1959* (Hong Kong: Kong Film Archive, 2003), p. 426.
30. Kwok, Ching-ling (ed.), *Hong Kong Filmography, vol. V, 1960–1964* (Hong Kong: Kong Film Archive, 2005), pp. 363–5.
31. Clayton, David, '"Water Famished Hong Kong": The International Political Economy of

Water Supplies in Hong Kong. 1960–64', pp. 12–13. Unpublished research paper by Dr David Clayton of the University of Bath, presented to Ian Aitken in May 2013.

32. Ibid. p. 7.
33. Ibid. p. 9.
34. Water Supplies Department of the Government of the Hong Kong SAR, *Milestones of Hong Kong Water Supply* (Hong Kong: Hong Kong Government Printer, 2011), p. 23.
35. Clayton, 'Water Famished Hong Kong', p. 7.
36. Ibid. p. 10.
37. Ibid. p. 11.
38. Water Supplies Department of the Government of the Hong Kong SAR, *Milestones*, p. 23.
39. 'Why Hong Kong Depends on the Dongjiang Water', *Ming Pao*, 8 August 2010.
40. Water Supplies Department of the Government of the Hong Kong SAR, *Milestones*, p. 27.
41. Clayton, 'Water Famished Hong Kong', p. 13.
42. Fonoroff, Paul, 'A Brief History of Hong Kong Cinema' (Hong Kong: Chinese University of Hong Kong), www.cuhk.edu.hk/rrt/pdf/e.
43. Kwok, Ching-ling (ed.), *Hong Kong Filmography, vol. VI, 1965–1969* (Hong Kong: Kong Film Archive, 2007), p. 284.

CHAPTER 3

Colonial Film: The Development of Official Film-making in Hong Kong, 1945–73, the Hong Kong Film Unit (1959-73) and *This is Hong Kong* (1961)

Colonial film-making, in the guise of British official film-making, as opposed to the early entrepreneurial British/US/French film-making of the 1898–1914 period, developed slowly in Hong Kong over the period from 1945 to the abolition of the Hong Kong Film Unit (HKFU) in 1973; and, in order to understand the reasons for that slow progression it will first be necessary to consider some problems and impediments that had already developed prior to and during the Second World War, problems which were related to an antagonism between a 'Colonial Office' (CO) and 'Griersonian' tradition. The term 'Griersonian' is often used as an abbreviation for the British documentary film movement of the 1930s and 1940s. There are problems associated with such abbreviation, principally, that the movement as a whole becomes subsumed under the name of its leader: John Grierson. Nevertheless, in order to be terminologically concise, and in the absence of suitable alternative terminology, the term 'Griersonian' will be employed here, but in a global sense, not to refer to matters very close to Grierson himself, but to the tradition of the British documentary film movement as a whole. Such employment is warranted here because this chapter is to a considerable extent concerned with an opposition between a general 'Griersonian' and 'CO' approach to official film-making. Put succinctly, if epigrammatically, the Griersonian approach involves making documentary films which attempt to advance the progress of democratic-liberal development across a broad filmic front, whilst the CO approach involves the production of much simpler films which make specific, pragmatic interventions, usually in order to consolidate a more conservative status quo. The two do not, and could not ever, square, and what we have here is, to an extent, an incongruity between reformism and conservatism.

The British documentary film movement of the 1930s was a social-reformist movement committed to using the documentary film as an instrument for social reform. If not outright socialists, the film-makers of the movement were at least liberals and social-democrats. They were not social or political conservatives. In the Empire Marketing Board Film Unit (EMB Film Unit) of 1930–4, and the General Post Office Film Unit (GPO Film Unit) of 1934–40, the film-makers of the documentary film movement made a number of important films which raised up the image of the lower classes, and promoted an agenda of social reform. However, this did not exactly endear them to the conservative (with both a lower and upper-case 'C') civil servants who employed them; and neither did it impress film producers within the commercial documentary film industry who regarded the films of the movement as an example of unnecessary government intervention within what ought to be a commercial market. As a consequence of these animosities, when the Second World War broke out in September 1939, the film-makers of the GPO Film Unit found themselves deliberately kept out of the newly formed Ministry of Information (MoI), which was then charged with supervising the production of propaganda, including film propaganda, as part of the war effort.

Whilst, the GPO Film Unit film-makers were initially kept out of the MoI, and despite their complaints over the matter, it quickly became clear to many that some sort of central film-making unit would eventually have to be established within the MoI. This caused the CO concern, because such a film unit might also have ultimate control over official film-making in the colonies. The CO was also particularly apprehensive here because, unlike staffing within the highly conservative CO, the MoI was staffed to a large extent by personnel from outside the traditional civil service. This departure from the standard model was also evident within the Films Division of the MoI, which, in addition to employing a 'glittering array of intellectuals', eventually housed the Crown Film Unit, staffed by Griersonians long mistrusted by civil servants.[1] In response to this situation, the CO attempted to inaugurate its own film unit, the Colonial Film Unit (CFU), in late 1939. However, the problem for the CO was that, because the MoI was now the central body responsible for propaganda and official information output, the CFU would have to operate under the aegis of the MoI, rather than the CO. The first director of the CFU, William Sellers, had, therefore, no choice other than to operate his Unit under the overall command, and alien terrain, of Films Division.

Initially, the fears of the CO were allayed by the fact that the first Head of Films Division, Joseph Ball, was a hard-headed conservative traditionalist who had also played a part in keeping the GPO Film Unit film-makers out of the MoI in the first instance. However, the abrasive Ball was dismissed in December 1939 and replaced by the more urbane Sir Kenneth Clark who quickly, and quite logically, initiated a process of incorporating the GPO Film Unit, then arguably the highest-profile film unit in the country, into Films Division, an event which occurred on 1 April 1940.[2] Then, in December 1940, the GPO Film Unit was given the new title of Crown Film Unit, and was formally recognised to be the central war-time official film-making organisation. The situation had now moved away from that desired by the CO. Both Crown Film Unit and CFU remained under the management of Films Division, but a Films Division within which authority had shifted in a Griersonian direction. Further rifts now developed between Crown and the CFU, principally over the type of official film that the MoI ought to make. The 'conservative' 'CO-CFU' position was that MoI films should have cost-efficient limited objectives. However, members of the documentary film movement held to the belief that the official film should employ an advanced array of filmic possibilities in order to 'present an apt picture of our democracy'.[3] To them, the CO-CFU position represented a betrayal of the reform-minded 'documentary idea'.[4]

Real enmities emerged here between the Griersonians and the CO-CFU, enmities which continued long after the war, and played a role in shaping the diffusion of the British official film into the colonies and dominions of the British Commonwealth. As part of that diffusion, and for a variety of reasons, the Griersonians tended to end up in the larger territories, the CO-CFU in the smaller. Whilst, therefore, the Griersonian 'documentary idea' inspired 'growing points in . . . Australia, India, Egypt, New Zealand and Malaya', no such growing point took root in the small, peripheral tropical colony of Hong Kong;[5] and it was, in contrast, the tradition represented by Sellers and the CFU which was to shape the growth of the official film within the Crown Colony. This growth was also directly and forcefully affected by the split which broke out between the CO-CFU and Griersonian camps in the early 1940s.

Prior to 1945 the colonial government in Hong Kong did not possess a public relations office. In addition, no official film-making took place within the colony, and no British official films were screened there either. Up to that point in time Hong Kong civil service mandarins were still possessed of the sort of old-school small-government mentality that has already been referred to several times in this book, and they saw no need for any kind of government-funded public relations organisation, much less film-making unit. That was, however, to change after 1945. During the immediate post-war period, and following the trauma of Japanese occupation and humbling reality of British imperial defeat, an enlivened local Chinese population was no longer prepared to tolerate the sort of colonial overbearance which had prevailed prior to the war. This new more impulsive situation then forced the old-style Crown Colony to respond in a number of ways, and one of these involved the establishment of a Public Relations Office (PRO) in May 1946. Between 1946 and 1950 the PRO dealt mainly with the press, though, from 1946 onwards, it also organised occasional showings of one-reel documentary films made by the MoI and the Central Office of Information (COI) (the organisation which replaced the MoI following the ending of the war).[6] Up to 1950 the PRO remained a relatively small-scale affair. However from late 1950 it entered a period of expansion. On 1 September of that year John Lawrence Murray was appointed as Public Relations Officer. Murray would be a crucial appointment, and would stay in post until 1963, bringing continuity, but also an acute antipathy towards the Griersonian tradition. Soon after his appointment as permanent Public Relations Officer, Murray looked into the possibility of establishing a film unit in Hong Kong. However, he quickly came under the influence of the CO-CFU and William Sellers. At that time, the largest official film unit in the South-East Asia region was the Malayan Film Unit (MFU). However, the MFU was then staffed by Griersonians. Murray, who, at that point, had no knowledge of Grierson's British documentary film movement, and, therefore, felt no antipathy yet towards the MFU, initially believed that the Unit could help him to establish an official film unit in Hong Kong. However, he was soon persuaded against this by Sellers and other officials at the CO.

When the CO learned that official film-making might start up in Hong Kong, and that the MFU might become involved in this, they became alarmed. At the time, the position of the CFU was financially precarious, and it had been hoped that Hong Kong might afford a new area of activity for the ailing unit. The CO was also keen to ensure that any film-making which did emerge in the colony would not fall under the influence of Griersonians at the MFU. Sellers probably started to correspond with Murray over these matters around January 1951, and, from that point onwards, Murray came to associate himself completely with Sellers. In June 1951 Murray travelled to London to meet Sellers and other CO officials. There he discussed the possibility of setting up a film unit in Hong Kong, and Murray's expectation was that a film-maker might be seconded from the CFU, an idea backed 'unreservedly' by Sellers.[7] Even at this point, though, Murray held on to the possibility of MFU involvement. Whilst he was in London Murray also received an unexpected offer of funding from the World Health Organisation (WHO) to develop Hong Kong into a hub for the production and dissemination of health-related documentary film. Murray rejected the offer, partly because he needed documentary film-making in Hong Kong to have a wider remit than that. However, the influence of Sellers was also a factor here, as becomes clear when, writing in retrospect in March 1952, Murray proclaimed that, with the WHO offer, he 'could see us being saddled with a young Crown Film Unit (or, perhaps worse still, Malayan F.U.) of our own . . . So I dug my heels in more firmly than ever'.[8] Murray did not want a large film unit staffed by experienced film-makers – possibly even recruited from Crown or – 'worse' – the MFU. Beyond that, the language Murray chose to use indicates that he had already, under the influence of Sellers, formed an antipathy towards the Griersonian approach.

This antipathy had also been stoked up a month earlier, in February 1952, when Murray met Tom Hodge. Hodge is the third most important figure in this story, and the 'troika' of Sellers, Murray and Hodge would come to have a crucial influence upon the development of the official film in Hong Kong. Hodge had joined the Foreign Office in 1939, and both he and Murray were part of the wave of new appointments taken on to support the war effort. Initially, Hodge worked at the MoI between 1939 and 1942. There he met both Sellers and the film-makers of the documentary film movement. From 1942 to 1951 Hodge worked for the MoI and the British Information Service, the latter charged with disseminating pro-British propaganda in America. Hodge was in charge of film publicity. In 1951 he was appointed in Singapore to co-ordinate official film production there. When he met Murray in February 1952, Hodge indicated that he had considerable respect for both Sellers and the CFU. Hodge and Murray also struck up an immediate rapport, Murray finding Hodge 'refreshingly realistic'.[9] The term 'realistic' is significant here, and Murray's understanding of Hodge's position as 'realistic' would come to shape the later development of the official film in Hong Kong. Hodge's 'refreshing realism' came with a warning:

> His warning was in effect: Beware that you don't employ some bright young director or producer who is more interested in making a name for himself than in producing the kind of film that you want in Hong Kong . . . who will want to produce one prize-winning documentary once a year in preference to a number of little films, none of them perhaps in the great cinema class, but which will do the job you want done . . . Hodge was full of praise for Sellers and the integrity of the CFU, but discouraging about the likelihood of recruiting an expert – particularly from the defunct Crown – who would put the job before his own career.[10]

So, Hodge warned Murray against appointing someone from Crown, and this reinforced the messages which Murray had been receiving from Sellers and others at the CO since 1950. Murray also fully took on board Hodge's comments about official film-making being about the production of 'a number of little films', when, in January 1955, and on being given the go-ahead to investigate the possibility of appointing a 'Films Officer', he wrote, in views indistinguishable from those expressed by Hodge in 1952, that:

I don't, above all, want a bright young arty Director who thinks he is going to make a little annual gem for the Venice or Edinburgh Festivals and lets the rest go hang. I want a real worker interested in films as a medium of propaganda and teaching who is prepared to make simple straight-forward documentary and educational films. And plenty of them! If, in the run of work, he happens once in a while to produce a little masterpiece, so much the better. But that is not the primary purpose of his appointment.[11]

Murray was eventually to put this CO-CFU and Hodge-derived stance on the production of 'simple straight-forward' films into practice in Hong Kong.

In 1955 Murray returned to London to attend a Colonial Information Officers Conference. There he again met Sellers to discuss setting up a Hong Kong film unit. The discussions proved inconclusive because of ongoing equivocation over the post by the Hong Kong financial authorities. Nevertheless, Sellers did introduce Murray to the person who would eventually become the first head of the Hong Kong Film Unit, Ben Hart, then working as a film director with the Federal Information Service Film Unit in Lagos, Nigeria. Further delays in appointing Hart then occurred, mainly caused by a reorganisation of the PRO, which eventually became the Government Information Services (GIS) in 1959, with Murray as its first Director. Just prior to that, in November 1958, Murray had presented a report on the proposed PRO reorganisation in which he expressed his opinions on the remit of government public relations operations in Hong Kong. Murray argued that such operations must now become more proactive, insistent and assertive. In terms of film, and in line with this more adamant stance, Murray proposed a Hong Kong film unit which would make:

prestige documentary films in colour, running time 15 to 20 minutes . . . at least one a year . . . We need initially a good general film dealing with the Colony as a whole, and this should probably be brought up to date and re-angled at least every three years. Our industrial expansion, specific aspects of that expansion, our tourist attractions, our achievements in resettlement and rehousing . . . can all be considered for either full length prestige films or as magazine items.[12]

The evolution of the PRO into a larger and better funded GIS now made it possible to establish a film unit able to make such public relations films, and the Hong Kong Film Unit that Murray had sought to establish from as early as 1951 finally limped into being, thirteen years after the formation of the nearby MFU, and eighteen years after the establishment of the first colonial film unit, the New Zealand Film Unit, in 1941.

THE HONG KONG FILM UNIT (1959–73)

From the outset, the HKFU had to contend with difficult financial and other restrictions, and this was particularly the case over the initial period of 1959–63. The grounds for those restrictions were also similar to those which had kept the Unit from becoming established until 1959: a civil service antipathy towards government public relations activity in general, and official film-making in particular; a continued emphasis upon small government and tight budgetary control; and hostility from the commercial film sector in Hong Kong. These limiting factors came from outside the HKFU. However, there were also internal constraints, largely emanating from the figure of Murray, whose conservatism and anti-Griersonianism continued to ensure that the HKFU produced 'simple straight-forward films'. In addition to this ideological bent, though, as a senior civil servant, one of Murray's chief responsibilities was to ensure that the HKFU operated within tightly controlled budgetery constraints, and his guide in this was also Tom Hodge, who, in 1954, had boasted that, in the MFU, he ran the 'cheapest film unit in the world'.[13] As a consequence of all these factors the basic output of the HKFU in its first few years were short, instructional black-and-white 16 mm sound films, in both English and Cantonese, which eventually came to be screened – under compulsion – in the colony's sixty-eight cinemas, after the commercials, and before the main feature presentations. In addition to such theatrical screenings, these films were also shown by mobile teams in the colony's immigrant-crammed sprawling resettlement estates. The evidence suggests that such screenings were relatively popular, as photographs taken at the time show large crowds of enthusiastic spectators. However, and despite a potentially large local audience, financial constraints were such that the films made over this early period could only cover their costs if such costs were kept to an absolute minimum.

In addition to these short and relatively limited films, the strategy for film production which Murray had laid out in his 1958 report establishing the GIS had also envisioned the production of one-off 'prestige films'. The idea here was that production of such longer more expensive films would be outsourced to commercial companies who would be better placed to both make them and turn in a profit, which might then be funneled back into the struggling, underfunded Film Unit. Murray had begun to explore this possibility from as early as 1959 and in doing so turned, perhaps inevitably, given the circumscribed film-making world that he operated in, to his old friend Tom Hodge, who, by then, had left the MFU to take up a senior position in the Singapore branch of the Cathay Organisastion. During the 1950s and 1960s Cathay developed into one of the major companies within the Hong Kong, Singapore and Malaysian film industries, and, by the early 1960s, Hodge was Director of both the company's feature-film operation in Singapore, Cathay-Keris Films, and its documentary film production arm, Cathay Film Services, which also had a branch in Hong Kong. Before he retired in 1963 Murray would oversee the production of the first 'prestige' film produced by the HKFU, *This is Hong Kong* (1961), which was outsourced to Hodge and Cathay Film Services.

Following Murray's retirement in 1963, his deputy, Nigel Watt, a long-standing Foreign Office civil servant, was appointed as head of GIS. Watt would come to play a quite different role in the development of the HKFU than had been the case with Murray, allowing the Unit more leeway, and appointing the sort of 'creative' people that Murray would never have countenanced. One of these was Brian Salt, who replaced Ben Hart as Films Officer around January 1965. It appears that Hart had largely worked conservatively under Murray's tutelage until the latter's retirement, and, after that, he continued to keep a relatively low profile until he left the Unit himself. Certainly, over the 1960–4 period, no major developments seem to have occurred within the Film Unit, and no major film appeared other than *This is Hong Kong*. That was, however, to change under Salt, who had a much wider background in film than had been the case with Hart, whose career had been almost entirely spent in the sequestered world of British official colonial film-making. Salt had been connected to Gaumont British Instructional Film in the early 1950s, directing two films shot in Singapore: *Citizen of Singapore* (1950), and *Study of a Port* (1951). These were shot in indirect association with the Malayan Film Unit during a period in which the MFU still retained a certain Griersonian character. In the early to mid-1950s Salt was also appointed to the National Film Board of Canada in an attempt to improve technical standards of film-making there, particularly in the field of animation.[14] The invitation came because Salt had earlier made a modernist animation film entitled *Equation: $X + X = o$*, in 1936.[15] Although there appears to be a Griersonian connection here, it seems that Salt was not particularly close to the Griersonians who then worked in the NFB.[16] As his career developed, it also seems that Salt turned away from the documentary film and towards fiction film-making. For example, in 1958 he made the drama-documentary children's film *Toto and the Poachers*, which was awarded a prize at the Venice Film Festival of that year; and, just before coming to Hong Kong, he was employed as a director on the British television police series *Gideon's Way*.[17] Salt was, in short, the sort of person (non-civil servant, non-CO or FO) that Murray would never have considered for appointment.

Salt's first major production at the HKFU – *The Magic Stone: A Legend from Hong Kong* (1965) – was an exercise in drama-documentary. Far removed from the general Griersonian style, and designed to be another HKFU 'prestige' film, like the 1961 *This is Hong Kong*, *Magic Stone* was a 24-minute colour film which could be compared in format to some of the 'story documentaries' produced by the GPO and Crown Film Units during the 1930s and 1940s.

However, there the comparison ends. With its mixture of quaint local legends, melodramatic scenarios, scenic backdrops and fictional characterisation, *Magic Stone* was intended to act as a means of attracting tourists to Hong Kong, and had no social, and very little aesthetic, significance.

Salt stayed at the HKFU until 1968. There are conflicting reports as to why he left. One source claimed that he was approached by Stanley Kubrick, who wanted him to join the team making *2001: A Space Odyssey* (1969). Kubrick apparently wished to set up an animation laboratory for the film in London in which Salt would have a prominent position. However, it has also been claimed that Salt turned down the Kubrick offer because he wanted to stay in Hong Kong, and left because he had reached official retirement age.[18] Another reason, though, may have been *Magic Stone*, which was not only panned by critics as a 'flop' and 'embarrassment', but also managed to recoup only $5,000 of its $40,000 production cost.[19] This was a huge loss for a British colonial official film and created a considerable scandal at the time, leading Salt, and, through him, also Nigel Watt, to come under considerable criticism and reprimand.[20] Whilst the reasons for his departure may remain unclear, though, there is no doubt that Salt oversaw some of the best years of the HKFU, from 1965 to 1968. During this period Salt moved the style of the HKFU significantly away from Murray's Hodge-influenced approach of making many routine films as cheaply as possible. For example, speaking about *Magic Stone* just before its release, he asserted that:

> Increasingly . . . Governments and other organisations who use the film as a vehicle for publicity recognise the need to interest the widest possible audience in a more general way than straightforward documentaries can do. This is the first experiment of this kind . . . Although Hong Kong has a tremendously successful film industry, its market is almost exclusively in Asia and mostly in South-East Asia. The potential of Hong Kong to provide interesting stories, first-class performers and skilled technicians has yet to be properly realised in the western world.[21]

Clearly, Salt had major aspirations for the HKFU, and his 'experimental' approach to official film-making was also very different to that endorsed during the Hart-Murray-Hodge era.

After Salt left, Charles Wang took over as Films Officer at the HKFU. Wang was an accomplished photographer who brought an enhanced visual documentary style to the films produced by the Unit. However, it seems that Salt's departure had a major impact on morale at the Unit, as Wang only stayed a few months in the job himself, resigning in late 1968. After this dual departure significant output at the HKFU declined. The final Films Officer, Albert Young – like Wang, Chinese – presided over this decline, which, according to one source, occurred mainly because the HKFU was then staffed by 'less talented personnel who brought to their task pedestrian skills that were producing diminished returns'.[22] However, and as will be argued later, this is not the whole story, and Young, in particular, was to make one of the most affective films to come out of the HKFU: the 1972 *The Sea and the Sky*.

It is not entirely clear exactly when the Film Unit was disbanded. It was certainly still making films as late as 1973, though that may have been the final year of the Unit. It may also be that *The Sea and the Sky* (1972) was the last substantial film to be made by the Unit. However, shorter films were also made in 1972 and 1973, and the Unit's newsreel, *Hong Kong Today*, was still being produced in 1973. For example, issue no. '68' of the newsreel, on the building of the new Hong Kong airport, was produced that year. In January 1972 the GIS also cites the Unit having a 'recurrent cost of $500,000', indicating a still substantial level of activity.[23] However, a significant amount of this expenditure now went into outsourcing films, and, by 1971, most major HKFU films were outsourced. The major production of 1971 was *Hong Kong Style*, produced by London-based Anthony Gilkison Associates. This film was, apparently, distributed 'worldwide'.[24] In 1973 *Teaching English as a Second Language* was also made by the Hong Kong-based Farkas Productions Company. This film, which, like *Hong Kong Style*, was expected to be 'used all over the world', may well have been the last film to be commissioned by the HKFU.[25]

The HKFU, which had taken so long to come into being, in the end only enjoyed a few years of real growth before its gradual 'decline' from 1968 to 1973. The central reason for its collapse was staffing. Although eventually well equipped technically, the Unit still only had a staff of four people when Salt took over in 1965. By 1968 Young was the only senior figure, and a staffing sheet from 1970–1 shows only Young, an administrator (by then the only Caucasian in the Unit, and probably installed to look after the Unit because Young was not an experienced manager), and four junior staff.[26] This was an impossibly small number to run the Unit. Thus, as television emerged in the late 1960s and early 1970s, the Unit contracted, and, whilst its annual running cost in 1972 remained as high as $500,000, this had already been overtaken by the television-based Education Television Unit and Radio Hong Kong Television, whose combined budget in 1972 was $1.8 million.

THE FILMS OF THE HKFU AND *THIS IS HONG KONG* (1961)

Whilst it is difficult to calculate the exact number, it may be that around 300 films of all types were made by the HKFU over the period between 1959 and

1973. GIS documents dating from 1963 claim that the HKFU had produced some 'thirty films' by that date.[27] However, beyond this figure, and up to 1973, only a rough approximation of the overall number can be made, and 300 appears a reasonable estimation. Three distinct kinds of output can also be identified here. The first category of output consisted of a large number of short films, some as brief as one minute in length, made entirely for local consumption. Some of these were made in both English and Cantonese, but the majority were in Cantonese only. The subject-matter of these short films – and also the newsreel which will be referred to shortly – illustrates Hong Kong government priorities at the time. For example, the largest group of films by far concerned issues related to security, policing and public order. After this, public construction projects, such as the building of reservoirs, bridges, housing estates and airports are prominent; whilst a third category concerned recreational activities of various sorts. In contrast, far fewer films were made on subjects such as public health, education and social welfare; this reflects the small-government model which still prevailed in Hong Kong during the 1960s. In this latter respect, whilst depicting government activities, these films also frequently stressed the role of voluntary agencies and religious societies, rather than government, in overcoming social difficulties.

From June 1967 the HKFU also produced monthly newsreel, ten minutes or so long, entitled *Hong Kong Today*. Occasionally, longer editions of up to twenty minutes were produced. The series ran up to at least 1973, producing, therefore, around eighty or so editions, and was, consequently, a substantial undertaking. From 1968 this was probably the main activity of the Unit. Evidence suggests that the newsreel was also popular as, by April 1968, local cinemas were asking for eighty copies per month.[28] As mentioned previously, mobile projection teams also took the newsreel to the resettlement estates, where it was also popular. Produced in both English and Cantonese, with even the English versions having Chinese subtitles, *Hong Kong Today* proved very effective as a means of both communicating information to the local public and helping develop a sense of more integrated Hong Kong identity. For example, issue number eleven, in April 1968, shows:

> The recent delivery by helicopter of an electricity generator to the remote island of Po Toi, which has never had electricity . . . [and] . . . a famous Chinese opera school rehearsing a Chinese opera about the legendary monkey Sun Hou Tse at the picturesque Tiger Balm Garden.[29]

This mixture of colonial news and items on local culture and society was typical of the approach adopted throughout *Hong Kong Today*, and it is possible that this series played some role in gaining support for the colonial government during the troubled years of 1967–8. Generally speaking, the overall subject-content of *Hong Kong Today* was similar to the 200 or so short films referred to earlier.

The third major form of output to emerge from the HKFU, and the one which this chapter is most concerned with, is a relatively small group of longer, bigger-budget films aimed at the overseas, as well as the Hong Kong, audience, which include the 'prestige' films which Murray had referred to in his 1959 memorandum setting out the future strategy and policy of the HKFU. Like *Magic Stone*, most of these films were made within the HKFU, at least up until 1970, after which more were outsourced. As mentioned, the Film Unit's first major effort, *This Is Hong Kong* (1961), was so outsourced. However, that year the Unit also made *Princess Alexandra in Hong Kong* (a film whose title is self-explanatory) in-house. This was followed by *Sea Festivals of Hong Kong* (1963), a 20-minute long film on sea and harbour activities in Hong Kong. Although largely celebratory in tone, an element of social-realism also arises when this film depicts the Hong Kong boat people: impoverished ethnic minorities who live and work on their ramshackle craft. The film premiered in London for two months and was distributed in the UK by MGM. Directed by Ben Hart, it deployed a commentary by Wilfred Vaughn-Thomas.[30] In 1963 the Film Unit also made *The Building of the Shek Pik Reservoir*, a film whose account of the process of construction of the reservoir from beginning to end brings it close to a Griersonian format. Following these two films in 1963 the HKFU made two 1965 films on the Hong Kong government rehousing programme: *A Race against People* and *Made in Hong Kong*. These two 13-minute films tackle the problem of housing shortage in a way that would become typical of the HKFU approach to the problem: emphasising the sheer numbers of people involved, the squalor of the squatter encampments, and the 'new life' emerging for the immigrants through the development of government-funded social amenities. However, and as will be argued in more detail in relation to *This is Hong Kong*, the picture presented here is somewhat misleading, as, even as late as 1965, government policy was still based on encouraging local organisations and charities to resolve the problem of the immigrants as much as possible, with government doing and spending the minimum necessary. One of the chief causes of the 1967 riots in Hong Kong was the poor housing situation, and it was only after the riots that the government took the housing issue as seriously as it clearly merited.

In 1966 the Film Unit made *Princess Alexandra and Lord Snowden Come to Hong Kong*, and a one-off review, *Hong Kong Today Review*, which provided a model for the regular monthly newsreel *Hong Kong Today*, which commenced in 1967. The year 1967 also saw the appearance of Brian Salt's two major and anachronistic efforts: *The Magic Stone*, and *Report to the Gods*. Both of these eccentric films are based on a drama-documentary style at odds with general HKFU output, and both attempt to link an informational remit to local

Cantonese legends and religion. Salt may be given credit here for attempting to engage with the local culture, but both films are mainly escapist, and it must also be remembered that they were both produced in the riot year of 1967. This was hardly an appropriate response to the crisis. Despite their large budgets, particularly for *Magic Stone*, these films also do not appear to be particularly technically accomplished. According to critics at the time, the HKFU was well equipped by 1967. However, those same critics also wondered why, given this, *Magic Stone* and *Report to the Gods* were so technically poor.[31] These films also bring to mind the sort of surreal sensibility that Alberto Cavalcanti brought to the British documentary film movement in the 1930s. However, Salt's films completely lack the ironic undertones of Cavalcanti's work.

The year 1967 also saw the appearance of *The Year of the Ram* (the ram being one of the signs in the Chinese calendar). However, this was not a single film but, rather, a collection of short, one minute or so long, review pieces. Much more substantial was *Suicide on H.P.* (Charles Wang, 1967), a film about drug addiction amongst the Chinese population, and possibly Wang's first film as director. Because of its subject-matter, this film was meant primarily for local consumption and was screened both in the local cinemas and by the HKFU mobile units in the resettlement estates. It was also – and curiously – put forward to be shown in film festivals outside of Hong Kong, despite being made only in Cantonese. In 1968 it appears that only two long films were made by the HKFU, and both encapsulate the colonial government's escapist approach to dealing with the political problems of that period via the official film. *Hong Kong Horizons* is a light-hearted look at the colony's landscape, whilst *Seeing Hong Kong in a Week* was specifically intended to distract attention away from the context of the 1967 riots. According to the *South China Morning Post*, *Seeing Hong Kong in a Week* was:

A fast-moving film, jazzed up both in tempo and musical background . . . produced during last year's troubles to prove the Colony was still a going concern.[32]

It is worth bearing in mind that, in addition to these two films, the monthly editions of the newsreel *Hong Kong Today* that appeared in 1967 and 1968 also failed to mention the riots. This can hardly be said to constitute an attempt to use the official film in an interventionist, reform-oriented, 'Griersonian' way.

The appearance of the successful *Hong Kong Today*, and financial debacle of *The Magic Stone*, both of which occurred in 1967, may have been responsible for the decline in overall production which took place at the Film Unit in 1968. As late as April 1968, however, that deterioration had certainly not been anticipated, as plans were then still in place to produce four new films that year: 'Village without Men', on problems relating to villages in which the male population had left to work elsewhere; 'Guardians of Law', on the Hong Kong Police Force; 'Flying High', on the building and housing industry; and 'A Look at the Port of Hongkong'. However, matters began to slide later when first Salt, then Wang left the Unit over mid to late 1968, and one consequence of the two departures was that these four anticipated projects did not see the light of day. In addition, no long films appear to have been made in 1969, and this clearly signals an overall falling away from the peak year of 1967.

When the next long film did appear, in 1970, it proved to be disappointing. Although *Festival of Hong Kong*, with Albert Young as both director, and, now, head of the HKFU, won an award for the 'best-planned documentary' (a minor award at the 17th Asian Film Festival in June 1970), it is entirely celebratory and sanguine in tone, and does not contain a trace of the social realism found in a film such as *A Race Against People*. *Festival of Hong Kong* portrays the 'Festival of Hong Kong' which was held that year. The Festival consisted of a myriad of events, performances and so on showcasing various aspects of the local culture; and the film shows a large number of these tableaux, one after the other. The result is a sort of frenzied montage, of slight quality, accompanied by either western pop music or 'westernised' Chinese music. Here, Hong Kong is depicted as 'gay' Hong Kong (in the old sense of the word): light-hearted and untroubled, and we are back here to the sort of superficiality found in Salt's two 1967 films. What *is* significant about *Festival of Hong Kong*, however, is the way that it, more or less inadvertently, portrays the emergence of a modern, westernised-Cantonese culture in Hong Kong Island and the Kowloon peninsula (the area of Hong Kong on the mainland, across the harbour from Hong Kong Island). The young people shown are dressed in a western manner, and listen to western pop music. They do not look traditionally Chinese. In contrast, when *Festival of Hong Kong* shows activities in the Hong Kong New Territories, adjacent to the border with China, we see far more traditional images of Chinese people and society. Unintentionally, therefore, *Festival of Hong Kong* provides a glimpse of the hybrid, western-influenced Chinese Hong Kong identity which was beginning to materialise in the late 1960s and early 1970s.

Following this the next long film to appear was *Hong Kong Style* (1971). However, this was not made by the HKFU, and, as mentioned previously, was outsourced to the London-based company Anthony Gilkison Associates. *Hong Kong Style* was championed at the time as a major achievement for the GIS, even though the film was not made by the Film Unit. The *South China Morning Post* thought it 'the best film yet on [the] Colony';[33] and its preview was attended by the then governor of Hong Kong, Sir David Trench.[34] Like its later companion film, *The Port of Hong Kong* (1972), which was also made by Gilkison as part of the same contract, *Hong Kong Style* suffers from a number of problems associated with the outsourced film, the most important being an unfamiliarity with the subject which leads to a degree of superficiality and ostentation. In the film, Hong Kong is portrayed as a bustling, energetic *modern* place, and this is conveyed through a fast-paced editing style and driving musical accompaniment. As Hong Kong is also portrayed as a new centre for the fashion industry here, this accompaniment also takes on an inconsequential 'pop-like' tenor. *Hong Kong Style* is pure public relations, with little or no critical social or political content, in which the colonial government is portrayed as playing a constructive and benevolent role in the affairs of a confident and gregarious colony.

Unusually for the films of the HKFU there are references to Hong Kong's relation to China in *Hong Kong Style*. However, the references are entirely soporific, and this may have been the line the government asked Gilkison to take. At the beginning of the film, for example, we are told that the frontier with China is 'built on mutual respect for each others' needs'; whilst, later in the film, we are informed that, because of the 'mutual benefit of Hong Kong and China to each other, Hong Kong is perhaps more secure today than at any time in her history'. This seems a remarkable statement to make only two to three years after the communist-instigated riots in Hong Kong, and whilst the Cultural Revolution was still ongoing in China. Neither was the contiguous region particularly secure in 1971, with China-supported communist victories looming in nearby Vietnam, Laos and Cambodia. It may, however, and paradoxically, have been precisely all this heat and light elsewhere that led the colonial government to the belief that Hong Kong was no longer top of the agenda for the PRC (if it had ever been), and that an attempt should be made to 'stabilise' the existing relationship. Certainly, notions of Hong Kong as secure and stable are very present *in Hong Kong Style*, and, intriguingly, also reappear almost verbatim in a contemporaneous review of the film in the *South China Morning Post*. According to the *Post*, the film 'aptly' points out that:

Hongkong and China have both in their 130-year-old relationship, profited from Hongkong and, even today, with the communists in power next door, the relationship not only continues to be profitable but becomes increasingly secure because of that fact.[35]

On the face of it, though, to say, in 1971, that Hong Kong is 'secure' with the communists in power 'next door' seems a remarkable evasion of political reality, and one of which the outsourced *Hong Kong Style* is also guilty.

It has been suggested by at least one critic that the HKFU went into steep decline after Albert Young took over as Films Officer in 1968.[36] However, it is worth investigating further what this idea of 'decline' might actually mean. Decline could mean institutional deterioration, relating to a fall in funding, output, manpower and resources; and the rise of a televisual alternative. If decline is understood in this sense, then it is an accurate description of what happened. After Salt and Wang resigned, there were only Young and a handful of junior apprentices left. However, it is also suggested that the *quality of the films* declined after 1968, and that much of the blame for this is to be placed not on resource issues but upon the shoulders of the 'less talented' Young.[37] However, a viewing of the films produced after 1968 reveals that this is not the whole story by any means, and this is particularly borne out by a comparison of two of the final films associated with the Film Unit: the outsourced Gilkison *Port of Hong Kong* (1972) (made, as mentioned earlier, as part of the contract for *Hong Kong Style*), and Young's *The Sea and The Sky* (1972). It will be argued here that, far from constituting evidence of decline, the latter film can, in fact, be associated with valuable elements of the Griersonian tradition.

Port of Hong Kong suffers from many of the problems which afflict outsourced official films, and these are problems which, it has been argued, also afflicted its sister film, *Hong Kong Style*. Because *Port of Hong Kong* was made by a company that did not possess an intimate understanding of Hong Kong the film is forced to rely on existing, stereotypical conceptions of the colony. The result is verbose generalisation about 'British pragmatism', 'Chinese common sense', and the idea that Hong Kong is now a modern 'international' port of consequence. Thrown into the mix here is also the usual presumption about Hong Kong being a mixture of 'old and new'. Lack of authentic knowledge of the subject forces the film to rely over-heavily upon statistics, whilst the jarring sound-track, which can only be described as a sort of hackneyed 'rock-Chinese', is also overly formulaic. Remarkably, a very long section of footage in the middle of the film is lifted directly, and without much apparent amendment, from *Hong Kong Style*. It is surprising that such plagiarism was not picked up by reviewers at the time. *Port of Hong Kong* shares many of the problems associated with its sister film; *The Sea and the Sky*, however, is quite another matter.

A consideration of *The Sea and the Sky* also sheds some light on what Government Information Services officials might have meant when declaring that Young had led the Film Unit into 'decline'. The original GIS briefing for the film sent out to the press suggested that it would show 'the changes that have taken place in the fishing industry in Hong Kong since the end of the Second World War'.[38] This sounds relatively routine and straightforward, and what comes to mind here, when reading such a briefing, were the similarly routine expectations aroused by another film, made a long time before, and in another place: John Grierson's 1929 film *Drifters*. The comparison with *Drifters* might appear far-fetched here. However, it is anything but. As with *Drifters*, the GIS officials who commissioned *The Sea and the Sky* were expecting what they believed had been commissioned, that is, a standard account and history of the local fishing industry. In both cases, those officials got nothing of the kind. *The Sea and the Sky* is, actually, strongly reminiscent of *Drifters*, and almost follows the same narrative model of Grierson's iconic film. As in *Drifters*, the focus is not on the fishing industry, but on *one* trawler. We also see the various stages of the process of fishing, beginning with the catching of the fish, then moving on to the selling of the fish at market, and later distribution of the product via vehicles of various sort. Like *Drifters*, *The Sea and the Sky* is focused on a few individuals, in this case the members of one family, and there are also montage-like edited sequences of the ships' engines and machinery which are very similar to those found in *Drifters*. It is not known whether Young drew directly on *Drifters* when making his film, but it is highly likely that he would have seen Grierson's ground-breaking and historically important film at some point.

The Sea and the Sky is definitely not an example of 'decline', though it is clear why the film would have disappointed government officials. Young's film does not really 'promote' anything very clearly. According to the *South China Morning Post*, the film covers 'the work of the Marine Department and the Agricultural and Fisheries Department'.[39] In reality, however, *The Sea and the Sky* hardly mentions these departments. *The Sea and the Sky* is actually a fine exercise in *film-making*, rather than promotion, and one which shifts well away from its remit, and also from the overbearing rhetoric of the outsourced *Port of Hong Kong*. This is an intimate, family-based study, showing sensitivity for the fishermen, their community and the natural environment. These film-makers are clearly *familiar* with Hong Kong, and this makes a difference. *The Sea and the Sky* is not only a charming vignette, however, it is also very well photographed, and a considerable achievement for the HKFU as late as 1972, when some commentators actually thought that the Film Unit had ceased to exist.

The films produced by the HKFU over the course of its duration also reveal one other matter of consequence: that the most significant film-maker to emerge within the Unit was not Brian Salt, or even Albert Young, but Charles Wang, and it is, in particular, Wang's cinematography which distinguishes some of the most interesting films to emerge from the Unit. A case in point here is the 1965 film *A Race against People*, which deals with the problem of population growth. The narrative of the film is fairly routine, and not particularly innovative or special in itself. We see sequences showing the immigrant masses, the squatter camps, and rehousing construction projects. However, and like the earlier *This is Hong Kong*, which will be discussed shortly, *A Race against People* makes no mention of the source of the immigrant problem, which is, of course, communist China. The film follows *This is Hong Kong* in both focusing on the problem of 'population' and using a well-known commentator, in this case a young Eamonn Andrews.

However, it is the photography which matters most in this film and much of it is of a very high order, with many individual shots possessing the detailed organised quality of still photography. Clearly, given that none of these scenes was rehearsed, Wang must have waited a while until he got the image he wanted, and he must also have had a fairly good idea of what he wanted from the outset. A particular kind of compositional structure also emerges within this photography: a divided shot (divided by the wall of a building, or such), with close-ups in the extreme foreground, and lines of direction leading to small areas of light and sky at the very back of the image. In addition to such composed, effective photography, Wang is also able to capture the rhythms of movement well, and set them within pictorial patterns. All of this is also reinforced by Wang's use of colour, which is both subtle and organised.

In addition to the photography, Wang is able to achieve the sort of local sensibility that Young was later to realise in *The Sea and the Sky*. At the level of narrative and plot, *A Race against People* may have been about what Andrews' commentary refers to as the 'gigantic project' of rehousing, and 'Hong Kong's industrial revolution', but Wang also focuses on the lesser, more human-oriented details of the Cantonese culture. Many shots, for example, show children playing or sleeping; and many others show women caring for these children whilst carrying out other everyday tasks. As was argued in relation to *The Sea and the Sky*, and as will shortly be argued in relation to *This is Hong Kong*, here, in *A Race against People*, the imagery does not really support the functional narrative of 'progress' in the way that the film's sponsors would have expected. Wang is clearly an individual whose work merits closer study. The same could be said for Young, because of *The Sea and the Sky*. However, the case is less clear here, because Young also made the forgettable *Festival of Hong Kong*. In many ways, *A Race against People* could be said to be superior to the supposed signature film of the HKFU: *This is Hong Kong*. Nevertheless, *This is Hong Kong was* commissioned as the early flagship film of the HKFU, and remained so after the failure of *The Magic Stone*. *This is Hong Kong* was, without a doubt, the most *historically* important film to be produced by the Film Unit, and, because of this, will now be the subject of a more detailed analysis than it has been possible to afford other films discussed in this chapter.

THIS IS HONG KONG (1961)

As argued, *This is Hong Kong* was intended to be the signature film of the HKFU, and the one which would launch the Unit on to the international stage. The film was made in Hong Kong by the Hong Kong branch of Cathay Film Services, a subsidiary of the Singapore-based Cathay Organisation, one of the largest film companies in the region. The head of Cathay Film Services was Tom Hodge, who joined the organisation in 1957, after leaving the Malayan Film Unit the same year. Under Hodge, Cathay Film Services would specialise in the production of documentary films with a commercial orientation, as well as a public relations remit. Hodge was also the named producer of *This is Hong Kong*. Apart from Hodge, the other notable contributor to *This is Hong Kong* was the film's director, scriptwriter and associate producer, Noni Wright. Wright (no relation to the Griersonian Basil Wright) was a New Zealander who had worked at the BBC in London during the war. She joined the MFU in 1953, shortly after Hodge, and left the MFU shortly after him, in 1958, to continue working under him at Cathay Film Services and Cathay-Keris. She died prematurely in a plane crash in 1964. *This is Hong Kong* was probably Wright's most important film. However, and despite her input, the resulting film clearly bears the overall imprint of the Hodge-Murray model set out earlier in this chapter. The evidence also suggests that, by at least 1964, and probably earlier, Wright and Hodge were in a personal relationship, further indicating the overall influence of Hodge on this signature film of the HKFU. *This is Hong Kong* was awarded the 'Best Picture Award in the Non-Dramatic Field' at the Asian Film Festival in Manila, in March 1961, and, from then on, was regularly touted as the Film Unit's most significant film. This was still the case even by as late as 1968, when, according to Nigel Watt, *This is Hong Kong* had been shown in '400 cinemas throughout the British Isles', and had also been made into 'nine different language-versions'. As Watt was speaking, in October 1968, a 'special showing of the film' was also being set up in Vancouver by the National Film Board of Canada.[40] *This is Hong Kong* clearly had some staying power.

   This is Hong Kong is divided into three main sections bracketed by an introduction and conclusion. The film opens with a nineteenth-century photographic view of Hong Kong harbour (Victoria Harbour). A dissolve then takes us to a modern-day film shot of the same view. The congruence of these two images implies continuity of past and present, and the co-existence of old and new, traditional and modern. These themes of continuity and co-existence are central to the film's ideological project, and are often deployed in order to justify a colonial presence which has been able to foster a stability not achieved at the expense of long-standing local mores and customs. The themes of continuity and co-existence set out pictorially in this opening sequence also set the ideological framework for the rest of *This is Hong Kong*, one which repeatedly depicts traditional, or authentic-indigenous Chinese ways existing alongside the forces of modernity. In addition to this evocation of connection and co-operation, the formal framing of the opening shot of the harbour, which preserves the art-photographic quality of the original nineteenth-century photograph, conveys a sense of lyrical seriousness from the outset, and this consequential tone, which implies the carefully achieved success of the liberal colonial project, is then imparted to the rest of this introductory section of the film.

In addition to being ideological, the themes conjured within the introductory section of *This is Hong Kong* are *stereotypical* conceptions of Hong Kong as – according to the commentary – 'a place where east meets west'; and, alongside the film's ideological project, there is also an accompanying generic dimension which the film-makers rely on from time to time in order to structure their film. It must be remembered that *This is Hong Kong* was made by people from outside Hong Kong, and this means that they had to rely on existing stereotypes of the city, to some extent at least. Whilst made – or at least shot – in Hong Kong (the full production and post-production details are unclear, but it is likely that post-production at least took place at the Cathay headquarters in Singapore), *This is Hong Kong* remains an essentially outsourced film, and this context shapes the film's generic vision of Hong Kong, a city which has commonly been perceived of as characterised by a sort of 'floating' and incongruous concoction of old and new.[41] Unfortunately, though, *This is Hong Kong* is rarely able to rise beyond such generalised suppositions: suppositions which also reinforce the film's ideological project (which the film is similarly unable to transcend).

After the picturesque opening dissolve the introductory section of *This is Hong Kong* continues with a voice-of-God commentary (by the then well-known Canadian-born British television presenter Bernard Braden), and the rest of the film also employs such commentary to help narrate its 'story' of Hong Kong. As we shall see, though, the construction of this story proved to be fraught with difficulties and elipses. The aim of the film's director, Noni Wright, may have been to articulate a 'balanced view of the colony – to put everything into perspective', but *This is Hong Kong* remains a *promotional* public-relations film, rather than a work of critical social-analysis, and a film whose 'perspective' is shaped by the need to both include and exclude matters held to be appropriate or not to the fabrication and rendering of the film's story.[42] As the commentary introduces us to Hong Kong, we see an airplane arriving at Kai Tak Hong Kong airport (now redundant). The aircraft carries a group of imaginary 'tourists' who will land in the colony and then be given a 'tour' by the disembodied narrator/tour guide: a pretended journey which will be articulated through the narration and which will furnish the 'balanced view' of and 'perspective' on Hong Kong the film seeks to construct for its make-believe visitors. This, of course, is a routine and familiar rhetorical device, which fits with what has been described earlier as the film's often bracketing-generic approach to its subject. However, this device of the 'guide commentary' also supports the film's socio-political story by enabling that interpretation to be put forcefully and confidently, and sometimes didactically. These 'tourists' are, after all, being *guided*, that is, they are inert recipients of a homiletic instructional *tutorial* on Hong Kong, which they will take away with them when they finally fly out of Hong Kong at the finale of the film, and which they will then communicate to the outside world. The fact that we never actually *see* these tourists also augments this idea of a future invoked outwards dissemination of the Hong Kong story, because, through this means, the film is able to avoid personalisation or individualisation, and, instead, suggest the existence of a reasonably held 'common sense' consensus on what Hong Kong *is*. In addition, the film also positions us – its spectators – as the accomplice-doppelgangers of the imaginary tourists, because we and the tourists occupy the same diegetic-address site within the film: the narrator speaks to us *through* the persona-space of the dreamt-up tourists; and, because we regard ourselves as level-headed and judicious spectators, we, like the seemingly contentedly-guided imaginary tourists, also come to – perhaps subliminally – accept the story that is being given of Hong Kong here as similarly level-headed and judicious. The interpolating subterfuge employed here is, therefore, quite a delicate one, and may have proved engrossing at the time. After working in the official public-relations business for over twenty years, Murray and Hodge had clearly learnt some shrewd tactical manoeuvres.

After this introductory sequence the main body of the film, consisting of three distinct sections, begins. The first of these deals with issues of production and commerce in the urban areas of the city, the second with agriculture in the countryside, and the third with the various social problems faced by the colony, mainly in the urban areas. This structure allows the film to carry through its project of depicting Hong Kong as a place in which indigenous continuity is evident, and in which the old (rural life) and new (urban life) persist, more or less harmoniously, side by side. The third section of the film also gives the impression that Hong Kong does have *some* social problems, as all societies do; and that *This is Hong Kong* is intent upon addressing these in a sober and responsible way. This third section thus affords *This is Hong Kong* a degree of insurance and simulation of warrantability. This comprehensive structure also affords a sense of *unity* to the picture of Hong Kong which is presented here: the *whole* society is purportedly shown, and relations between the various groups in that society are also depicted. What we have, therefore, is an attempt at *organic* presentation of the sum of parts and relation between parts. However, and as will be argued later, *This is Hong Kong* does *not*, in fact, show the whole society, and some significant exclusions are made.

The first section of *This is Hong Kong* begins with a brief potted history of colonial Hong Kong from 1842 to the present day (in 1961). There is little that is contentious here, rather just a basic outline-chronology, though, of course, from an underlying reassuring British colonial point of view. As we reach the present day, the narration then settles on to the issue of economic change within the colony, and, specifically, the emergence of a light manufacturing sector from the 1950s onwards. Here, the commentary and accompanying illustrative imagery portray the colony as a modern metropolis, and also as an increasingly important international economic hub. The sheer extent of the industrial and modern transformation of the city is conjured up through Promethean rhetoric here, as we hear that 'mountains are torn down to make runways'. The central role of the colonial government is also stressed in this part of the film, as we are told that such 'development' continues apace under the eyes of a munificent and 'far-seeing government'.

As the brief history lesson, with its account of the contemporary, fast-modernising, government-led situation, comes to an end, we realise that we have encountered one of the film's main areas of exclusion: China has not been mentioned at all, and, in fact, throughout the rest of the film, China exists as an invisible presence, hardly ever pointed to. As already mentioned, *This is Hong Kong* is a *promotional* film, designed to advance the international image of the city, and it would not have been advantageous to raise the spectre of potentially dangerous monolithic neighbours. In addition, at this point in time, sandwiched between the cataclysmic events of the Great Leap Forward and the Cultural Revolution, Hong Kong was not experiencing significant problems with China; and this further enables the film to leave the mainland as much out of the picture as possible. Nevertheless, this tendency to make the 'China problem' invisible does create difficulties within the overall narrative logic of *This is Hong Kong*, given that so much of the colony's development was shaped by that problem. These difficulties become particularly evident, and anachronistic, whenever the issue of population growth is addressed. The main cause of such enlargement was, of course, immigration from China. However, this is not referred to, and instead, we are eventually told later in the film that Chinese people have 'the fifth-highest birth-rate in the world', leaving the misleading impression that population growth in Hong Kong stemmed from a general Chinese propensity for mass reproduction *within* the colony. Here, the film refuses to face the political and historical reality, and paternalistically places the cause of the problem upon the colony's Chinese inhabitants, both officially resident and illegally immigrant.

A background of paternalism also appears in the account of the development of the manufacturing sector in Hong Kong given here. In *This is Hong Kong* 'the population' is depicted as both the main 'problem' facing Hong Kong, and also – in tandem with colonial guidance, of course – the main driving force of economic modernisation. These masses, and the additional waves of offspring soon to emerge on the scene, must have jobs to go to, and must be able to earn an income to support their extended family structures. Industries must be developed by government in order to cater for this, and the impression is given that the colonial power can and does help imperatively here. We then see sequences showing modern, large-scale, colonial-owned enterprises of various sorts. However, such sequences are few in number, and are very quickly followed by others showing the smaller-scale, local, manufacturing community. *This is Hong Kong* is not meant to display colonial authority but, rather, depict a paternalistic provider, and, images of regal–industrial muscle are kept to a minimum – though they are deployed from time to time as bracketed interjections, in order to remind viewers where power truly lies within the city. During this period large-scale industry remained firmly in British hands and attempts were also made to ensure that the rising Chinese enterprises did not compete with colonial corporations. This was not exactly free and fair, and was resented at the time by the rising Chinese middle class. However, *This is Hong Kong* expresses no sense of there being any issue here, and passes over the matter in order to show a generally contented and hard-working Chinese community fully accepting of the existing situation.

The ideological trope of colonial policy – or propaganda – at the time, of providing the foundations for economic activity and then letting the local community get on with things, is evident in this part of *This is Hong Kong*, as, in sequences set in the small-scale manufacturing sector where no Caucasians are to be seen at all as locals go about their business. These Chinese workers also *smile* as they carry out their apparently repetitive tasks. Here, the focus is also on family-based enterprises, and on what the commentary refers to as 'craft skills, handed down through the generations'. A classic Griersonian approach emerges here, in this un-Griersonian film, of portraying craft and working processes from beginning to end (think of *Night Mail* (1936), or any choice of films made by the documentary film movement in the 1930s and 1940s); and this is particularly exemplified in sequences which look at the textile manufacturing industry and begin with the production of the fabric and end with finished garments displayed by a (western) model.

Whilst the print of *This is Hong Kong* available for viewing today is somewhat washed out, it is obvious that this section of the film places considerable emphasis on the display of vibrant colour. Made in dazzling (sometimes garish) Eastmancolour, the screen is often completely filled with the bright and contrasting colours of fabric and garments, as *This is Hong Kong* attempts to maximise this colourful visuality. The editing and photography here is often highly composed and organised, with diagonal organisations of settings, and classical shot-reverse shot sequences predominating. Many of the images here – as in the opening shots of the film – give the impression that a stills photographer was involved in the film at some point, as many shots are 'photographed', as it were, in a formal manner. All of this, together with the effective use of colour photography, speaks of the *professionalism* employed in *This is Hong Kong*; this professionalism was one of the main reasons for the film's perceived success at the time. Both Wright and Hodge had considerable experience under their belt by 1961, and managed to achieve a degree of technical quality within the film's relatively large budget of $116,000.[43] This opening section of *This is Hong Kong* is principally concerned with industrial and commercial development within the urban areas, and with the fabrication of a modern infrastructure. The section ends with a – characteristic – return to the issue of 'the population', and on the need to reclaim land from the sea in order to house that population. As we approach the end of this first section of the film, the commentary takes on a more lyrical tone, evoking the scale of the enterprise involved in creating this city out of the surrounding land, and its struggle with natural limitations.

The lyrical tone adopted here sets the scene for the second section of the film, which is set in the northern agricultural areas of the colony. Whilst the first section of the film depicted contented factory workers smiling as they carried out their highly repetitive tasks, this second section shows us similarly contented peasants living in a rural idyll, and at one with nature and the peacefulness of country life. The poetic tone adopted towards the end of the first section of the film now enlarges, and a slower pace of editing also becomes apparent, as the film attempts to depict this more traditional side of local life and culture. The area of Hong Kong shown here is near the border with China, but, significantly, the film plays down the consequence of that proximity, and also the border itself. In fact, this border is depicted as an almost abstract, simulated thing, with there being no discernible difference between the ordinary Chinese people on either side of it. This is, again, in accordance with the film's attempt to play down the notion of problems associated with the nearness of the PRC.

However, these sequences depicting the border area do, at last, force *This is Hong Kong* to at least *mention* China, and also to address the 'China problem'. We are informed, for example, that this border is 'the frontier between two different ideologies which divide the world'. However, in the spirit of political neutrality which characterises the film, there is no claim made that one of these ideologies is better or worse than the other; and, as we are shown scenes of peasants peaceably entering Hong Kong from the Chinese side, we are informed that 'in the goings and comings of these people there are no signs of conflict'. Problem: what problem? It is as though *This is Hong Kong* is trying to deny the existence of the issue, and that China was, in fact, the cause of the most severe social problems facing Hong Kong. One reality was, certainly, that small-scale cross-border trade existed; and the way that the border-crossing itself is portrayed here as almost open, easy to cross, without any sense of a high-security presence, at precisely the point where the 'different ideologies which divide the world' meet, certainly endorses this existing reality. However, the *other* reality, of mass-scale illegal exodus from China into Hong Kong over the overall 1937–61 period, is obfuscated. In this sense, and once again, *This is Hong Kong* turns itself away from political reality in order to fulfill its public-relations mandate.

In this section of the film we also see a reiteration of the ideology of benevolent but arm's-length colonial paternalism which is evident in the first section of the film. This is also sometimes delivered in a rather heavy-handed manner here, as, for example, when, in a sequence showing nursing staff introducing new medical and hygienic practices to villagers, we are told that the colonial authorities are 'teaching' the local women 'how to be better mothers'. The point that is being made here is appropriate in itself. Advances in medicine and hygiene practice will undoubtedly improve the quality of rural life, particularly in relation to issues of infant and maternal mortality. However, the implicit paternalism within the commentary adds an unfortunate note. Similarly, in a risible sequence showing officials bringing British-bred boars to villages in order to increase and improve the pig population (pork being the staple Cantonese meat, alongside fish) we are told, again unhappily, that 'crossing local breeds with pedigree English boars produce fine, stronger litters each year'. Some pigs are, of course, better than others, at least from the point of view of them ending up on the dinner plate, but here we are told that British pigs are better than Chinese pigs. In both of these sequences we can see an underlying sense of colonial imperiousness, but we can also see the policy of *arm's-length* liberal interventionism which the colonial authorities preferred, as they intercede temporarily in order to 'improve' some situation (in this case the pig situation), and then withdraw from the scene. This policy of intervention–then–withdrawal is also alluded to later in these sequences, when the commentary stresses that the local community, aided and abetted by voluntary bodies and charities, should and does play 'the principal role' in the organisation of daily life, and not the state.

As mentioned earlier, this 'agrarian' section of *This is Hong Kong* has a different tone to the first section of the film, and, here, a pastoral idyll is generally evoked. However, another contradiction emerges here, and, once more, that contradiction relates to the imperceptible presence of China. We are told that the food grown in the rural areas is sufficient to 'supply 50 per cent of Hong Kong's needs'. On the face of it this sounds an affirmative statement, and it is backed up by convincing images of plentiful crops. However, the fact is that, during the 1950s and 1960s, food and water shortages were common in Hong Kong. Water shortage was the bigger problem, but water is also necessary in order to grow crops. The confirmatory tone adopted in this sequence over this issue is unable to address this problem, or the fact that, at that time, Hong Kong was actually *dependent* upon China for a large proportion of its food. Again, as elsewhere in the film, China remains the great unmentionable, and the corroborating cornucopia evoked here is at odds with the environmental, never mind political, reality of severe water – and food – shortage.

Until this point *This is Hong Kong* has largely celebrated the achievements of the colony of Hong Kong. However, such celebration could hardly make up the whole of the film given the evident problems faced by the colony, and the final section of the film now addresses some of these. This final section has a different tone to the previous rural section: more sober now, less pastoral; more pragmatic, as we return to the problems and issues associated with the *urban* areas of Hong Kong. Characteristically for *This is Hong Kong*, with its constant reference to the role of the colonial government, the socio-economic order portrayed here is not shown as dominated by free-market competitive capitalism, but by a government which intervenes actively and substantively in promoting social, economic and infrastructural development. So, for example, we are told that 'Much is being done to improve living conditions by the Hong Kong government'. Here, once again, the film is referring to the housing situation. As mentioned earlier though, this is misleading, as adequate and necessary intervention on this front did not take place until after the 1967 riots. Another unfortunate glimpse of colonial insensitivity also creeps in here. As we see shots of the sprawling, forsaken squatter communities, we are informed that 'These shacks spread like an ugly disease across the beautiful face of Hong Kong'. The tactlessness here – poverty as an 'ugly disease' – is also compounded by the choice of music used to accompany this commentary and these images of abject poverty: elegaic wistful music which is at odds with the stark social reality on view.

Following this, *This is Hong Kong* makes another of its frequent China ellipses. As argued, the reason for the population explosion in Hong Kong was immigration from communist China, particularly during the disastrous Great Leap Forward of 1958–61, in which around 20 million people died of starvation within China. But no mention is made of this catastrophe in this overly cautious film, and, as mentioned earlier, the only explanation for the population growth we are given is that Chinese people have the 'fifth highest birth-rate in the world'. This retreat from political reality, and the attempt to place an implicit but never directly stated responsibility upon the immigrant poor, is one of the most unlikeable aspects of *This is Hong Kong*. It should be remembered that *This is Hong Kong* was not made long after the period of the Great Leap Forward but actually just about *within* it; and it bears some responsibility to make reference to this catastrophe.

Having established the point that the problem of 'the population' lies in a Chinese predilection for over-procreation, *This is Hong Kong* goes on to set out ways in which the colonial government is trying to deal with what the film refers to as the 'gigantic problems of Hong Kong people'. We are then shown the resettlement estates and building programmes, the erection of schools, and the provision of social services for the immigrant community. By this time it has become clear that *This is Hong Kong* posits the existence of three distinct communities in Hong Kong. The first is the seemingly contented workforce in the urban areas, the second the equally seemingly contented rural population, and the third the immigrant masses, who are, clearly, not very content at all with their situation. *This is Hong Kong* now focuses on this itinerant community. However, in doing so, the film encounters a problem in that it fails to make these sequences dealing with the immigrants fully work because the image-track comes into contradiction with the sound-track. For example, we are told that the government is trying to organise the immigrants into a structured community, and we see long lines of children waiting to receive sustenance as evidence of such ongoing consolidation. The overall impression which the film seeks to give here is of compliance with and acceptance of the government's actions. However, the faces of the children tell a different story: dejected, apprehensive, anything but happily patient. Here, the image-track simply does not support the commentary as the camera moves closer into its subject-matter, and, instead, provokes a question not accommodated or intended by that commentary: for exactly how long has this interminable column of miserable-looking children been standing out there, in the baking tropical sun? There is also a further incongruity here, at the level of *both* commentary and image-track this time, when we discover what the children are waiting in line for: milk. There were probably some sound medical reasons for dishing out milk to young Chinese children. On the other hand, milk was not a regular part of their diet, and a great many Chinese people are lactose-intolerant. The impression comes across of injudicious colonial incursion here, rather like the earlier mentioned provision of British boars to Chinese pig farms in the rural section of *This is Hong Kong* (bringing a foreign breed into another country has, to say the least, not always proved to be an ideal strategy in the past).

This section of *This is Hong Kong* presents a picture of a well-drilled Chinese immigrant population apparently agreeing with the commentary's mantra that 'It is on economic stability and progressive social services that the peace and happiness of the colony depends'. The film ends on this uncritical note, as, for almost the first time, we see the *colonial* community. It will be remembered that *This is Hong Kong* displays three main community groups, all of which are Chinese. In contrast, the colonial community is largely absent from the film, even though the commentary repeatedly invokes the colonial government. Of course, other communities are also absent (Indian and Nepalese, in particular). Now, however, as the film nears its finale, we begin to see colonial buildings, and so on. The film thus begins its finale by, finally, showing us the seat of power; as commentary and image-track unite. After this, the narrator allows his imaginary tour group to fly out of Hong Kong, and the film comes to an end.

This is Hong Kong was a film of its time, and, in some respects, one of the last of its kind, occupying a moment when this sort of conservative, British-influenced official colonial film in South-East Asia had reached the end of its possibilities, or utility. Nothing so *packaged* as this was made at the HKFU again until the final years of the Unit, and, when the model did reappear, as in *Hong Kong Style* and *Port of Hong Kong*, the results were predictably disappointing. *This is Hong Kong* is really a promotional object: a manufactured, almost made-to-order entity, albeit a professionally produced one. It certainly does not conform to the Griersonian 'documentary idea' of invoking the ordinary and pursuing a liberal-progressive agenda. So, it does not, in the end, matter too much that the film's director, Noni Wright, claimed that 'government gave me a free hand', or that 'Government . . . made very few changes to the film after it had been shot'.[44] The 'Government' knew it was in safe hands with Murray and Hodge, and that it would have no need to intervene in the film's portrayal of the colony.

Whilst Wright's contribution should not be discounted, ultimately, *This is Hong Kong* really represents the continuation of the conservative CO–CFU vision of the official film into the 1960s, as that vision is refracted and refined through the equally conservative attitudes of Murray and Hodge. This is, without question, and with all due respect to Wright's contribution, basically a Hodge-Murray film. However, and as has been argued earlier in this chapter, *This is Hong Kong* is not genuinely characteristic of the spirit of film-making which evolved within the HKFU after 1961, and, in particular, after the departure of Murray, and, through that departure, the disappearance from the scene of Hodge. The spirit of film-making which developed within the Unit thereafter *did* invoke the Griersonian ideal to some extent, and is epitomised in films such as *A Race Against People* and *The Sea and the Sky*, and in the contributions of Wang and Young. Nevertheless, *This is Hong Kong* still remains of importance in the way that it illuminates a particular context and nexus of the British-influenced official film in South-East Asia in the early 1960s. In this respect, it remains a historically significant film whose conditions of production and reception and forms of representation still merit further consideration.

CONCLUSIONS

In many ways, film-making at the HKFU was afflicted by the same problem that affected the British official film everywhere. The overall mandate given to the Unit was a public-relations one, and the Unit was not expected or allowed to make a critical, analytical intervention. The remit of the HKFU was to communicate approved information on the various issues affecting the colony, with a view to acquiring and developing public support for the colonial government. It was, therefore, not possible for the HKFU to complete films which were socially or politically controversial, even when controversial events had actually been filmed. This is made clear when the events of 1967 are taken into account. As argued, the HKFU did not make a specific film about the riots of 1967, and, in fact, the main series of short films to emerge that year, entitled *The Year of the Ram*, focused on various programmes of road construction, the maintenance of public order, police training, the tracking down of illegal immigrants, and the building of new public facilities such as roads and tunnels. Nevertheless, extensive footage of the riots *was* actually shot, but not used, and this suggests that the film-makers initially wanted to, and perhaps even expected to be able to, turn this into a film. However, they were not allowed to.

The films made by the HKFU could not, therefore, deal directly with controversial subject-matter. What they could do, however, was portray the physical, social and cultural fabric of Hong Kong, and especially so at the level of the image. There is also, as argued, a Griersonian focus on the people at the bottom of the social ladder: the fishermen, boatpeople and squatters. Here and there, one also finds sequences of high aesthetic quality, and these sequences are more often than not set in the everyday world of ordinary, local people. What is also striking here is the way in which these films are highly visually *realistic* in the extent to which they portray the rich visuality of the local milieu. It could be argued that the films of the HKFU have been previously ignored, or discounted, on the basis of preconception: the preconception that there could not be much of significance in Hong Kong bureaucratic official film-making of the 1960s; a period in which the colonial mentality still held sway, and a tradition of independent documentary film-making had yet to emerge. But this is a prejudice based on lack of knowledge, and, as this chapter has shown, there is much of value here.

NOTES

1. Pronay, Nicholas and Croft, Jeremy, 'British Film Censorship and Propaganda Policy during the Second World War', in Curran, James and Porter, Vincent (eds), *British Cinema History* (London: Weidenfeld and Nicolson, 1983), p. 153.
2. Clark, Kenneth, Sir (later Lord) (1903–83), art historian; Director of the National Gallery during the Second World War; Surveyor of the King's Pictures (1934–45); Chairman of the War Artists Advisory Committee during the War; Head of Films Division of the MoI (December 1939–April 1940); Chairman, Arts Council of Great Britain (1955–60), and of the Independent Television Authority (1954–7); wrote and presented *Civilisation* (1969).
3. Fox, Jo, 'John Grierson, His "Documentary Boys" and the British Ministry of Information, 1939–42', *Historical Journal of Film Radio and Television*, vol. 25, no. 3 (2005), p. 355.
4. Ibid. p. 360.

5. Ibid. p. 364.
6. HKRS 41-1-1603, 'Notes on Organisation of an Information Office', 14 November 1946, p. 3.
7. HKRS PRO 204, 6/516/52, Murray, Letter to Carstairs, 19 March 1952, para. 5.
8. Ibid. para. 7.
9. Ibid. para. 15.
10. Ibid. paras 16–17.
11. HKRS 160/1/23, 'Reorganisation of the Public Relations Office', PRO 1/2, Murray, Letter to S. H. Evans, CO, London, 19 January 1955, para. 9.
12. HKRS 160, 5/7C, PRO Staff – General, Murray, 'Government Publicity in Hong Kong: A Report by the Public Relations Officer', November 1958, paras 29–30.
13. 'Top Critics Praised Malayan Film Unit Productions', *The Straits Times*, 3 October 1954, p. 9.
14. Graham, Gerald G., *Canadian Film Technology 1896–1986* (Newark: University of Delaware Press, 1989), p. 114.
15. Moss, Peter, *No Babylon: A Hong Kong Scrapbook* (New York: iUniverse, 2006), p. 39.
16. Graham, *Canadian Film Technology*, p. 114.
17. 'Speed is the Watchword of G.I.S. Film Unit', *China Mail*, 8 May 1965.
18. Moss, *No Babylon*, pp. 39–40.
19. 'Squeezing the $ out of the Magic Stone', *China Mail*, 28 April 1969.
20. Moss, *No Babylon*, p. 38.
21. HKRS 70-6-580 (i) 1961–73 (untitled), 7 January 1966.
22. Moss, *No Babylon*, p. 41.
23. 'Govt Replies to Film Unit Queries', *South China Morning Post*, 14 January 1972.
24. HKRS, 'Memorandum', 7 July 1971.
25. HKRS 'Memorandum', 8 January 1973.
26. HKRS 160-3-13, ISD 1/64 (CR), 'HK Government Film Unit Staff Costs 1970–1', undated.
27. HKRS 'GIS Press', 70-6-580 (i) 1961–73, 'Five Hundred Films Available for Lending at Government Library', 29 October 1963.
28. HKRS 'GIS Press', 70-6-580 (i) 1961–73, 'Film Unit Produces Series of Newsreels on Hong Kong to Keep Public Informed of Interesting Local Happenings', 5 April 1968.
29. Ibid.
30. HKRS 'GIS Press', 70-6-580 (i) 1961–73, 'Film on Hong Kong Makes Impact on London Cinema Audiences. Hong Kong's Sea Festival Enters Sixth Week of World Premiere, General Release throughout Britain', 23 February 1963.
31. 'Squeezing the $ out of the Magic Stone', *China Mail*, 28 April 1969.
32. 'New G.I.S. Travel Film should be a Winner', *South China Morning Post*, 10 April 1968.
33. 'Hong Kong Style – the Best Film yet on Colony', *South China Morning Post*, 30 August 1971.
34. 'London Sees Film on Colony', *South China Morning Post*, 8 July 1971.
35. *South China Morning Post*, 30 August 1971, op. cit.
36. Moss, *No Babylon*, p. 41.
37. Ibid.
38. HKRS 70-6-580 (1) 1961–73, 'GIS Press', 'Film Record of Changes in Fishing Industry, GIS Film Unit Starts Production', 30 September 1971.
39. 'New Films Show a Changing Pattern', *South China Morning Post*, 10 August 1972.
40. 'Film Unit Productions' World Successes', *South China Morning Post*, 16 October 1968.

41. Abbas, Ackbar, *Hong Kong: Culture and the Politics of Disappearance* (Hong Kong: Hong Kong University Press, 1997), p. 4.
42. 'This is Hong Kong Receives Oscar Award for Best Film', *South China Morning Post*, 14 March 1961.
43. Ibid.
44. Ibid.

CHAPTER 4

Public-service Broadcasting in an Authoritarian Setting: The Case of Radio Television Hong Kong and the Development of Television Documentary Film in Hong Kong

HISTORICAL SUMMARY: THE ROAD TO THE HANDOVER

During the 1970s, agitation for political reform remained muted amongst the local population in Hong Kong, and no substantive political leadership emerged from within that population to promote such reform. This was partly due to the fact that the local community and its leaders had been kept out of governance and executive authority by the colonial regime for so long that they had become habituated to that circumstance. However, it was also partly because, by the 1970s, the colonial regime was administering Hong Kong fairly well. Following the confrontation of the late 1960s some action had been taken against corruption through the inauguration of the Independent Commission against Corruption in 1974. The rule of law remained sovereign, and largely independent of government. Necessary if still inadequate welfare reforms had been enacted. Social stability now seemed reasonably assured, and the colonial government was finally proving more responsive to the needs of the population. By the mid-1970s Hong Kong was also becoming incrementally more prosperous, and the evidence suggests that this led large sections of the local population to preoccupy themselves more with matters related to family situation and pecuniary advantage than with suffrage. Of course, the colonial presence was still widely resented, but the small-government model which prevailed meant the local community did not have to encounter its existence too recurrently. If that presence also created the framework for local business to succeed, and wealth to accumulate, as seemed to be the case, then the local community were prepared to tolerate it. The indenture which had shaped Hong Kong since the colony's inception continued to hold.

In addition, and important to some local Hongkongers, was the fact that, however undemocratic it may have been, the Hong Kong colonial government was still ultimately controlled by a democratic metropole which, in a post-colonial age, closely supervised the affairs of the Crown Colony. Many educated Hongkongers recognised this and then chose to associate themselves psychologically with Britain, rather than with a communist China which, during the 1970s, appeared to be perpetually riven by internal schism. By the mid-1970s many middle-class Chinese in Hong Kong were sending both themselves and their families to Britain for education, training and western enlightenment. As a stable society continued to develop in Hong Kong following the riots of the late 1960s, and as a local culture was increasingly disseminated through the new medium of television, and other media, a degree of stasis settled on the population in relation to demands for democratic reform. The population in Hong Kong were, to all effects and purposes, experiencing many of the benefits usually associated with a working democracy without such a democracy actually existing, and this experience helped sustain diffident recognition of the colonial condition.[1] However the perception of stability and permanence that was developing within this insular setting was to prove false very soon, as the local community began to realise that a fundamental and disquieting change was underway.

It was the opening of negotiations between Britain and China over the future of Hong Kong which finally engendered a widespread local demand for democratic reform and representation in government. During the 1970s and early 1980s the Hong Kong population – and also elements of the colonial regime – still retained an anticipation that an extension of the British lease of the New Territories – due to expire in 1997 – could be successfully negotiated. After all, it was believed, Hong Kong was economically useful to China, and given this it seemed improbable that the struggling communist regime would act in such a way as to jeopardise said utility. Extension of the New Territories lease was the principal objective of British policy towards the future of Hong Kong when covert discussions with the Chinese government began in 1979. The official reason given for the visit to Beijing that year of the then governor, Sir Murray MacLehose, was the pressing need to discuss issues of land-lease and mortgage terms in the New Territories leading up to 1997. However, MacLehose also sought to have the termination date for the British lease on the New Territories amended, or at least blurred. MacLehose first broached the subject with the Chinese leader, Deng Xiaoping, by insisting that the predetermined date was creating long-term investment problems within Hong Kong in relation to land arrangements, and then by suggesting that a degree of flexibility over the date would ease such problems. However, Deng assured him that the PRC would not interfere with existing and ongoing commercial arrangements up to and after the handover, and that there was, therefore, no need to amend 1997 on these, or any other grounds. A deflated MacLehose then returned to Hong Kong, informing the public that Deng had given assurances over investment, but failing to bring out clearly enough the fact that the Chinese leader had also insisted on 1997. MacLehose's disingenuous account of Deng's declarations created a false sense of 'euphoria' amongst the public and mass media.[2] However, the British government now knew the full truth of the matter: the depletion of natural resources in Hong Kong which would follow on from any forfeiture of the New Territories would make the Crown Colony unsustainable and retrocession to the PRC inevitable.

Formal negotiations with Beijing over the future of Hong Kong took place for the first time in 1982. The British negotiators, led by Prime Minister Margaret Thatcher, knew they had little room to manoeuvre, and were not surprised when Deng reaffirmed his 1979 position on the New Territories. However, this time the truth could not be kept from the Hong Kong population, as it had been in 1979, and the shock felt by that population upon receipt of the unwelcome news was palpable. The local people may have disliked their colonial rulers but they were also 'petrified' at the thought of being handed over to this communist dictatorship.[3] There is no doubt at all that, at the time negotiations began in 1982, the overwhelming majority of the local population did not want Hong Kong to be handed back to the PRC,[4] and, when such an outcome began to appear inescapable, a sense of anxiety and hopelessness began to grow, further augmented by the fact that PRC negotiators would not allow Hong Kong residents any role in the negotiating process. The PRC would only deal directly with Britain. As negotiations continued after Thatcher left China, the PRC did not even acknowledge the formal position of MacLehose's successor, Sir Edward Youde, as Governor of Hong Kong. As far as PRC officials were concerned, he took part in the negotiating process as a member of the British delegation, and no more than that.[5] When the British Government realised that there was no prospect of retaining sovereignty over Hong Kong after 1997 it began negotiating with the objective of creating an institutional framework which would survive the handover, and preserve as much of the rule of law, freedom of expression, and human rights, as possible. This it felt it had achieved with the Sino–British Joint Declaration of 1984.

Amongst other matters, the Joint Declaration stipulated that Hong Kong would remain much as it was after 1997, and for at least fifty years, under the principle of 'one country two systems'. The Joint Declaration also stipulated that a degree of democratic development would take place, in that a legislature with an elected element would be instituted in 1997. Faced with the prospect of handing over a British colony to a communist dictatorship, the British Parliament supported the Joint Declaration on the basis that democratic development would be instituted in Hong Kong in 1997, and that the rule of law and protection of civil and human rights would be preserved for a lengthy period of time after that. However, details concerning exactly how a post-handover Hong Kong would be run in terms of democratic accountability were left extremely vague within the Joint Declaration. The key text relating to this can be found in paragraph I of Annex I: 'Elaboration of the People's Republic of China of its Basic Policies Regarding Hong Kong'; and the crucial wording in this paragraph goes as follows:

> The legislative of the Hong Kong Special Administrative Region shall be constituted by elections. The executive authorities shall abide by the law and shall be accountable to the legislature.[6]

However, the question of precisely what kind of 'election' would be 'constituted' was not addressed at all in the Joint Declaration, and this meant that, when it came, the election, could, potentially, be thoroughly undemocratic. Nevertheless, the people of Hong Kong preferred to see in that wording the promise of a future democracy operating under the rule of law; and the anxiety which pervaded the colony after 1982 began to recede in some measure. It seemed, then, that the pragmatic British negotiating stance had proved to be at least operative.

Whilst negotiations over the Joint Declaration were continuing, and under pressure from the British Parliament and media and Hong Kong public opinion, Britain belatedly attempted to institute a limited degree of democratic reform within the colony, and, as a consequence of this, a Hong Kong Government Green Paper was published in July 1984 which proposed both the creation of a number of indirectly-elected seats within the Legislative Council for 1985, and possible inauguration of some directly-elected seats in 1988. The proposals inspired considerable debate within Hong Kong, further boosting a now fast-growing attentiveness to issues of political reform that had been first stimulated by the beginning of bilateral talks in 1982. The Green Paper was published before the Joint Declaration was signed in order to give the Chinese side the opportunity to look at and comment on it. The objective was not to undercut negotiations taking place over the Joint Declaration, which London believed would, in any case, eventually endorse a process of democratisation which would in general accord with the proposals put forward in the Green Paper. Initially, PRC negotiators did not object to the proposals, though they remained mistrustful of British intent. However, when the final text of the Joint Declaration appeared, no mention was made in it of any democratic reforms occurring prior to the 1997 legislature, and, in 1985, and in contrast to the position initially adopted in 1984, PRC negotiators unexpectedly (as far as the British were concerned) accused Britain of violating the negotiation process, and insisted that direct elections proposed for 1988 be postponed until after the promulgation of the Basic Law in 1990. The Joint Declaration of 1984 was a formal agreement, but the Basic Law would be the instrument of governance, and would set out the details of Hong Kong's future from 1997, and for a period of at least fifty years thereafter.

What occurred here in this largely unanticipated dispute can best be defined as a misapprehension between two legal and political traditions, rather than any wilful jockeying. As far as the British were concerned, and under British common law, if individual reforms taking place within an agreed general framework were not specifically prohibited, they ought to be allowed, or at least advocated; whereas, for the Chinese, if those reforms were not directly specified, they ought simply to be prohibited. The Chinese side also suspected the British of attempting to advance democracy in an underhanded manner, though the British felt they were merely responding constructively to public opinion within a largely agreed framework. In addition, the British believed that, even though retrocession in 1997 had been agreed, in the meantime, the colonial government remained in charge of Hong Kong, and had the right to reasonably advance democratic reform which would help safeguard civil and political liberties. Once the dust had settled and Chinese suspicions had been mollified, a compromise was reached. The British agreed to postpone the 1988 elections till 1991, and the Chinese agreed to allow a process of democratic reform organised within the framework of the Basic Law to move forward up to that date. However, the Chinese also believed that they had obtained an informal agreement from the British that the latter would adhere closely to Chinese positions over remaining reforms after 1991, and up to 1997; and this belief was to prove a considerable bone of contention later. Nevertheless, as a consequence of these settlements the British continued with their reform process, and a White Paper of 1988 proposed that elections for ten directly elected seats to the Legislative Council should go ahead in 1991. Once again, the British believed that they were working within the terms of the Basic Law, as it had been known by 1988 that the PRC intended to allow at least that number of directly elected members to be admitted to the first Special Administrative Region (SAR) legislature in 1997. These seats would now be brought forward to 1991. PRC negotiators could have quibbled over the number of these seats for 1991, but they did not do so.[7]

However, the fact that the PRC had successfully vetoed the introduction of political reform in the 1988 fuelled further anxiety within the local population in Hong Kong, and this increased much further following the release of proposals by a PRC-dominated Basic Law Drafting Committee (BLDC) that same year. The BLDC proposals called for a degree of representation, as had been promised in the Joint Declaration, but, and crucially, also averred that no referendum for full democracy could take place until at least 2011.

These proposals 'provoked vehement attacks' from the Hong Kong media, which regarded the date of 2011 as too distant, and which also believed that a considerable degree of democratisation had been promised for 1997 under the Joint Declaration. Here, the vague wording of the Joint Declaration about a 'legislature constituted by elections' took its toll, and wording which had appeared hopeful in 1984 seemed much less so in 1988. By that time a clamorous demand for democracy had developed within Hong Kong, and the realisation that the PRC might not allow any substantive degree of democratisation until – at least – 2011 came as a considerable shock; and one which was soon to be further intensified by unfolding horror in China.[8]

The Tiananmen massacre of 4 June 1989 in Beijing left the people of Hong Kong, who were already fearful of the PRC, 'utterly devastated'.[9] However, in addition to such desolation, the massacre led to the rapid growth of a widespread and vibrant pro-democracy movement, which demanded a much greater degree of political reform than was currently being promised. This demand, and pressure from the British Parliament and media, forced the British to accelerate the process of democratisation in Hong Kong. British negotiators then applied forceful pressure on Beijing to amend and further liberalise the existing draft of the as yet un-promulgated Basic Law, and this eventually led to an agreement with the PRC to extend the degree of democratisation endorsed by the Law. Here, the British managed to convince an extremely reluctant PRC, then reeling under international condemnation of the Tiananmen massacre, that it was necessary to calm fears in Hong Kong by showing flexibility, greater liberality and some willingness to negotiate. The agreement, which was inserted into the draft of the Basic Law in late 1989 as Annex II, provided for twenty directly elected seats in the Legislative council in 1997 (up from the ten proposed in the previous draft of the Law), rising to twenty-four in 1999, and thirty in 2003. Nevertheless, and despite this enlargement, an extensive pro-Beijing majority within the legislature remained assured: a fact that British officials, eager to reach the best agreement they could with the PRC, tried to play down when putting the deal before the Hong Kong public and British Parliament.

Following this, elections due in 1988, but postponed until 1991 because of opposition from the PRC, took place. During the negotiations just referred to, in addition to the figure of twenty directly elected seats for 1997, British negotiators had also managed to obtain the concession that eighteen of those twenty seats could be contested in the 1991 elections. Again, the intention, as far as both the British and Chinese were concerned, was to calm fears in Hong Kong whilst remaining within the covenant of the Basic Law. The first direct elections to the Legislative Council to take place in the history of Hong Kong led to the formation of an expanded Legislative Council of sixty seats, of which almost one third were directly elected. The election also resulted in a sweeping victory for the pro-democrats in these seats, and concomitant comprehensive defeat for pro-Beijing candidates.[10] The PRC government was dismayed, but was nevertheless constrained to accept the results.

In 1992 the last Governor of Hong Kong, Sir Christopher Patten, took office. Patten, a politician rather than career civil servant, arrived determined – and with a clear mandate from the British Government – to push forward democratic reform to the full extent provided for under the terms of the Joint Declaration and Basic Law.[11] By 1992 the British Government, now led by Prime Minister John Major, had come to feel that the previous Hong Kong Governor, Lord Wilson, had been too conciliatory towards the PRC, and that, as one consequence, Britain had made too many concessions towards an opponent perceived to be intransigent and narrow-minded. The intent now was to reverse some of that, and Patten arrived on the back of such sentiment, and determined to extend the process of democratisation. The Basic Law did not specifically prohibit any additional reform taking place after 1991 and prior to 1997, but neither did it contain any provision for such reform, and the British knew that, however modest their proposals for reform might be, they might still be opposed by Beijing on the latter grounds. However, the British were fully aware of the strong post-Tiananmen demand which had emerged in Hong Kong for the pace of democratisation to be quickened, and meeting that demand as much as possible now became the priority. For the British there was also a moral imperative at stake here. Given the events at Tiananmen, the British Government felt it had a duty to protect its citizens in Hong Kong as much as it feasibly could. The problem was, however, that the Chinese believed they had obtained an agreement in 1985 that, ideally, no further reforms would be proposed after 1991 and prior to the handover, and that, less ideally, any that were so proposed would be discussed closely with Beijing and would be agreed by Beijing before being made public. This 1985 'understanding' would now prove to be of considerable consequence.

Patten's plans for reform were both small-scale and legitimate within the terms of the Basic Law. However, a suspicious PRC did not fully grasp this and came to the conclusion that Patten was surreptitiously instituting counter-proposals to aspects of the Basic Law, or even to just the spirit and structure of the Law. Following the pattern of the previous governorship the PRC expected that Patten would come to Beijing early in order to enter into confidential negotiations over the management of the remainder of the transition period; it also expected that any reforms he might propose would more or less submit to stated Chinese positions. However, Patten and the British Government had no intention of continuing to behave in such a subservient manner, and also believed that, following Tiananmen and the 1991 elections, a strong demand for augmented reform had emerged within Hong Kong. In close contact with London, and without seeking Chinese consent first, or even going to Beijing,

Patten put forward his proposals in the face of increasingly volatile Chinese objection. The PRC then initiated a campaign of personal denigration against him, and also tried to have him removed as Governor. However the campaign backfired, as Patten came to be seen by Hongkongers as a Governor who would at last stand up for their rights and interests. London also made it clear to the PRC that Patten would not be replaced. It was, in fact, a major failure of diplomacy on the Chinese part to insist on the removal of Patten, as it would have been quite impossible for a British Parliament and government to meet that demand. It is also difficult to believe that the PRC demonisation of Patten was anything other than a propaganda strategy, and that the PRC was not fully aware that, although Patten may have designed the detail of the reforms, he did so as a consequence of covenants reached at the highest levels of the British Government. Patten was no maverick figure, as the PRC tried to show him to be, but a British political heavyweight with direct access to the British Prime Minister and Foreign Secretary. In addition, it would have been near impossible for the British Government to abandon a further reform process begun in the wake of 1989 and 1991, and based on extensive pressure from British and Hong Kong public opinion: to have done so would have made Britain appear a thoroughly emasculated force in comparison with an indurate PRC.

The Patten reforms were put before the Legislature in November 1993 and passed into law in June 1994. They were then implemented in September 1995 in preparation for municipal elections which took place in 1996 and led to yet another crushing defeat for pro-Beijing candidates. In December 1993 the PRC terminated negotiations with the British over the administration to be formed for 1997 and proceeded to develop its own plans for that administration. In December 1996 the PRC also established an appointed Provisional Legislative Council to take power in 1997. This fully appointed council violated the terms of both the Joint Declaration and the Basic Law, which clearly stipulated that one third of the legislature should be elected in 1997. The PRC took the view that, because of Patten's reforms, which did not violate the Basic Law, they could now violate that law as they saw fit. The British were now cut completely out of the picture, as also were the people of Hong Kong.

On 1 July 1997 a PRC-appointed Chief Executive, Executive Council and Legislative Council assumed power in Hong Kong and the Patten reforms were annulled. The election results of 1991 and 1995 were also overturned, and the twenty directly elected seats created in 1991 – eighteen of which had sitting members by 1997 – were suspended. The extensive pro-democracy victories of 1991 and 1995 were invalidated and many of the pro-Beijing candidates who had been soundly defeated in these elections were placed on the appointed Legislative Council. Nascent democracy in Hong Kong had disappeared. Hong Kong entered its post-colonial era as a Special Administrative Region (SAR) allowed to run a capitalist economy. As part of 'one country two systems' Hong Kong was, supposedly, granted considerable autonomy to run its own affairs. The SAR was also, according to the Basic Law, supposed to have an independent judiciary, and final jurisdiction. However, this proved not to be fully the case, as the judiciary discovered as early as 1999, when the first Chief Executive of the SAR, Tung Chee-hwa, refused to accept a judgment on foreign domestic helpers delivered by Hong Kong's highest court. Instead, Tung sent the judgment to the central authorities in Beijing, who overturned it. In this case the Chief Executive and Central Government believed that they were effectively above the Hong Kong law, and had the power to interpret that law in such a way as to counter decisions made by Hong Kong's highest court. Mainland officials also understood this in the post-colonial era, and, as Radio Television Hong Kong (RTHK) was soon to find out to its cost, believed that they had the right to intervene not only in legal matters, but also in matters relating to other aspects of the Hong Kong 'system'; and particularly where such matters involved an allegedly 'colonial' broadcaster such as RTHK.

THE HISTORICAL DEVELOPMENT OF TELEVISION IN HONG KONG

For present purposes the development of television in Hong Kong can be traced back to May 1957, when the Hong Kong branch of the British television company Rediffusion established the first television station in the colony. Initially, Rediffusion operated only a few subscription channels in English, and, as English was not the main language spoken by the majority of the Hong Kong population, the station had a very small audience, mainly consisting of expatriates and better-educated members of the local elite. However, in 1963 Rediffusion introduced a Chinese channel which was to become not only the first Chinese television channel in Hong Kong but also the world. In April 1973 Rediffusion was granted a free-to-air broadcasting licence and transformed itself into a terrestrial broadcasting service, with the title of the company also changing to that of Rediffusion Television Limited (RTV). In 1982 RTV was again renamed, this time as Asia Television Limited (ATV), offering two free channels: the Chinese 'Home' channel and the English 'World' channel. ATV remains today as one of the two terrestrial broadcasters in Hong Kong.

As Hong Kong's first and only television station, Rediffusion initially exercised monopoly control over the television industry in the colony. However, the company's decade of hegemony came to an abrupt end in November 1967 when Television Broadcasts Limited (TVB) was established as the first free-to-air terrestrial commercial television service in Hong Kong, offering services in both English and Cantonese. The launch of TVB provided an opportunity for the rapid and enhanced dissemination of local, popular Cantonese culture.

However impecunious sectors of the audience may have been, the purchase of a low-cost television set was now all that was required to view a considerable volume of soap operas, variety programmes, chat-shows and filmed Cantonese operas. Just as Cantonese commercial film was disappearing from the cinemas under pressure from a dominant Mandarin cinema, therefore, Cantonese popular culture found a new mode of mass-media expression in television.[12] TVB offered, and still offers today, two free-to-air channels: the Chinese 'Jade' and English 'Pearl' channels; and Jade, in particular, quickly came to dominate the local television market, sometimes securing up to 90 per cent of prime-time ratings.[13] In September 1975 a third commercial television channel, Commercial Television (CTV), was established. However, the presence of three commercial channels during the 1970s created intense competition, and CTV soon went out of business in August 1978, in part because of that competition, and in part because, unlike the other two broadcasters, it was required by the colonial government to broadcast some relatively unpopular 'educational' programmes. During the 1970s television became a mass medium in Hong Kong, with over 90 per cent of the population possessing a television set by 1976; and television had now also become the most important means of shaping and facilitating a growing sense of Hong Kong culture and identity amongst the local population.

TVB and ATV remain the only two free-to-air terrestrial broadcasters in Hong Kong to the present day. Both are widely considered to be pro-Beijing institutions at the level of their management, with ATV the more so, and TVB also earning the ironic designation of 'CCTVB' (CCTV being the official mainland broadcaster). From 1977 onwards TVB made individual documentary films at the estimated rate of two per year. Films winning international awards include *The Elderly* (1977), *Which Child is This* (1978), *I Quit* (1979), *Bless The Wives and the Children* (1985), and *China Reforms* (1985). A film such as *China Reforms* also provides an insight into the already partisan alignment of TVB at this time. *China Reforms* only tackles the issue of political reform in China in a marginal way, and is mainly concerned with the impact of economic reforms instituted in the early 1980s. The picture that emerges here is a reassuring one for the Hong Kong establishment: China is modernising, and developing an economy that is increasingly business-friendly; with new, relatively autonomous managers taking over previously parochial state-run monopolies. Various problems arising from these developments are discussed in the film, and leftist resistance to the economic reforms is touched on. However, the film does not criticise the central PRC authorities in any way, and does not, for example, address controversial issues of the day such as far-reaching corruption and nepotism. This is all the more surprising in that the film does mention that, as the reforms proceed, the new managers who are being shoehorned into important economic and political positions are actually the progeny of elite communist families. *China Reforms* does not indicate that there might be a problem with this, from any ethical or equitable point of view, and this lack of indication also reaches levels of high irony when one of the elite cadres is introduced. We are presented with a youthful Bo Xilai and informed that, as a member of one of the leading communist dynasties, he is being showered with a considerable number of high-ranking positions. Today, at the time of writing in 2013, Bo is under house-arrest awaiting trial, whilst his wife languishes in prison, convicted of murdering a British businessman. Part of the irony here is also that Bo did not encounter the wrath of the Central Government in 2012 because he was trying to institute modernising reform, as *China Reforms* claims he was in 1985, but because he was attempting to reinstate a pre-reform period 'red' Maoist system within the province of which he was governor.

It will not be possible to cover the documentary films of TVB in any depth in this chapter due to limitations of wordage, and because the principal focus of the chapter is RTHK. In addition, and for similar reasons of unavoidable restrictions on scope, the focus here will be on the films rather than the individuals who made the films. There are many such individuals involved, and they cannot all be considered here, though this is not to gainsay their achievements. In addition, these films are the product of teamwork, rather than individual authorship, and this provides a further rationale for regarding them as texts which have a relationship to their parent institution and historical context, rather than individual authorship. However, one point that needs to be made here in relation to this issue, and as regarding TVB, is that whilst the organisation itself may be evidently pro-Beijing, it does not necessarily follow from this that the documentary film-makers who work for the station are similarly so. Rather, it is more often a case of film-makers attempting to secure a requisite degree of editorial freedom within a sometimes unpropitious framework. Having said this, though, the evidence over the years does suggest, for one reason or another, a certain tendency to be 'respectful' rather than overly critical of the PRC. This attitude is clearly signalled in *China Reforms*, and can also be found in other films, including some – but not all – made on the subject of the Tiananmen massacre.

TVB documentary film-makers made a number of films on the China student protest movement just before and shortly after the massacre of 4 June 1989, and one film which deserves special mention here is *Spring of Discontent*, which appeared just before it, on 2 June 1989. *Spring of Discontent* is a remarkable and grippingly effective example of direct cinema, in which the film-makers interact, and also identify, with the student demonstrators. Unusually for TVB, the film contains virtually no commentary, and, instead, allows the protestors to speak for themselves. The passion and resolve of the demonstrators is vividly captured here, as they demand 'freedom' 'democracy' and the rule of law; and as they ridicule a 'senile' Deng Xiaoping. What also comes through here is the mammoth scale of the demonstrations, with over a million people marching at one point. *Spring of Discontent* is one of the foremost achievements of the Hong Kong documentary film, and would have a considerable impact were it to be shown today. Nevertheless, things changed quickly. *The Long March* (July 1989) (that is, the 'long march' of the student demonstrations from early 1989 to 4 June, not the Maoist 'Long March' of 1934), made only one month after the massacre, provides a history of the demonstrations, but hardly mentions the massacre, and contains no criticism of the military crackdown; whilst the over-arching tone of another film, *June 4th: One Year On* (June 1990), is of the PRC seeking 'stability' and social 'improvement'. In place of the visceral direct-cinema cinematography of *Spring of Discontent*, we now have a conventional studio discussion, in which comfortably seated guests coolly discuss the aftermath of massacre. As with *The Long March*, there is little criticism of the PRC or the military crackdown here.

From the mid-1990s onwards TVB appears to have ceased to make significant one-off documentary films and today mainly relies on its weekly current affairs programmes, *The Pearl Report* and *Sunday Report*, approximately 20 minutes long and in English and Cantonese respectively, which mainly cover social and sometimes political matters in Hong Kong, but which, by virtue of a pressing itinerary, are rarely able to cover subjects in great or incisive depth. In the earlier period, shortly after Tiananmen, a pronounced pro-Beijing bias also appears evident in at least some of these films. For example, *Patten v China* (1992) covers the debate over the reforms instituted by the Governor, Sir Christopher Patten, in 1992. The programme, a studio discussion involving three guests and a presenter, is, overall, critical of the reforms. For example, at one point the expatriate presenter, departing from a neutral position, suggests that 'Britain was changing the goalposts here', and, later, the same presenter opines that the reforms do 'not honour the spirit of the 1984 Accord'. One of the guests, an expatriate representing one of the elite financial corporations in Hong Kong, reinforces this position by claiming that the Patten reforms had 'fundamentally moved away from the 1984 agreement' and were 'tantamount to full democracy'. This latter charge, which is patently untrue, is not challenged. Another example that could be cited in this respect of apparent institutional bias is *Human Rights in China* (1993), which gives the general impression, and one not backed up by much evidence, that human rights abuse was decreasing in China in the early 1990s. *Human Rights in China* focuses mainly on suppression of religious, rather than political, rights, and this emphasis has the effect of diverting the programme away from issues related to political dissent. What these two films also illustrate is the growing polarisation taking place within Hong Kong society at the time between the business elite, who mainly wanted economic stability and continuance and therefore increasingly aligned themselves with Beijing, and the colonial administration and pro-democrats, who insisted upon the need for democratic reform.

It is also important to note that whilst the two TVB films just mentioned display an apparent China favouritism, this was not necessarily true of all the documentary films produced by TVB after 1990, and a change to this does seem to have occurred around 1994. Having said earlier that the contribution of individual figures within the film-making process would not be covered in this chapter, an exception does nonetheless have to be made here in the case of Diana Lin. In 1994 Lin was the presenter in a *Pearl Report* film featuring interviews with both Chris Patten and Lu Ping, the then Director of the Hong Kong Macau Affairs Office. The contrast with the 1992 *Pearl Report* film *Patten v China* is stark here as Lin fires questions at a visibly discomforted Ping, who is clearly not used to this sort of treatment. After a while Ping abruptly declares that he has had enough and walks out of the room, leaving a still-seated Lin gazing fixedly at the floor. In contrast to the haughty Ping, Patten comes over as a sophisticated, relaxed politician in his interview, and even looks relatively youthful. However, in a later 1996 *Pearl Report* film, in which Patten, with only '500 days' of his governorship remaining, is interviewed in depth, things have clearly changed. By this time the PRC has broken off negotiations, and, in two years, Patten appears to have aged considerably. Now grey-haired and with pronounced bags under his eyes, he appears both defensive and defiant in denying that his 'remaining 500 days will be only ceremonial'.

By 1996 Diana Lin had become both presenter and executive producer of the *Pearl Report*, and her impact comes through strongly in both the 1996 interview with Patten and a 1997 film made just months before the handover, entitled *RTHK's Future*. This 60-minute *Pearl Report* 'special' examines the prospects for RTHK following the retrocession, and, although one prominent pro-Beijing newspaper owner appears to be given more air-time than any pro-democracy figure, the programme remains commendably balanced in the face of the many criticisms being levelled at RTHK by pro-Beijing figures at the time. Whether or not Lin's superintendence was responsible for the equitable approach evident in *RTHK's Future* can only be a matter for speculation. However, in a 2004 film entitled *Doomed Democracy*, which deals with Beijing's refusal to grant Hong Kong universal franchise to elect the Chief Executive and Legislative Council in 2007–8, Lin is not even-handed at all. Far from echoing the pro-Beijing partiality of the 1990–3 period, she is, in contrast, forthrightly partial here in asserting that the decision of the Central Government has rung 'the death knell to Hong Kong's hopes for democracy' (though such forthrightness has also to be set against the context of the widespread anger and gloom felt in Hong Kong following the decision to rescind the elections). Lin would go on to lead the *Pearl Report* from 1996 to the present day of writing, and her impact has been considerable.

In addition to one-off programmes, the *Pearl Report* and its Cantonese counterpart have, over the years, clustered films together to form mini-series on subjects such as Tiananmen, the handover, SARS, Taiwan and reform in China. For example, in terms of the last of these, TVB made a four-part series on it in Cantonese in 1992, and, in 2009, a three-part series in both Cantonese and English. Although it will not be possible to explore these and other series in this chapter, a brief outline of the English series on reform in China will provide a serviceable summary of what the *Pearl Report* was able to do in the recent past, and what it is able to do today. *60 Years a Nation* consists of three programmes: *Born in 1949*, *The Absolute Principal*, and *Beyond Propaganda*. In *Born in 1949* a number of individuals born in 1949, including intellectuals, workers and rural farmers, are interviewed in their own living spaces. However, the oral-history approach adopted here tends to emphasise the human interest rather than political aspects of the stories. The overall feel of the film is nostalgic, lyrical, and safely uncritical of the present-day PRC. The phrase *The Absolute Principle* is a reference to Deng Xiaoping's statement that 'development' was the 'absolute principle' which superseded all other concerns in modern China governance. However, whilst the film covers the impact of rapid economic development on ordinary people and shows us examples of human suffering arising from such development, there is no great criticism of the authorities here, and no evident tragedies; and, in contrast to such criticism and evidence, and through numerous interviews with government functionaries, parts of the film even appear to eulogise the massive economic development taking place. The third film in the series, *Beyond Propaganda*, on the development of China 'soft power' as a public relations instrument, is mild indeed, and could never trouble any governing official in either Beijing or Hong Kong. This is the sort of relatively low-key path which the *Pearl Report* must still travel today, and another good example of this approach, also from 2009, is a film which purports to mark the twentieth anniversary of Tiananmen. Rather than focus on the profound political issues involved here, *Passing the Baton* focuses on a non-conforming President of the Hong Kong University Students Union, and the attempt by the student body to impeach him on account of his revisionist views on the Tiananmen massacre. This quirky and low-key stance towards such an important subject does not serve the *Pearl Report* particularly well, and there is even a hint of TVB pro-Beijing bias here, as the youthful impeached President is seen to be, to some extent, the 'victim' of an entrenched and 'closed-minded' view of Tiananmen as PRC atrocity.

However, and to reiterate, a film such as that just referred to, and other examples also given here, do not ineludibly indicate that the film-makers involved have compromised, and the reality is that they continue to do what they can within restrictive frameworks, whilst also working within an institution which is increasingly pro-Beijing and increasingly prone to inter-ference in matters of journalistic editorial judgment. As with ATV, which will be discussed next, film-makers (and News Office staff) at TVB have, from time to time, also strongly and publicly objected to the partisan approach adopted by their employer, and have exposed what they took to be unfair practices and unacceptable interference in editorial autonomy. In 2004, for example, a number of staff in the ATV newsroom resigned in protest at such practices and interference, creating a considerable amount of negative publicity for the broadcaster as a consequence. Finally, and also to restate once again, this time in the past tense, it has not been possible to cover the documentary films of TVB in any depth in this chapter, though it is expected that will take place in later publications.

ATV has produced a number of current-affairs documentary film series over the years. As with TVB, it will not be possible to explore these in depth here, and neither will it be possible to discuss the roles and achievements of particular film-makers, for the various reasons already given in this chapter. However, an overall study of the output of ATV has been carried out, and will be presented in outline. In addition, some films will also be explored in a degree of depth where possible. ATV's *News Magazine*, the Cantonese equiva-lent of the TVB *Sunday Report*, has been produced since 1988, but a number of the films produced in this series have been lost, and are not available for scrutiny. An English-language version (and/or equivalent) of *News Magazine* entitled *Vision Today* appeared in 1989 and lasted until 1992, when that series was replaced by *Monday Monitor*, which then ran until 1993. *Monday Monitor* was then replaced by *Inside Story*, which runs to the present day. Some of the films made in the early *Vision Today* and *Monday Monitor* series are available for viewing today, but others are not; whilst the copies of *Inside Story* available appear to date only from around 2009. In other words, there are many gaps here. As the title indicates, *Inside Story* films generally covered matters *inside* Hong Kong and seldom ventured beyond that. As will be discussed later, when some of these films are touched upon, a decidedly pro-establishment orienta-tion is evident within many of the films, and especially the later ones. Beyond this series, though, and over many years, frequent accusations of overt pro-establishment political bias have been levelled against ATV as an institution.

The documentary films of ATV tend to be more generic than those of TVB and were regularly made in extensive series, with few changes from film to film. Many of these series were also bought in. For example, *Touching Stories Hong Kong*, from 1998 to 2004, contains some 150 episodes of interviews with Hong Kong personalities or celebrities, but all share the same format from episode to episode. The same is true of a series such as the interview-based hagiographic *HK 100 VIPs* (privately sponsored, 2011–12, 100 episodes). It is, though, debatable whether these series could even be classed as 'documentary films' as they consist almost entirely of interviews. Other longer series which can be more clearly categorised as 'films' include *Macau 500 Years* (2010, twenty episodes), which was a commissioned series; and *One Hundred Years of the Republic* (2011, twenty episodes), which again appears to have been bought in but given some added post-production treatment, including a hosted commentary, by ATV current-affairs personnel. Whilst relatively objective in the recounting of the history of the China 'republic' from 1911 to 2011, the added ATV narration to this commissioned series nevertheless manages to imbue it with the – for ATV – requisite 'loyalist' tone. In addition to these longer series, ATV has also made a few short series of films in-house, including *Deng Xiaoping and Hong Kong* (2004, five episodes). Even rarer than these, but similarly under-critical, are one-off productions such as *Donald Tsang: A Man and His Mission* (2006) and *Wen Jiabao's Work Report* (2010). It is worth pausing for a while to consider both of these, and particularly *Donald Tsang: A Man and His Mission*, given what happened to the lauded subject of this film later.

Donald Tsang Yam-kuen was the second Chief Executive of the Hong Kong SAR, and one of the most striking things about the opening sequences of *Donald Tsang: A Man and his Mission* is the extent to which the film criticises the first Chief Executive, Tung Chee-hwa. For example, we are told in no uncertain terms and quite scathingly that Tung was 'a poor . . . indecisive . . . leader', and this surprisingly strongly expressed sentiment – from a decidedly pro-Beijing broadcaster – is reiterated several times later in the film. It is true that by 2005 the Tung administration had become unpopular, but what is also happening here is that ATV is taking a modicum of reckoning on Tung, whose populist policies affected the interests of the Hong Kong tycoon class of which ATV was a prominent member. At the time Tsang was seen by the tycoons as someone with whom they could do business, in contrast to Tung, who was viewed as being more closely associated with mainland elites. However, Tsang's closeness to the Hong Kong (and, in some cases, also mainland) tycoons would eventually bring him into disdain. In this highly forgettable film, which is little more than an affirmative public-relations exercise, Tsang mentions that nobody can become the leader of Hong Kong 'without Beijing's blessing', and that he is happy to work with an 'enlightened and supportive Central Government'. Most ironic, however, is Tsang's assertion, in response to a question on how he would like his legacy to be perceived, that he wanted to be remembered for having done 'an honest job'. Tsang's close connections with the tycoon class eventually led to his departure from office in ignominy in 2012 (at the end of his term) when it was revealed that he had accepted gifts and privileges for which civil servants below his rank would have been strongly disciplined, if not sacked. The contrast between the confident, blasé 2006 Tsang of *Donald Tsang: A Man and his Mission*, and the 2012 Tsang seen weeping before an animated Legislative Council is cogent. *Wen Jiabao's*

Work Report (2010) is in many ways a more interesting film than the Tsang film because it is so peculiar. The film's presenters first set out an entirely affirmative account of Wen's Report to the National People's Congress, and show NPC members giving the report their unqualified enthusiastic endorsement. However, back in Hong Kong an invited commentator, a straggle-haired female 'noted Sinologist' from Sweden, then proceeds to systematically demolish almost every clause of the great Report, to the evident embarrassment and surprise of the presenter. As with the contrast between the Tsang of 2006 and 2012, the dissimilarity between the stage-managed and ATV/mainland-lauded 'Report' and this exposé of it is glaring.

ATV used to store its films in a warehouse near the sea. However, it appears that the company did not take too much care of these as, unfortunately, the severe humidity destroyed a considerable number of them. Then, and by way of contrast, in 1987 a fire at the ATV Kowloon Tong Broadcasting House base destroyed yet more. Thankfully, though, some Hong Kong university libraries started copying ATV film broadcasts from the mid-1990s, and some of these (now badly deteriorating) tapes are available for scrutiny. What survives appears to show a clear pro-establishment orientation. In the early period this is less obvious, though, with a 1992 film on the Patten reforms entitled *Constitutional Changes of the Governor* managing to achieve balance, and little evident bias. *Constitutional Changes of the Governor* was part of the ATV *Monday Monitor* series, which only ran from 1992 to 1993. It also seems that both this series and its brief-lived predecessor, *Vision Today* (1989–92), were able and prepared to tackle some subjects which later programmes would shy away from. For example, two other *Monday Monitor* films from 1992 – *Self-censorship and the Media*, and *June 4th . . . Three Years On* – are anything but pro-Beijing. *Self-censorship and the Media* makes the point strongly that the problem of self-censorship in Hong Kong is increasing, as media editors become increasingly nervous about retaliatory measures that might be taken by Beijing, and as pro-Beijing businessmen start to buy up media outlets. *June 4th . . . Three Years On* contains interviews with a number of young people whose lives have been affected in one degree or another by the Tiananmen massacre, and makes no attempt to be other than sympathetic to the cause of the student protestors in Tiananmen Square. One interviewee, for example, recounts receiving a phone call from her sister, who had witnessed events unfolding in the square, in which her sister claims to have seen 'tanks rolling over students'.

However, from 1994, and after the demise of *Monday Monitor*, ATV's Cantonese *News Magazine* and English *Inside Story* gradually moved away from such a critical approach to China. The picture is, however, still a varied, if not muddled, one, both in relation to China and imperative subjects; and films made between the mid-1990s and the late-2000s clearly display a determined commitment to maintain necessary measures of balance and objectivity. Here, credit must be given to the news staff and film-makers, and, bolstering this, anecdotal and other evidence also suggests that during this period the relationship between news staff, film-makers and management at ATV was sometimes tense, as programme-makers sought to preserve editorial autonomy in the face of intercessionist management. Such attempts at preservation came to a head from time to time. For example, in 1994 management intervention to cut footage of the Tiananmen massacre from a programme marking the fifth anniversary of the atrocity led to the resignation of several senior programme staff. By the time we arrive at the late 2000s, though, a pro-establishment/Beijing bias appears more evident in the material coming out of ATV. For example, a 2012 *Inside Story* film on the introduction of national education, entitled *National Education and Liberal Studies*, clearly weighs in favour of national education; whilst another *Inside Story* film from 2012, entitled *Chief Executive Leung Chun-ying*, is set solidly within the pro-establishment camp. This latter film explores tensions within the said camp and 80–90 per cent of those interviewed in the film are from that camp. In contrast, the pro-democrats are granted only token coverage. This is fully in line with ATV's covert policy of promoting the pro-establishment, pro-Beijing cause. However, and as with TVB, ATV does not occupy a central place within this chapter, which, instead, focuses on Radio Television Hong Kong (RTHK). The remainder of this chapter will now cover the debates which have arisen around this broadcaster, whilst the next chapter will explore the films of RTHK.

RADIO TELEVISION HONG KONG

Radio Television Hong Kong (RTHK) was, and remains today, the public-service television service of Hong Kong. It is also a government department, and therefore quite unlike the two commercial broadcasters (ATV and TVB). The history of RTHK can be traced back to as early as 1928. In June of that year an amateur broadcaster with the acronym of GOW came on air. In 1929, recognising the need to establish its authority over radio in Hong Kong, the colonial government stepped in, and GOW was given the new acronym of ZBW, and supported with the aid of a government grant. Five years later, in 1934, another broadcaster, ZEK, was established to provide radio broadcasting in Chinese, whilst ZBW continued to broadcast in English.[14] In January 1939, and against the background of both looming war in Europe and the ongoing Sino-Japanese War, both ZBW and ZEK were placed under the direct control of the Postmaster General, whilst an advisory body, the Broadcasting Advisory Committee, was also established.[15] However the Committee was, as its title suggests, only 'advisory', and the two broadcasters remained firmly under the control of the Postmaster General, who was in turn directly responsible to the Governor.

ZBW and ZEK ceased operation following the occupation of Hong Kong by Japanese forces in December 1941. Then, after the liberation in August 1945, a group of amateur enthusiasts took possession of the broadcasting apparatus, operating it as best they could until it was re-appropriated by the Office of the Postmaster General in 1947, one year after British colonial civilian rule had been restored to the colony. In August 1948, and partly in celebration of the twentieth anniversary of the birth of radio broadcasting in Hong Kong, ZBW and ZEK were renamed Radio Hong Kong (RHK), a title which clearly and openly established the station as the official radio broadcaster.[16] In April 1951 the station then came under the control of the Government Public Relations Office (PRO).[17] The PRO had been established in 1947. However, and as argued in the previous chapter of this book, it did not expand its operations significantly until 1950, when John Lawrence Murray took over as Public Relations Officer. The change of affiliation of RHK to the PRO was driven and influenced by that expansion. However, the growing importance of radio during the 1950s, and the need to provide public-service radio with at least the semblance of independence, meant that inclusion within the government propaganda and public relations department proved unsatisfactory, and in July 1953 RHK was reconstituted as a separate government department under a 'Controller, Broadcasting'. Despite such augmentation, however, RHK was not able to carry out all-day broadcasting in Chinese until 1957, and, in English, until as late as 1960.[18] These dates are revealing. Broadcasting in English had begun in Hong Kong in 1928, and did not take place in Chinese until five years after that date. However, in the 1950s it was comprehensive Chinese broadcasting that came first. During the chaotic 1950s radio had now become a crucial means through which the colonial government would attempt to maintain order and social stability in Hong Kong, and that is largely why the Chinese service was given the go-ahead first.

In 1968, eleven years after the appearance of commercial television in Hong Kong, the colonial government finally initiated a process that would lead to the establishment of a government television unit. The unit, which was based within RHK and given the title of Radio Hong Kong Television (RHKTV), was belatedly established in April 1970, though it was not fully operative until 1972. The formation of RHKTV was a controversial event, as will be discussed in greater depth shortly. The main point to make for the moment is that the broadcaster was not inaugurated as a comprehensive organisation with a dedicated broadcasting platform. Instead, RHKTV made programmes which were broadcast – under government obligation – by the two commercial broadcasters.

The relationship between public broadcasting and the colonial government in Hong Kong was a contested and controversial one. Hong Kong was not a democracy, and some influential voices within the colony were of the opinion that public-service broadcasting should not have the same sort of self-determining relationship to government that obtained within democratic countries such as Britain. Radio in Hong Kong had been under government control since 1929, and RHK was formed in 1948 as a government office, if not yet department. The transfer of RHK from the Office of the Postmaster General to the PRO in 1951 was merely a transfer from one government department to another, and did not signify that any greater degree of autonomy for the broadcasters had taken place. However, broadcasters working in RHK often came from a background and training in Britain or Commonwealth territories such as Australia, and expected a very different model of relations between public broadcaster and government: one epitomised by and enshrined within the institutional structure of the semi-independent 'public-corporation'. Here, as with the British Broadcasting Corporation (BBC), which was granted public-corporation status as early as 1926, the public broadcaster was not controlled directly by a government minister or department, but by a professional authority advised by a (theoretically) autonomous board of governors. By the 1950s it was increasingly appreciated by some within the colonial government in Hong Kong that official communications, and particularly news reporting, would be more easily received by the local population if that communication and reporting had at least the semblance of being disinterested and of stemming from a reasonably autonomous professional source. Fuelled by such a gathering appreciation, guarded discussions then began on the pros and cons of making RHK more autonomous from government, and these discussions eventually led to a government review of RHK in 1956 which proposed a:

> Transfer [of] the station to the control of a public corporation which will combine the advantages of independent management with a responsibility to the public for the provision of balanced programmes of a reasonable standard without the need to show a profit to shareholders.[19]

Then, in 1960, and following up on the 1956 review, a working party chaired by the then Director of Broadcasting proposed that a public corporation be established to take over RHK for the production of both radio and a later television service.[20] However, this proposal was not adopted. Whilst some within government accepted the logic of the public-relations argument here, other, more senior officials did not, and remained reluctant to give up direct government control of the broadcaster.

Having said the above though, a distinction must be drawn at this point between the debate on whether or not RHK should become more independent of government and the less contentious perception that the institution's reporting and communication could or should be as 'objective' as possible. The notion that RHK should practise unprejudiced journalism was, in fact, largely acceptable to government on public-relations grounds, and, given this level of acceptability and also given the government's pressing requirement for help and expertise in ultimately establishing television broadcasting within the colony, it was reasonable that it should look towards the much-admired BBC in Britain for such help and expertise. Consequently, in 1970, an experienced BBC broadcaster, James Hawthorne, was appointed to the post of 'Controller, Television'. However, whilst government officials may have thought Hawthorne would be able to institute the sort of impartial programming that they, the officials, deemed to be necessary (or just unavoidable), those same officials underestimated Hawthorne's commitment to the model of institutional autonomy represented by the BBC.

The decision to develop what was first referred to as a 'Government Television Unit' (GTU) was first made in late 1969. Initially, there were no plans to replace the Hong Kong Film Unit (HKFU) with the GTU, and, in fact, HKFU staff even joined a consultation on creating a 'Film Section' within the GTU for the production of documentary films. For example, the head of the HKFU at the time, Albert Young, took part in such a meeting on 12 March 1970.[21] Discussions then continued through 1970 and 1971 over the organisation of the GTU, and, in June 1971, the nascent unit was given the appellation of Radio Hong Kong Television (RHKTV). However, although apparently linked to Radio Hong Kong through title and location, RHKTV was actually placed under the control of the Government Information Services department (GIS). RHK was not part of GIS at this time and was already a separate government department. As part of GIS, therefore, the confusingly named RHKTV was, at least initially, expected to carry on playing the same role that the GIS HKFU played, though in relation to television rather than the cinema.[22] For example, government correspondence at the time makes it clear that RHKTV was to broadcast government policy and public information through short information bulletins, with more contextual – though still government-related – documentary films emerging at some as yet unspecified point in the future. Though much of this is confusing, and must have appeared so at the time, one thing remains evident: RHKTV was not founded as a public-service broadcaster in the usual sense of that phrase, but as a government instrument; and this envisioned functionality was reinforced by the fact that RHKTV was placed under the auspices of GIS, rather than RHK.

The initial positioning of RHKTV within GIS was also linked to an ongoing struggle for control of official information which had accelerated following the riots of 1967. Essentially, two schools of thought were at odds with each other here. The first of these contended that, following the riots, tighter regulation of government information must be exercised; the second maintained that, given the ultimate widespread public support for the government evident during the riots, information supervision should now be eased, and also possibly decentralised. Whilst, however, two schools of thought may have been in evidence over this matter, at the time it was the former of the two which held sway, and, for the most part, and as during the 1950s, senior officials remained staunchly of the view that close command should be maintained over the production and dissemination of government publicity and information. One imperative example of such a stance can be found in the intercession in this matter of Nigel Watt, the then Director of GIS.

In a memo and proposal to the government dated 11 December 1967 Watt called for public information units to be set up in all government departments. Watt believed that following general public opposition to the communist-inspired riots the public should be consulted and informed more fully, and he also believed that because an increase in the propagation of communist propaganda in Hong Kong was to be expected, official information services would have to be expanded exponentially (and, here, for Watt, an undertaking to apprise and a responsibility to manipulate information go effortlessly, and unreflectively, hand in hand).[23] However, and crucially, in addition to calling for such additional operations, Watt also insisted that GIS retain its existing ultimate authority over all official information output, and this meant that, in practice, all departments would remain dependent upon GIS for such output, and overall regulation from the centre would be retained. However, this created a contradiction, because such an arrangement implied that GIS would continue to both produce 'objective' information *and*, as Watt put it, ensure 'that Government always appears in the best possible light in the minds of local people'.[24]

The fact that GIS was having to perform – and insisted upon so performing – both these functions, and was, in addition, in control of all official information and news output, created problems and anomalies, not only for GIS, but for other government departments. These difficulties were most keenly felt at RHK, and, later, RHKTV. RHK was a government department which broadcast what the organisation hoped the public would take to be accurate and impartial news bulletins. However, in fact, RHK was entirely dependent upon GIS, the government mouthpiece, for those bulletins. The Director of Broadcasting at the time, Donald Brooks, objected to this on the quite reasonable grounds that he was being made accountable for news broadcasts that he had no control over. In contrast to Watt, Brooks wanted RHK to distance itself from GIS, and to eventually generate its own news output. By 1968, however, senior colonial officials still continued to back the stance taken by Watt rather than that of Brooks, arguing that 'there might be doubts as to the degree of control which could be exercised over a RHK news team'.[25] The stand-off between Watt and Brooks over control of news output continued up to 1972, and also became particularly heated that year, with Brooks asserting, in a memo to the Colonial Secretary (second only in standing to the Governor), that Watt and GIS had 'strangleholds over operational matters' at RHK.[26]

The arm-wrestling and impasse finally ended in October 1972, with the appointment of an 'Information Secretary . . . responsible for Government's total information and public relations effort'. This appointment meant that there would now be senior oversight of RHK and RHKTV operations, and, therefore, no need for GIS to also continue with such oversight.[27] Nigel Watt lost this particular battle because, late in 1972, senior government ministers, including the governor himself, Sir Murray MacLehose, finally came to the conclusion that both RHK and the newly created RHKTV would work more productively, and be more acceptable to the public, if they were seen to possess at least a modicum of self-determination. Consequently, in late 1972, RHK obtained its newsroom, and RHKTV was moved out from under GIS control to come under the purview of a newly-established Film and Television Department, which itself came under the oversight of the Secretariat for Home Affairs, within which the newly created post of Information Secretary was located. Like RHK, RHKTV remained within a government department, but was now at least some distance from the government mouthpiece (though, in practice, some RHKTV activities continued to take place within GIS premises, as well as at the studios of RHK – all very confusing). Nevertheless, the colonial government still remained concerned over the possibility that RHKTV might become semi-detached from government imperatives, and, in 1973, moved Watt from his position in GIS in order to establish him as Hong Kong's first Commissioner for Television and Films, and first Director of the newly established Film and Television Division. The newly promoted and, from the government point of view, highly trusted Watt, previously Director of GIS for ten years, could now continue to monitor the situation on behalf of the government, and keep the broadcasters in plain view.[28]

In addition to such supervision by Watt, however, the colonial government also developed legislation which would ensure that RHKTV, and RHK, remained closely connected to official imperatives and under ultimate government control. In 1971, one year prior to the separation of RHKTV from GIS, a government working party was established in order to take submissions and submit recommendations to government on the future organisation and structure of radio and television broadcasting in Hong Kong. In their own submissions to the working party, Hawthorne and Brooks argued strongly that RHK and RHKTV should become constituent elements of a new public corporation which would be independent of government. However, the 1971 working party rejected this proposal because, as has been shown, many within government remained firmly opposed to the idea. Hawthorne then publicly, and vocally, disassociated himself from this decision, and, in doing so, set a precedent for other and later confrontations between leading figures within the public broadcasting service and government officials.[29] Nevertheless, and despite Hawthorne's protestations to the contrary, at the conclusion of the working party review, RHKTV remained the official television unit within the government department of RHK, and, as previously mentioned, also remained linked in various ways to GIS.

This situation continued up to 1975, when another committee was assembled to discuss the reorganisation of the department of RHK, and the merger with it of the existing small-scale Education Television service (ETV), which was then located within the Department of Education. The reorganisation and merger eventually took place in 1976, and the newly restructured department was given the new and still current title of Radio Television Hong Kong (RTHK).[30] After 1976, therefore, RTHK remained a government department. It was, however, an unusual one. The public-service broadcasting ethos and editorial autonomy inherited from the BBC, and sanctioned – however reluctantly – by the colonial administration, meant that, unlike other government departments, the broadcaster was not charged with communicating government policy unequivocally and categorically. RTHK was given more latitude than other departments were able to enjoy largely because of the imperative need to convince the public that the broadcaster was reporting the news as impartially as it was able. RTHK was also in the public eye all the time, and this distinguished the broadcaster from other government departments, which may have had only marginal contact with the public and public-opinion leaders. The make-up of RTHK also differed from that of other departments in that only around 60 per cent of those appointed to the broadcaster were civil servants. The rest were contracted professionals who were employed without civil service pension entitlement. All of this meant that RTHK existed at the periphery, rather than the centre, of government, a fact which helped the organisation to develop a sense of its own particular identity, but also gave rise to conflict with government officials wedded to the belief that it was important for the colonial administration to fully control 'its own [broadcast] propaganda organ'.[31]

In February 1984 a Broadcasting Review Board (BRB) was established to review the state of broadcasting in Hong Kong and present recommendations to government. However, 1984 also marked both the signing of the Sino-British Joint Declaration on the future of Hong Kong and a considerable escalation of apprehensive debate within the colony on what that future might consist of. Any consideration of the future of broadcasting in Hong Kong would, therefore, inevitably be framed by this much larger and contentious context, and considerable importance then became ascribed to the BRB, whose recommendations would be judged by many in relation to the extent to which they might enhance or deplete the ability of broadcasters to report on that context. The BRB was, in addition, a substantial committee, whose composition – chaired by a High Court judge, rather than a government official, and also containing eight unofficial members alongside eight officials – suggested that it had been given a mandate to explore significant change to the existing broadcasting system, including that which might relate to the role of RTHK.

The final BRB report was released in September 1985, and one of its major recommendations, that a Broadcasting Authority be established to regulate the broadcasting industry, was quickly accepted by government.[32] However, the BRB recommendation that RTHK cease to be a department of government and become an independent public-service broadcaster was merely placed under consideration. The BRB recommendation on RTHK attempted to address the difficulties that the Board felt RTHK was facing by the mid-1980s, difficulties which stemmed from a still widespread perception that the broadcaster was largely a mouthpiece of the colonial government. The BRB believed, for example, that:

> RTHK sometimes encountered difficulties stemming from public perception of the station as a government department. [Staff of RTHK] . . . expressed concern that RTHK was regarded by many government officials and members of the public as a propaganda instrument serving the interests of the Administration, that the editorial independence of the staff was not fully respected, and that this was detrimental to staff morale.[33]

The BRB took the view that this was an unsatisfactory situation, and recommended that in order to counteract such perceptions RTHK should be made more clearly and openly independent.

As discussions continued between the various parties over the BRB recommendations, RTHK appointed a new Director of Broadcasting, Ms Cheung Man-yee, who succeeded the veteran Hawthorne in January 1986. Like Hawthorne, Cheung was committed to the belief that RTHK should become a public corporation, and, in February, just one month after taking up her position, she made a submission to the government supporting the 1984 BRB recommendation on RTHK.[34] In November 1986, in response to this and other contributions, the government decided in principle to increase the autonomy of RTHK further, and allow it to be run by a Board of Governors, as was the case with the BBC. However, the government again rejected the call for RTHK to be disestablished from government and become a full-blown public corporation.[35] Finally, in December 1986, the government passed into law a Broadcasting Authority Ordinance and created a Hong Kong Broadcasting Authority to implement the Ordinance. Under the terms of the Ordinance, RTHK would achieve a greater degree of corporate autonomy, and be advised by a nine-member Board of Governors who would also report to government. A degree of financial autonomy was introduced in the form of a block grant which could be used by the broadcaster as it, not government, saw fit.[36]

However, and as far as RTHK was concerned, the new arrangements came with attendant difficulties. RTHK would not have full independence as a public corporation, and would remain a government department, albeit one with a very unusual and devolved management structure. Journalists and other staff in RTHK were also concerned about the level of autonomy which would in fact be achieved under the new scheme, and, in particular, with the issue of who the government would place on the Board of Governors.[37] The situation was, after all, very different from that of the longed-for British one, in which a democratically-elected government was obliged to place figures from a wide range of walks of life on the Board of Governors of the BBC, under the keen scrutiny of Parliament. In contrast to that, in Hong Kong the Governor was absolute ruler, and could place whoever he wanted on the Board of RTHK. These appointees might then come to play a substantial role in shaping, and possibly interfering with, editorial and journalistic practice within the institution. In addition, the members of the Broadcasting Authority itself were chosen by the government, and, although not a government institution but, rather, a government-appointed advisory body, the new and inexperienced Authority was heavily reliant on a particular government department, the Television and Entertainment Licensing Authority, for expert advice and guidance.[38] This all meant that the relationship between RTHK and the government remained both close, and uncertain; and the problems associated with such a relationship were then foregrounded further, and in dramatic form, in 1989.

The machinery of colonial government in Hong Kong sometimes moved slowly during this period, and one consequence of this was that, whilst the Broadcasting Authority was established in 1986, no significant change occurred to the organisational structure of RTHK, and no board of governors was established, either that year or in 1987–8, even though change had been agreed upon. This situation of drift and delay then continued on into the crucial year of 1989. As mentioned previously in this chapter, the Tiananmen massacre of 4 June 1989 created widespread alarm and shock in a Hong Kong which was by then only eight years away from forced retrocession to the PRC. However, the anxiety caused in Hong Kong by this terrible event also led to a widespread demand within the colony for more accurate and truthful information about the unfolding situation, irrespective of the needs, policies and objectives of a colonial government which, otherwise, might wish to tone down such information. The forceful Director of Broadcasting at RTHK, Cheung Man-yee, also took the opportunity presented by the events at Tiananmen to once more press for the independence of RTHK, claiming that, if this did not happen with immediate effect, 'after 1997 people may regard it as [a branch of] Central Television' (CCTV, the Communist Party controlled television organisation on the mainland).[39] As a result of this intervention and others, some of which took the form of heated debates within the Hong Kong Legislative and Executive Councils, an unequivocal government decision was taken in July 1989, just one month after the Tiananmen massacre, to finally turn RTHK into a public broadcaster which would be genuinely independent of government. However, and even so, it was not until October 1991 that the Executive Council decided to formally disestablish RTHK and set up an independent corporation, with full 'corporatisation' expected to be achieved by 1992.[40]

This relatively long timetable from 1989 to the expected end-date of 1992 was partly conditioned by the various administrative hurdles which the disestablishment exercise was expected to have to overcome. However, it was also influenced by the political confusion that broke out in Hong Kong after the events at Tiananmen. As previously argued in this chapter, the Tiananmen massacre provided the colonial government with the momentum and strength of mind necessary to override Chinese objections and finally implement elections in 1991 which had been suspended in 1988. As argued earlier, these 1991 elections had been agreed in principle by the Chinese, and did not contravene the 1990 Basic Law. However, PRC negotiators remained suspicious of any attempt made by the colonial government to introduce further democratisation measures in Hong Kong prior to the 1997 handover, and were, in addition, particularly alarmed by the outcome of the 1991 elections, which handed clear victory to the pro-democracy camp. The colonial government was also fully aware that any attempt to make RTHK independent would not go down well with authorities in the PRC, and might be perceived as an exercise in underhand democratisation. In July 1991 British and Chinese negotiators had also signed a 'Memorandum of Understanding' that, though specifically aimed at clarifying shared responsibilities and costs for the building of a new airport in Hong Kong, also laid down the general principle that both sides would consult and co-operate with each other over any significant developments taking place within the colony prior to 1997 (and this also reinforced the 1985 informal 'agreement' mentioned earlier in this chapter).[41] Amongst other things, this meant that, if the Chinese objected, it would be difficult for the colonial government to press ahead with the corporatisation of RTHK.

The PRC did object, and repeatedly. For example, in a visit to Hong Kong in February 1992, a senior official at the Hong Kong and Macau Affairs Office of the Chinese Central Government insisted that the future Hong Kong Special Administrative Region government must have its own broadcaster – that is, RTHK – to broadcast and promote government policy.[42] Quickly following this, in March 1992, Lu Ping, the Director of the Office, insisted that only minimum changes to the existing political system in Hong Kong, including, by implication, any to the role of the government broadcaster, should be made during the transition period to 1997.[43] Finally, in the same month, the Chinese representatives of the Sino–British Liaison Group, which was then making preparations for the 1997 handover, refused to give approval to any proposed corporatisation of RTHK. A political impasse had now been reached, and the colonial government was forced to shelve its plans to make the broadcaster independent.[44] The window of opportunity which had opened after 1984, and, in particular, after 1989, had closed.

On 1 July 1997 Hong Kong was handed over to the PRC and became a Special Administrative Region (SAR) of the PRC. However, although the concession of 'one country two systems' provided assurance – albeit conjectural – that the Hong Kong way of life would continue as it had before the handover, that did not necessarily apply to RTHK, a public-service broadcaster which mainland officials regarded as an unwelcome vestige of colonialism. To those officials there was no doubt that a public broadcaster should be controlled by the state, and that public broadcasters were there to support and communicate government policy, and little beyond that. It was, therefore, inevitable, that mainland attention would turn to the 'problem' of RTHK, and this turned out to be the case from as early as March 1998, when Xu Simin, a Standing Committee member of the Chinese People's Political Consultative Conference, argued that RTHK was a 'remnant of British rule' and was 'against the SAR Government and Mr Tung [first Chief Executive of the HKSAR] under the pretext of editorial independence'.[45] Tung himself was more than happy to respond considerately to this intervention, asserting that, 'while freedom of speech is important, it is important for government policies to be positively presented. I will look into this matter'.[46] Tung's language implies a degree of warning here. Under the Basic Law the Hong Kong media was also supposed to be the responsibility of the Hong Kong government alone. Yet the intervention here by a senior PRC official so soon after the handover suggested otherwise. Xu's comments may have been those of one individual, but Xu was also a senior party official and this gave the impression that the party was speaking through him. As mentioned earlier in this chapter, the majority of the people of Hong Kong had preferred to approach the predestined and unavoidable handover in a spirit of resigned though anxious hopefulness. However, interventions such as those by Xu gave pause for thought and cause for concern; and also much for the Hong Kong media to talk about.

Xu's position on RTHK stemmed from a totalitarian conception of the relationship between the state and the media which had been entrenched within the PRC since its founding, and in which the media – and particularly public broadcasters – were expected to act as the communication arm of the state. Given this, Xu would not have understood how RTHK, as a government department, could be allowed to adopt an editorial and journalistic practice which sometimes appeared to question government policy. However, by the time that Xu had made his comments in 1998, and after many public debates reaching as far back as the 1970s, the largely self-directed (or at least precariously semi-autonomous) public-service role of RTHK had been widely accepted within Hong Kong civil society. Such a role would have riled authoritarians such as Xu and Tung, but it also posed difficulties for less authoritarian figures in Hong Kong because, in a public-service broadcasting system, there is no clear dividing line to determine to what extent the broadcaster should support the state on any particular issue and to what extent it should not. Public-service broadcasting carries this difficulty unavoidably as an integral and characteristic aspect of its day-to-day operations. On top of this difficulty, though, there is, in the case of RTHK, an added fundamental contradiction, and one pointed out frequently by supporters of RTHK, between RTHK as a public-service broadcaster modelled intellectually on the highly autonomous BBC, and RTHK as a government department within an authoritarian regime. And this contradiction could only be genuinely overcome by either of two means: through making RTHK independent of that regime, or making the organisation subordinate to the regime. Otherwise, the future could only be one of ongoing tension.

These difficulties, and the lack of resolution on this point, made RTHK vulnerable. RTHK broadcasters walked a tightrope, and had to be cautious about arriving at decisions on how far they could go in apparently contradicting, or even just questioning, SAR and PRC officials, policies and ideology. The problem, though, is that tightropes are inherently unsteady, and, inevitably, some of the decisions reached by RTHK were bound to be seen, and were seen by government officials at the time, as going beyond the broadcaster's proper remit. Nevertheless, RTHK remained an influential institution which retained public support, and could not be easily subordinated. And, after all, the situation was a tense one: Hong Kong had been appropriated by a totalitarian dictatorship against the will of its people, and, against that context, public demand for RTHK to remain a source of accurate and truthful information about SAR and mainland government activities remained high. This meant that, however much they may have wished to ostracise RTHK, government and mainland officials were unable to challenge the organisation in any fundamentally direct manner. As the first Chief Executive of the HKSAR put it in 1998, the 'problem' of RTHK would have to be dealt with 'slowly-slowly'.[47]

The unexpected intervention of Xu in March 1998 also caused something of a backlash in Hong Kong, leading to further calls to protect the editorial autonomy of RTHK. Later in March, and shortly after Xu's intercession, the long-serving and forthright Director of the broadcaster, Cheung Man-yee, also restated her well-known stance of 1989 that RTHK must not become a mere government mouthpiece. Following that, in April, the Legislative

Council passed a motion affirming the editorial independence of the broadcaster.[48] The 1997 Government may have been hand-picked and unelected but many of its members were nonetheless locals embedded within a Hong Kong civil society in which RTHK was still regarded as an important institution, and this regard bore on the April affirmation. With this support in mind, RTHK then also issued detailed production guidelines to its staff in September 1998 designed to further consolidate the broadcaster's editorial and journalistic autonomy. All of this irritated and confused authoritarians such as Xu and Tung. However, what RTHK did next annoyed them much more, and also infuriated the mainland government.

By the mid-1990s Beijing had managed to gain extensive indirect control of the media in Hong Kong. By then, for instance, most newspapers were either openly pro-Beijing, or unprepared to criticise Beijing.[49] At the same time, media tycoons in Hong Kong were also increasingly gravitating towards and establishing alliances with their counterparts on the mainland. Economic reforms on the mainland which had begun in the early 1980s had produced a new and wealthy class of corporate entrepreneurs in China by the late 1990s, and Hong Kong media tycoons saw these individuals as their natural business collaborators and even benefactors. The fact that these entrepreneurs were also often closely linked to leading communist families and figures also led Hong Kong tycoons into ever closer allegiance with Beijing. One consequence of this convergence was that, by the late 1990s, a culture of self-censorship had emerged in Hong Kong within which the media increasingly avoided issues, or terminology, that mainland authorities might be sensitive to. For instance, all reference to a Tiananmen 'massacre' virtually disappeared from media outlets after the handover,[50] whilst any reference to the Tibet or Taiwan 'problems' was also discouraged. In general, mainland officials expected the Hong Kong media to focus on local, everyday Hong Kong matters, rather than address contentious issues of significance to the PRC.

Against this growing, forced 'consensus' on the configuration of self-censorship, RTHK continued to be viewed as an irritant by government and mainland officials, but one which, as mentioned earlier, they felt could be dealt with gradually and quietly. However, in July 1999, the 'slowly-slowly' strategy advocated by Tung imploded when, in the RTHK radio programme *Letter to Hong Kong*, RTHK presenters invited Taiwan envoy Cheng An-kuo to express his views on the 'two-states theory' put forward by the then President of Taiwan, Lee Teng-hui. As the title of the 'theory' suggests, Lee had argued that Taiwan and China should be regarded as two separate sovereign entities.[51] However, this contradicted the Central Government 'One China' position that Taiwan was not a sovereign state but an inalienable part of the PRC. The RTHK broadcast also covered issues of foreign policy here, and, under the vaguely worded terms of the Basic Law, could be regarded as a matter on which mainland officials and pro-Beijing loyalists felt they therefore had a right to comment. And this they duly did. For example, Tsang Hin-chi, a National People's Congress Standing Committee member, immediately called for action to be taken to stop RTHK becoming a conduit for the expression of 'splittist' views.[52] The Central Government's vice-premier, Qian Qichen, then warned the media in Hong Kong not to promote Taiwanese separatism, and insisted that open deliberation on the two-state theory would constitute a violation of media guidelines on Hong Kong-Taiwan relations.[53] Qian went on to declare that, 'under the one-China principle, one can't promote such matters in Hong Kong'.[54] However, Qian did not only mean that promotion of the two-state theory should be forbidden, but also that *discussion* of it should be similarly prohibited. All that was allowed was affirmation and restatement of the Central Government position on the issue – or no comment at all.

Following what became known in Hong Kong and China as the 'Cheng An-kuo Incident', the mainland and HKSAR governments continued in their attempts to curb media discussion of the Taiwan issue in Hong Kong, and one of these attempts then affected RTHK directly. In October 1999, and only a few months after the Cheng An-kuo incident, Cheung Man-yee was removed from her post as Director of Broadcasting at RTHK. Cheung had been a target of pro-Beijing criticism ever since the July 'Incident', because, as Editor-in-chief, she was held to have ultimate responsibility for the transmission of the broadcast. In October Cheung found herself suddenly transferred out of RTHK to a trade-related Government representative position in Tokyo, leading many to believe that she had been punished for the broadcast, particularly given the fact that the announcement that she was to leave RTHK was made while she was abroad on vacation.[55] Following Cheung's departure, pressure on the Hong Kong media over the Taiwan issue continued. In April 2000 Wang Fengchao, the representative of the Hong Kong Liaison Office of the Central Government, told a meeting of journalists that Hong Kong media should not publicise opinions supporting the independence of Taiwan,[56] declaring that the media had a duty to 'defend the sovereignty and integrity of the country', and that the implementation of self-censorship on this issue had 'nothing to do with press freedom'.[57] By 2000, therefore, and only three years after the handover, the Hong Kong media, including RTHK, were being confronted with demands to restrict the free flow of information within the city in order to advance the general interests of the authoritarian state.[58]

Following this, RTHK continued to be targeted by SAR and mainland authorities. In a 2000 policy review of coming digital terrestrial television an RTHK request to be granted a digital channel was passed over,[59] whilst the submissions of the two – now very evidently pro-Beijing – free-to-air television broadcasters, TVB and ATV, dominated the outcome of the review.[60] Then, in June 2001, Claudia Mo Man-ching, the weekly host of the RTHK radio programme *Open Line, Open View*, was axed, allegedly because some government officials found her approach to be too critical of the Central Government.[61] These events also occurred against a more widespread background of anxiety inside and outside Hong Kong that freedom of expression was being curtailed within the territory. For example, a 2001 Report by the US State Department found that practices of self-censorship within Hong Kong's media organisations were becoming more prevalent, particularly in relation to reports concerning the Central Government, Taiwan, Tibet, and the relationship between the governments of Hong Kong and China.[62] Within Hong Kong itself, a 2002 survey carried out by the Chinese University of Hong Kong showed that 82 per cent of those interviewed believed the Hong Kong Government was intervening continuously to restrict press freedom,[63] whilst 50 per cent believed the Central Government was also intervening regularly to the same end.[64]

In the light of all this growing concern that journalistic integrity was being compromised, voices were once again raised demanding that RTHK be granted its own dedicated television channel. This was not, however, a view shared by the HK SAR Government, which continued to distrust RTHK. In 2006 the then Chief Executive, Donald Tsang (the second Chief Executive of the SAR), announced his displeasure with RTHK, arguing, as had Xu during the time of the previous Tung administration, that RTHK had a duty to explain, not critique, government policies.[65] Tsang then decided to establish a review of public-service broadcasting in Hong Kong which, to most extents and purposes, meant a review of RTHK. Raymond Roy Wong, a veteran journalist and previous head of the TVB newsroom, was assigned to form a seven-member Committee for the Review of Public-Service Broadcasting (PSB Committee). Though asked to consider the whole issue of public broadcasting within the SAR, the committee was inevitably concerned with the role of RTHK. The committee eventually published proposals in September 2006. Prior to that, however, in April 2006, RTHK had appeared on the government radar again, this time over the state of its finances, when the Audit Commission released a report about poor financial management of salaries, overtime pay, and entertainment expenses at the broadcaster. Apparently, RTHK had allocated HK$6 million for staff overtime and HK$750,000 for 'entertainment expenditure' from the HK$400 million government funding tranche allocated to it in 2004–5. On the face of it, these figures do not and did not to many at the time seem particularly unreasonable, and some within RTHK felt that the Audit Commission intervention was connected to the overall government dislike of RTHK.[66] Nevertheless, the audit figures caused a stir, and made uncomfortable headlines for RTHK. A further blow to RTHK was then also dealt in June 2006 when four people, including two RTHK employees, were arrested by the International Commission Against Corruption as a result of fraud and misconduct allegations related to the production budget of RTHK programmes over the 1995–2001 period.[67] The image that was being projected to the public now was that of impaired and faulty governance within RTHK, and, as the organisation looked ahead to the September release of the PSB Committee proposals, it found itself in a debilitated position.

Just prior to the publication of the PSB Committee Report information began to be leaked (or inferred) that the committee intended to take an unexpectedly bold stance over the issue of public-service broadcasting in Hong Kong, and this created a good deal of speculation in the local media. For example, a Hong Kong Journalists Association publication suggested that the final report of the committee would argue that 'there is a consensus that a public broadcaster should be outside the government structure and staffed by non-civil servants'.[68] The dissemination of this supposed affirmation, which, taken at face value, appeared to support independence for RTHK (though this would also mean that many RTHK employees would have to forfeit their civil-service status), then proved to be the catalyst for a series of other interventions in support of RTHK which appeared within the local media. Writing in the newspaper *The Standard*, Chan Yuen-ying, Director of the Journalism and Media Studies Centre of the University of Hong Kong, echoed earlier declarations in arguing that the main problem with RTHK was that it was both a media organisation and a government department, and that, therefore, de-linking RTHK from the government – as it appeared that the PSB Report would advise – would solve this problem.[69] The *South China Morning Post* also supported this position, arguing in its editorial column that RTHK should be akin to the BBC, which has a 'genuinely independent executive board'.[70]

However, these media interventions misinterpreted the import of discussions taking place within the PSB Committee. It is true that, when it finally appeared, the main and most radical recommendation of the final report related to the need to establish an independent public broadcaster. However, the media had already jumped to what turned out to be the premature conclusion that the 'statutory body independent of the government' which the report would endorse would be RTHK.[71] This prior assumption – a thoroughly reasonable one it has to be said – then generated more excitement when linked to another startlingly radical proposal leaked from the committee, that no members of the Executive Council, Legislative Council, National People's Congress, or Chinese People's Political Consultative Conference should be placed on the proposed Board of Governors of the new statuary body.[72] For those advocating democratic change in Hong Kong it appeared that the PSB Report intended to advocate that RTHK might be transformed into something resembling the BBC. However, media commentators at the time should have taken more note of the fact that the leaks and hints from the committee did not specifically mention that RTHK should be the independent broadcaster it referred to, and that, in addition, the committee – most revealingly – intended not to back the request from Chu Pui-hing, the Director of Broadcasting at RTHK after the (probably) forced departure of Cheung Man-yee, that RTHK should have its own television channel.[73] This decision not to support was askew of media assumptions that the committee would argue for RTHK to be the new independent broadcaster. Moreover, those assumptions were also treated with greater caution within RTHK, and by groups such as the Hong Kong Journalists Association. In its 2006 *Annual Report* the Association criticised the fact that the PSB Committee did not contain any member with substantial public-service broadcasting expertise, and also found the lack of reference to RTHK in the committee's terms of reference 'intriguing'.[74] According to the Association, there was:

> considerable suspicion about the motives for the review, given the intense criticism of RTHK by Hong Kong-based pro-Beijing politicians over the past ten years and more. They argue that the broadcaster should better reflect the views of the government, or simply become a propaganda mouthpiece for the administration.[75]

It seems, therefore, that the PSB Committee, and both RTHK and the Hong Kong Journalists' Association, were occupying different corners in this engagement.

The PSB Report was eventually submitted in March 2007. And it was not at all to the liking of RTHK and the institution's supporters. However, it *was* a progressive document in itself which, on the face of it, stood against authoritarian control of public broadcasting. The PSB Committee did indeed propose that there should be a statutory independent broadcaster, to be called the 'Hong Kong Public Broadcasting Corporation' (PBC). However, the committee also argued that turning RTHK into such a body was bound to encounter significant problems, and that as a consequence the broadcaster should not become the proposed PBC, which should, in contrast, commence operations with a clean slate, and without the considerable baggage of RTHK. That baggage, as far as the committee was concerned, was the product of RTHK's uncomfortable and dual role as both official organ and independent liberal voice, and, rather than argue that the way out of the difficulty of RTHK being both was to de-link RTHK from government, as so many were arguing at the time, the PSB Report argued that RTHK should more or less cease to be the main public broadcaster, and revert to being a government instrument. If this were to happen, RTHK would eventually become indistinguishable from Government Information Services, and the situation would return to what it had been in 1970, when RHKTV was formed as a serving 'Government film unit'. On the other hand, if the PSB Report recommendations were accepted by government, Hong Kong would, in theory at least, have a new and perhaps genuinely independent public-service broadcaster.

The recommendations of the PSB Committee as those recommendations related to RTHK were both unambiguous and acerbic. Despite the fact that RTHK had been the de facto public broadcaster since the early 1970s, the committee took the view that the institution was not actually qualified or suited to be so:

> Turning to RTHK, it is funded fully by the public, and tasked to provide programmes that inform, educate and entertain. However these attributes are insufficient to qualify RTHK as a public broadcaster, or ensure that its services satisfy public needs for PSB . . . RTHK is part of the executive branch of the Government, managed and staffed by civil servants who are duty-bound to implement government policies and comply with government-wide rules and regulations. RTHK's status as a government department casts a shadow of doubt over its independence, and cannot help but reinforce, however unfairly, the perception of doubt on the impartiality of its programmes. This is an inherent problem that applies to RTHK radio and TV programmes alike.[76]

The logic involved here, that the actual-existing official status and history of RTHK precluded the organisation from becoming a different sort of broad-caster, one more independent of government, seems only partially argued through, and raises a number of questions. Why, for example, should it be taken as a sine qua non that RTHK *must* and *ought* to remain a government department under all conditions, instead of being allowed to rise phoenix-like from government edict as so many had called for previously? Why would the organisation be *constitutionally unable* to become an independent broadcaster, given that so many of its staff wished that to be the case and had been educated to that end? However, whilst questions such as these appear to be warranted, their substance was given short shrift in a substantial number of clauses within the PSB Report which asserted to the contrary that the 'culture' of RTHK made the broadcaster fundamentally unsuited to be the future PSB of Hong Kong. According to the committee, RTHK had 'an entrenched structure and a strong corporative culture',[77] and:

> In short, a sea change in RTHK's status is bound to be fraught with prac-tical and insurmountable problems, and not conducive to the start-up of a new public broadcaster.[78]

RTHK comes over as a peculiarly local hybrid organisation in these assertions, different from other public-service broadcasters around the developed world.

And in stating that RTHK film-makers were 'duty bound' to 'comply' with 'government-wide rules and regulations', a sleight of hand is also revealed. Yes, of course, government rules applied to RTHK; but what is also implied here and in the earlier assertions by the committee that RTHK was 'an executive part of the Government' is that RTHK films might or did function like GIS Items of Public Information (IPOs). As this chapter has shown, as will the next, this would be a misreading of the history of RTHK.

The main recommendations of the PSB Report were radical and liberal enough. They were: (1) that an independent statutory broadcaster, the 'Hong Kong Public Broadcasting Corporation', be established; (2) that this broadcaster should *not* be the existing RTHK; (3) that the broadcaster should have an autonomous board of fifteen members; (4) that the broadcaster be led by an independent management team with a Chief Executive officer; (5) that the broadcaster be primarily funded by government; (6) that it should run at least one free-to-air TV channel, plus a number of radio stations; and (7) that it should have a committee which would receive public feedback. In addition to this commendably BBC-like model, the new broadcaster would also have a liberal and progressive remit. Its purpose would be to (1) sustain citizenship and civil society, (2) foster social harmony and promote pluralism, (3) promote education and lifelong learning, and (4) stimulate creativity and enrich multicultural life.[79]

However, the PSB recommendations stood virtually no chance of being enacted. However much the authoritarian government of Hong Kong may have disliked the troublesome RTHK, that government was hardly likely to replace the organisation with an even more institutionally independent one. In addition, by 2006–7 around 780 staff worked within RTHK, a third of whom were civil servants. Terminating their official status prematurely would involve compensatory costs of hundreds of millions of dollars. Of course, many existing RTHK staff might be expected to apply for positions in a newly created PBC. However, under the PSB proposals there was no guarantee that they would be so re-employed, and, indeed, the PSB Report was equivocal on this, stating that some personnel 'could be drawn on'. Hardly a ringing endorsement! And if RTHK were not to be abolished, but just turned into a more directly functional government department, it would have to downsize considerably. The PSB Report made no bones about this outcome, and, leaving aside all questions of compensation as outside its remit of consideration, bluntly declared that:

> Subsequent to the proposed transfer of RTHK's existing PSB functions to the PBC, the reduced role of RTHK could hardly justify the allocation of seven radio channels and TV airtime on the domestic free TV channels.[80]

And here, perhaps, we have at least one root of the apparent antipathy between the committee and RTHK. The committee was, to an extent at least, reacting to pressure applied on it by the existing commercial broadcasters, broadcasters who did not want the burden of hosting RTHK on their platforms, or of competing with RTHK in what they thought ought to be a commercial market. If RTHK were to be downsized, these difficulties would be reduced. However, the notion of a newly established PSB which did not have many RTHK staff on its books also raises the question of where the new staff would come from, and, more imperatively, where the new *management* personnel would come from? Some would come from abroad, certainly. But the bulk could only come from the existing broadcasters, ATV and TVB; both of which were unfalteringly pro-Beijing (though, and as has been argued earlier, not all their film-makers were similarly so). So it seems that a likely outcome would be the inauguration of a public-service broadcasting institution which would be more management-friendly to the government than the existing RTHK was.

In coming to its conclusions, the PSB Committee had in fact arrived at what was probably the most disruptive option possible. The committee could have suggested that RTHK become the new public broadcaster. Instead it suggested both the creation of an institution over which government would have less control and the attenuation of RTHK: an institution which many Hongkongers still deemed to be important. In October 2007, in an attempt to distance itself from what it considered to be an insupportable PSB Report, the government stated that it felt the need to launch a further public 'consultation' exercise on the future of public-service broadcasting. However, on 17 January 2008, Chief Executive Donald Tsang announced the postponement of publication of the consultation paper because, according to him, the issue was still too 'sensitive and complex' to be put before the public.[81]

In September 2009 the government finally abandoned the PSB Committee recommendations on the setting up of a 'newly minted' public-service broadcaster and decided instead to unambiguously make RTHK the Hong Kong public broadcaster. The government could not countenance setting up a structurally independent public-service broadcaster, and was unprepared to face the media storm that would have broken out had RTHK been significantly downsized. RTHK was now to become an 'independent department' within the government, though this might seem to be a contradiction in terms. In August 2010 RTHK was granted a new Charter, and a Board of Advisors, similar to that proposed by the PSB Committee. However, this Board was smaller in number, and did not possess executive powers. And whilst RTHK was now a supposedly 'independent' government department, it was also placed under the 'policy purview and housekeeping oversight of the Commerce and Economic Development Bureau' (CEDB).[82] Although the Charter made clear that RTHK would have editorial independence (as the original Charter had), it also stipulated that the Secretary of the CEDB would provide the Director of RTHK with 'policy guidance' including 'reviewing policy aspects of each programme area'.[83] The Director of RTHK was, in other words, responsible to the Secretary of CEDB as his or her superior, and such responsibility could be a moveable feast. The Charter did point out, on page four of the document, that RTHK was expected to be 'accurate and authoritative in the information that it disseminates', and also be 'impartial in the views it reflects, and even-handed'.[84] However, on page two, and much more imperatively, under a section which sets out the 'Public Purposes and Mission' of RTHK, the broadcaster is also charged with 'promoting understanding of the concept of "One Country Two Systems" and its implementation in Hong Kong' (this was also a central recommendation of the 2006 Review Report).[85] Clearly, this amounts to a contradiction, in that such 'promotion' is neither 'impartial', nor 'even-handed'. As will be shown in the following chapter of this book, which looks at the documentary films of RTHK, from as early as the mid-1980s, when the 'concept' of 'one country two systems' was first devised by Deng Xiaoping, many people in Hong Kong simply did not believe in it.

CONCLUSIONS

RTHK came into being under the dominion of one authoritarian regime and was then passed on to another, completely different one. In one sense, therefore, RTHK was unlucky. Not many modern liberal broadcasting organisations within the 'developed' world are passed from authoritarian government to non-democratic autarchy in this manner. There are, of course, many countries in the world in which broadcasters work within an authoritarian media system and are habituated to that. This is the case, for example, with mainland China, in which broadcasting is controlled by the Central Government and Chinese Communist Party. However, this was never really the case with Hong Kong. Colonial Hong Kong may have been an authoritarian Crown Colony, but, and as argued previously in this chapter, it was also linked to a democratic government and society in the metropole. When RTHK appeared in the 1970s, colonial Hong Kong was also in the process of casting off the autocratic form of the Crown Colony, and developing into something of a more liberal, representative, welfare state. RTHK was influenced by this new, more liberal environment, but what led the broadcaster to go even beyond this new consensus was the influence of the British public-service broadcasting system. In Britain conservative and other politicians regularly expressed frustration at the BBC, and did not believe that the public broadcaster should be able to question government policy in the manner in which it did. However, the broadcaster always tried to resist such criticism, and affirm the importance of editorial independence. In Hong Kong RTHK was strongly influenced by the BBC model from the outset, and aspired to become a similar sort of autonomous organisation. However, if British politicians living and working within a democracy often questioned the role of the BBC, it is hardly surprising that conservative civil servants – and others – living and working in a non-democratic Crown Colony regularly came to question the role of RTHK.

When the first 'Controller, Television' of RTHK, James Hawthorne, had his staff trained at the BBC, he helped create a situation in which professional broadcasters within RTHK and conservative officials within the Hong Kong government would inevitably find themselves at odds with one another. This situation continued after 1997, when Hong Kong ceased to be a Crown Colony. From that date the policy of the pro-Beijing government in Hong Kong was to deal with the 'problem' of RTHK 'slowly-slowly', as the first Chief Executive of the HKSAR had put it, rather than seek open confrontation. Today, the government is trying, 'slowly-slowly', to increase more civil-service control over the professional broadcasters, to the extent even that the current Director of RTHK is a career civil servant with no experience in broadcasting. This Director is also the first 'administrative officer' to run RTHK since its separation (as RHK) from GIS in the mid-1950s. This appointment was, unsurprisingly, met with admonishment by RTHK staff who also rolled out a black carpet to welcome him on his first day at his new post.[86] According to one commentator, the appointment 'reinforced the image of RTHK as official media. The government's pledge of editorial independence for RTHK is a sham'.[87]

In 2006 the Hong Kong Journalists' Association had made the case for an independent RTHK strongly and clearly. According to the Association:

> The question of RTHK's future is of vital importance. The broadcaster has over the past twenty years become a symbol of the state of media freedoms in Hong Kong – as Beijing has tried to impose its way of thinking on the local media . . . These developments highlight the vital importance of Hong Kong having a truly independent broadcaster. It should be structurally independent of the government and free of government interference and pressure. The HKJA believes that the existing public service broadcaster is in the best position to take on this role.[88]

Today, however, there are divisions within RTHK, as the governing regime attempts to 'impose its way of thinking' upon the broadcaster through a process of insistent bureaucratic appointment and control; and the broadcasters, or, at least, some of them, attempt to fight against this. Even up to the present day of writing, in late June 2013, such controversy continues, with quite senior RTHK staff openly accusing the RTHK Director of imposing 'political missions' on broadcasters and interfering with editorial independence.[89] RTHK remains a government department now as it did in the 1970s, but its top personnel no longer call for institutional autonomy, and its filmmakers no longer make too many films that shake society. As we will see in the following chapter, however, that was not the case in 1989, when the RTHK film *The Hong Kong Case* portrayed the aftermath of the Tiananmen massacre.

NOTES

1. Tsang, Steve, *A Modern History of Hong Kong* (Hong Kong: Hong Kong University Press, 2009), p. 208.
2. Ibid. p. 215.
3. Ibid. p. 220.
4. Ibid.
5. Ibid. p. 222.
6. *A Draft Agreement Between the Government of Great Britain and Northern Ireland and the Government of the People's Republic of China on the Future of Hong Kong* (known as the Joint Declaration), Annex I Paragraph I: 'Elaboration of the People's Republic of China of its Basic Policies Regarding Hong Kong' (1984).
7. Tsang, *A Modern History*, pp. 232–4.
8. Ibid. p. 243.
9. Ibid, p. 246.
10. Ibid. p. 252.
11. Ibid. p. 251.
12. See Chapter 2 of this book for more on the decline of Cantonese cinema during this period.
13. Ma, Eric, Kit-wai, *Culture, Politics and Television in Hong Kong* (New York: Routledge, 1999), p. 29.
14. It is unclear what these initials stand for, if anything.
15. Commonwealth Broadcasting Association, *Commonwealth Broadcasting Association Handbook* (1981–2), p. 106.
16. RTHK, 'Things about RTHK', http://rthk.hk/about/80book.htm, p. 6.
17. *Public Relations Office Annual Report* (Hong Kong: Hong Kong Government Publications, 1951), pp. 110–11.
18. Moss, Peter, 'GIS through the Years', http://www.info.gov.hk/isd/40th/2.html.
19. Cheung, Anthony, B. L., 'Reform in Search of Politics: The Case of Hong Kong's Aborted Attempt to Corporatise Public Broadcasting', *Asian Journal of Public Administration*, vol. 19, no. 2, (December 1997), p. 280.
20. Ibid.
21. HKRS 72 4–1, 'Government Television Unit', 12 March 1970.
22. The Public Relations Office was renamed 'Government Information Services' (GIS) in 1959.
23. ISD 5/71C, Watt, Nigel, Draft Executive Council Paper: 'Government Information Policy', 11 December 1967, p. 3.
24. Ibid. p. 2.
25. HKRS TC 211/68, 'Notes of a Meeting on Radio Bulletins held in DC's office at 11.30 a.m.', 23 November 1968.

26. HKRS RHK (A) 1/3/68 (C) Memo: 'Director of Broadcasting to Hon. Colonial Secretary', 23 June 1972.
27. HKRS 670-1-9, ISD 4/60 (CR), 'Memo', Director of Information Services to Deputy Colonial Secretary, 'Radio News', 5 October 1972, para. 1.
28. HKRS 72-4-1, Colonial Secretariat, General Circular no. 19/73, 'Government Publicity by Means of Television', 24 May 1973, para. 3.
29. Cheung, 'Reform', p. 280.
30. RTHK, 'Historical Background', *RTHK – History and Development* (Hong Kong: RTHK/Hong Kong Government Printer, 1984), p. 5.
31. Cheung, 'Reform', p. 281.
32. Yan Mei Ning, 'The Role of Academic Research in the Making of Broadcasting Policy: The Case Study of Hong Kong', *International Journal of Communication*, vol. 2 (2008), p. 396.
33. Hong Kong Government, Broadcasting Review Board, *Report of the Broadcasting Review Board* (Hong Kong: Hong Kong Government Printer, August 1985), Clause 48, p. XXI.
34. Cheung, 'Reform', p. 284.
35. Ibid. p. 287.
36. RTHK Programme Staff Union Newsletter, vol. 1 (1987), p. 9.
37. Ibid. p. 10.
38. Yan, 'The Role of Academic Research', pp. 397–8.
39. Cheung, 'Reform', p. 288.
40. Ibid.
41. Cheung, 'Reform', 293.
42. Ibid. p. 294.
43. Ibid.
44. Hong Kong Journalists' Association. *2006 Annual Report*, p. 7.
45. Choi, Linda and Yeung, Christopher, 'Tung Sparks RTHK Autonomy Fears', *South China Morning Post*, 3 May 1985.
46. Ibid.
47. http://rthk.org.hk/mediadigest/md9911/nov_01.html.
48. Lo, Alex, 'Show Ends for Heavyweight Defender of Independence', *South China Morning Post*, 20 October 1999.
49. http://rthk.org.hk/mediadigest/md9911/nov_01.html.
50. Choi and Yeung, 'Tung Sparks RTHK Autonomy Fears'.
51. Hong Kong Journalists' Association. *2006 Annual Report*, p. 7.
52. Li, Angela, Yeung, Jimmy and Ng, Kang-chung, 'Qian Instructs Media Not to Back Calls for Taiwan split', *South China Morning Post*, 20 August 1999.
53. Ibid.
54. Ibid.
55. Hong Kong Journalists' Association. *2006 Annual Report*, pp. 7–8.
56. 'Comments' section, 'Beijing's Stamp on Hong Kong', *South China Morning Post*, 27 October 2000.
57. Ibid.
58. Schloss, Glenn, 'Pressing Times for the Media', *South China Morning Post*, 6 July 2002.
59. Yan, 'The Role of Academic Research', p. 401.
60. Ibid.
61. 'Focus' section, 'When You Talk Back Too Much', *South China Morning Post*, 16 June 2001.

62. Hon, May Sin-mi, 'Journalists Endorse Self-censorship Fears', *South China Morning Post*, 28 February 2001.
63. Ng, Kang-chung, 'Majority Believes Government Meddles with the Media', *South China Morning Post*, 22 October 2002.
64. Ibid.
65. Hong Kong Journalists' Association. *2006 Annual Report*, p. 5.
66. Kwoh, Leslie and Ng, Michael, 'RTHK Controversy Grows', *The Standard*, 27 April 2006.
67. Hong Kong Journalists' Association. *2006 Annual Report*, p. 10.
68. Ibid. p. 9.
69. Kwoh and Ng, 'RTHK Controversy'.
70. Editorial', 'Broadcasting Review Can Learn from BBC', *South China Morning Post*, 19 April 2006.
71. Ching, Frank, 'The Future RTHK Takes Shape', *South China Morning Post*, 12 October 2006.
72. Ibid.
73. Chu Pui-hing, 'End the Confusion in Broadcasting', *South China Morning Post*, 28 June 2006.
74. Hong Kong Journalists' Association. *2006 Annual Report*, p. 5.
75. Ibid.
76. Hong Kong Government, Committee for the Review of Public-Service Broadcasting, *Report on Review of Public-Service Broadcasting in Hong Kong* (Hong Kong Government Printer, March 2007), clause 66, p. 13.
77. Ibid. clause 90, p. 19.
78. Ibid, clause 96, p. 19.
79. Chung, Jimmy and Lee, Claudia, 'Panel under Fire over RTHK's Future', *South China Morning Post*, 29 March 2006.
80. Hong Kong Government, Committee for the Review of Public-Service Broadcasting, *Report*, clause 251, p. 69.
81. Fung, Fanny and Hung, Denise, 'Public Broadcasting Delay Surprises Lawmakers', *South China Morning Post*, 18 January 2008.
82. Hong Kong Government, 'Status and Responsibilities of RTHK and Relationship with CEDB and the Secretary', *Charter of Radio Television Hong Kong* (Hong Kong: Hong Kong Government Printer, 1 August 2010), p. 4.
83. Ibid. pp. 5–6.
84. Ibid. p. 4.
85. Ibid. p. 2.
86. Cheung, Gary, 'Into the Lion's Den', *South China Morning Post*, 20 September 2001.
87. Ibid.
88. Hong Kong Journalists' Association. *2006 Annual Report*, p. 3.
89. Luk, Eddie, '"Whistle-blower" Left Out as RTHK Reshuffles Deck', *The Standard*, 28 June 2013.

CHAPTER 5

The Documentary Films of Radio Television Hong Kong (RTHK) and *The Hong Kong Case* (1989)

Although established in 1970 Radio Hong Kong Television (RHKTV) did not produce anything that year, and, by 1971, the unit was still only producing some short information bulletins derived from Government Information Services (GIS) sources. The unit did not actually become fully operational until 1972, when it moved into new studios made ready for it at the new Radio Hong Kong (RHK) centre, Broadcasting House, in the Kowloon Tong area of Kowloon. However, although RHKTV was able to develop its own news bulletins from late 1972, the unit did not succeed in freeing itself entirely from dependence upon well-established GIS sources, and this situation continued after the founding of Radio Television Hong Kong (RTHK) in 1976. It was, apparently, not until the early 1980s that RTHK developed full editorial autonomy over its news broadcasting.[1] RHKTV, under Controller, Television, James Hawthorne, began to recruit staff from 1971. In 1973 RHKTV began to broadcast its first film series, *Home in Hong Kong*. Broadcast once a week on the platforms of the two commercial broadcasters, *Home in Hong Kong* lasted for half an hour, and, with its magazine format, can be regarded as successor to the Hong Kong Film Unit's *Hong Kong Today*, a newsreel programme which was screened in the cinema rather than broadcast on television. *Home in Hong Kong* was released predominantly in Chinese, and remade in English-language version on a few occasions. The series lasted only a few years and was eventually replaced in 1977–8 – after RHKTV had become part of RTHK – by a current-affairs series which still runs in the present day. The series in question, which began as *Common Sense*, was later renamed *Hong Kong Connection*. From 1985 *Hong Kong Connection* was led by Dominica Siu as executive producer. Siu was to stay in position until her retirement in 2003, and, under Siu, *Hong Kong Connection* would often take forthright stances on the subjects it dealt with, rather than just conforming to safer journalistic edicts.[2]

Hong Kong Connection films won around fifty international awards under

Siu's watch, and she and her team brought to the series a sometimes cinéma vérité-like, documentary approach, in contrast to the earlier years of *Common Sense*, in which re-enactment and actors were often employed. Of the three directors initially employed on *Common Sense* two had a drama and film background, and often preferred to employ re-enactment using actors in dramatic narratives. For example, the first episode of *Common Sense*, *Golden Bowl* (1978, also known as *Civil Servant*) concerned a woman's change of career from actress to civil servant working at RTHK. The film, which was completely re-enacted, set out the pros and cons of being a civil servant. In addition to the dramatic element here, *Golden Bowl* illustrates how, in the early stages of *Common Sense*, the films produced were functioning much like the films that had come out of the HKFU, in that they frequently promoted government public-information messages and stories, or even just redelivered messages that were then also coming out of GIS through other channels. *Common Sense* did not free itself from this role until the mid-1980s, when the films became more investigative and critical against the context of growing debate about Hong Kong's future generated by the Sino-British negotiations.[3] By the mid-1980s, the style of *Common Sense*, and then *Hong Kong Connection*, also began to change, and the drama-documentary format gradually gave way to a more naturalistic one. One of the influences upon this change may have been the success of one of Dominic Siu's first films as director-producer, *Temple Street* (1982). *Temple Street* is a mainly commentary-less observation of street life in a Hong Kong night market which merges together the fluid activities taking place within the marketplace in collage-like form. With its intersecting, boundary-blurred sequences, *Temple Street* is reminiscent of some of the direct cinema films which appeared in France and America during the 1960s and 1970s. *Temple Street* was awarded the Asian Broadcasting Union Television Prize for Best Documentary in 1982, and is a little-known but noteworthy film in the history of the Hong Kong documentary film. Although the name of Dominica Siu has been mentioned several times here, it is, at this stage, nonetheless necessary to introduce the same rider employed in the previous chapter when discussing the films of Television Broadcasts Limited (TVB) and Asian Television (ATV): that this chapter will not focus on the film-makers of RTHK, as this would be beyond its remit and wordage. In addition, and as with ATV and TVB, a focus on individual film-makers in relation to the films of RTHK would be difficult because these films are the result of teamwork, rather than individual authorship. In many cases, for example, the key player is not the director but the executive producer, or presenter. Because of all this, this chapter will focus on the films as product of RTHK, and their relationship to historical context. Again, this is not done to gainsay the achievements of the individual film-makers involved, but to mark out clearly the course to be followed.

Hong Kong Connection is still, today, producing around fifty or so 20- to 25-minute films per year broadcast on the platforms of one or other of the two free-to-air television broadcasters, TVB and ATV (as mentioned in the previous chapter, RTHK does not have its own dedicated channel). Each year around thirty of the original Chinese films are also translated into English and broadcast on the English channels of the two stations: 'Pearl', for TVB, and 'World', for ATV. Each individual film in the series tackles a particular issue and normally consists of commentary and information backed up by interviews. These interviews are, predominantly, with ordinary people, rather than important figures or government ministers. In part, this approach stems from the difficulty of gaining access to such people on the sort of regular basis that the series requires, but it is also influenced by the production team's desire to report on the grass-roots and condition of Hong Kong civil society. This approach also leads to a great deal of location-shooting, a characteristic of the series since the mid-1980s. Since the early 1980s, when the Sino-British negotiations began, the production team of *Hong Kong Connection* has been asked to make one quarter of its yearly output (around thirteen films per year) on China. In addition to this, *Hong Kong Connection* produces around ten or so films per year on international matters.

Although it will not be possible to review the entire output of *Hong Kong Connection* from the 1970s to the present date in this chapter, an admittedly schematic overview of the general approach and coverage adopted by the series may be obtained by observing programme output for the latter half of 2012. Although a snapshot, what appears here does to a good extent reflect the characteristic range of *Hong Kong Connection*. There are two China stories here, one on repression of gay rights in the present, the other a historical study of the great famine of 1959. In addition to these, there are films on minority rights in Hong Kong and on environmental pollution. Other films have a more directly political orientation. For example, there are films on divisive legislative elections; on the notion of a Hong Kong 'identity'; and on the issue of 'national education', in which pro-Beijing factions attempted to introduce a topic into the school curriculum which would teach schoolchildren about the 'nation' – that is, the communist state. The attempt to introduce a national education subject into the school curriculum proved to be highly contentious, leading to mass protests and the eventual withdrawal of the subject. Despite the controversy over this issue though, RTHK did not shy away, although the programme attempted to be balanced in its approach. In September 2012 a one-hour 'special' was also broadcast entitled *Fifteen Years of 'One Country Two Systems'*, which reviewed the state of Hong Kong fifteen years after the handover. This programme will be discussed in more depth later in this chapter. Amongst other matters, the above brief survey of films appearing in 2012 makes it clear that, despite pressures emanating from the pro-Beijing/

pro-establishment sector (pressures extensively documented in the previous chapter of this book), *Hong Kong Connection* remained able and more than willing to tackle big political issues. However, a distinction can nonetheless be made between Hong Kong and China here, and, in general, the series has more leeway to address political issues related to the former than the latter.

In addition to one-off films, the *Hong Kong Connection* team, and, possibly, others within RTHK, makes occasional series of films. Some of these are produced over a long period of time and include *Success Stories* (1997–2008), a series of biopics of successful Chinese people including property tycoon Li Ka-shing, ex-Singapore Leader Lee Kwan-yew, martial arts novelist Louis Cha, and Chinese opera master Pak Suet-sin. Other series include *My Childhood* (1999, ten episodes), which investigates the diaspora of overseas-born Chinese whose families left their hometowns or countries due to war or political instability. Countries involved here include Indonesia, Australia, Cambodia, Taiwan, Singapore, Thailand, Japan, South Korea and Hong Kong. Similar to this is a much longer series of films on the problems of childhood, some of which deal with childhood issues in China. This series ran from 1999 to the present, whilst another, *The Outsiders*, covered issues related to mainlanders and minority groups within Hong Kong, and ran over the period 2004–6. It will not, however, be possible to explore all of these and other series of films made by RTHK in this present chapter, and, given that, the approach adopted here will instead be to focus on films and film series made about three of the most controversial events to have occurred in Hong Kong: the 1989 Tiananmen massacre, the 1997 handover; and the attempt to implement so-called 'national security' legislation in 2003. Consequently, this chapter will focus on the following films and film series: *Four Years On* (1993) and *Twenty Years On* (2009), both of which concern the Tiananmen massacre; *Ten Years On* (2007) and *Fifteen Years of 'One Country Two Systems'* (2012), which concern the handover; and *Article Twenty-three of the Basic Law: The Lawyer's Last Ditch Battle* (2003) and *Article Twenty-three of the Basic Law: Fear not, Only Believe* (2003), which are concerned with the attempted implementation of national security legislation. The chapter will then conclude with an account of another film made on Tiananmen, and one of the most important films to be made by RTHK, *The Hong Kong Case* (1989).

FOUR YEARS ON (1993)

Four Years On was made four years after Tiananmen, and, in the film, five people with differing viewpoints are interviewed on why they decided to stay in Hong Kong following the event, even though many others had left the city for Canada, the United Kingdom and elsewhere. The individuals concerned here are a lawyer, a surgeon, a university lecturer, an actress and a journalist cum political editor. The views expressed by these individuals cover much of the political spectrum. The lawyer is semi-detached from the political context, enjoys her affluent middle-class lifestyle in Hong Kong, and is prepared to grudgingly accept looming mainland rule if she is able to retain that lifestyle. She is also lukewarm on the issue of democracy, believing, in accordance with the predominantly pro-Beijing promulgators of the Basic Law, that only 'gradual change is suitable for Hong Kong'. Beyond this, she takes the view that she will continue to function sufficiently well as an individual and family member after the handover, putting up with the political context as well as she can, and keeping it as distant from her as she can. The surgeon is also wedded to his Hong Kong middle-class status. However, he displays a greater sense of mission than the lawyer, believing that it would not be right for him to run away and 'leave the patient' (Hong Kong) to fend for itself. Nevertheless, he is suspicious of the manipulative activities of the Chinese government, and feels that China will attempt to control Hong Kong as much as it possibly can. In contrast to these two, the university lecturer is deeply pessimistic about the future of Hong Kong, believing that the city would become 'just another kind of colony after 1997'. Of all the characters presented here, he is also the one who came closest to leaving Hong Kong after Tiananmen. In contrast to him, the actress is most aligned to a pro-Beijing viewpoint. She argues that an over-emphasis on the need for democracy might lead to internal division to 'such an extent that our society crumbles'. She also expresses confidence in the coming Chinese rule, arguing that democracy itself is a flawed notion and that the majority 'did not know or understand' enough about things to be allowed to make important decisions. Finally, the journalist positions himself as a fatalistic Hong Kong Chinese proto-activist, arguing that Hong Kong is a pawn of both Britain and China, and that 'both will win' whilst 'Hong Kong people will be the only losers'. The journalist foresees turbulent times ahead as Hong Kong civil society attempts to resist the coming of the authoritarian state.

Four Years On follows a standard format for the interview film in that it begins with a brief introduction which is then followed by the interviews. The interviews take up most of the body of the film and also divide the film into five sections, a strategy that does not add to the film's overall cohesiveness. Because *Four Years On* is mainly concerned with the political opinions of the interviewees, the visual background and context shown in the film is of marginal importance, and mainly consists of depictions of the interviewees engaged in everyday activities which have little or nothing to do with their political convictions, or even with what they are saying. There is little of interest here at the level of film form and the film makes no real attempt to be filmic. It is primarily, or even wholly, a piece of televised interview-journalism. The interviewees are also, at one level, lacking in appeal, or, at least, are difficult to empathise with. None of them is courageously idealistic and all lead fairly comfortable middle-class lives. RTHK may have been targeting its core audience here, but the contracted range of individuals presented detracts from the overall purpose of the film, which is, according to the narration, to understand – through interviewing these five people – how the populace of Hong Kong in general feel about Tiananmen and the looming handover. Yet despite such an objective, there are no working-class people in this film, and nor, for that matter, is there any member from the upper or 'tycoon' class. These people are the bourgeoisie. They are not public-opinion leaders, radicals, dissidents, or the very poor; and the narrow spectrum presented here, inevitably, leads to the articulation of a relatively tapered range of ideas and comments. One is left with a sense of a general and truncated consensus being enunciated based around suspicion of the Chinese government and anxiety over the future of democracy in Hong Kong, but no real apprehension that personal livelihoods or interests will be significantly affected by the handover. The one person who departs from this consensus is the pro-Beijing actress, but that departure is only on the basis of her support for Chinese rule, and, like the others, she looks forward to a relatively comfortable personal future. *Four Years On* could almost be interpreted as an ironic critique of self-satisfied materialism and small-mindedness incongruous with the apocalyptic events of Tiananmen; or as a disclosure of how a self-protective retreat into the domestic and professional environment had taken place as a consequence of those events. However, this would be a misreading of the film, which does not operate at such an erudite level, either intentionally or unintentionally. Tiananmen itself also has a somewhat ghostly presence in the film, as something in the past which is currently being expunged from the consciousness of these individuals because its true nature cannot be contemplated by those who will soon be forced to live under the regime which perpetrated it.

The producers of *Four Years On* decided to let the film's characters 'speak for themselves' rather than enable their film to articulate an incisive account of the Hong Kong situation in relation to Tiananmen through analysis, and, whilst this approach does allow a range (though, as argued, a constricted range) of voices to speak, the overall strategy results in a lack of investigative depth. There are no complex arguments set out here, only the unrounded and sometimes contradictory commentaries of the various interviewees. The film also ends rather lamely with a statement that each of the five people featured had 'set out their own opinion on democracy, and their own expectations for the future of Hong Kong'. However, given that the film appeared in 1993, when the Hong Kong media were vibrantly engaged in political debate against the background of the Patten reforms, and the negative – not to say vituperative – Chinese communist response to those reforms, this seems a rather slight note upon which to end the film. The mild tone adopted here may have been influenced by the institutional context of RTHK in 1993, as well as by the political context. The planned corporatisation of RTHK in 1992 had fallen through and a government letter to RTHK in January 1992 noted the 'frustration and uncertainty' felt by RTHK staff.[4] By 1993 that 'frustration and uncertainty' had not diminished, and criticism of RTHK from the mainland continued. One can, however, only speculate on whether this state of uncertainty affected the subdued tone and position of *Four Years On*.

TEN YEARS ON

Ten Years On is a six-part series made in 2007 to mark the ten-year anniversary of the 1997 handover of Hong Kong to China. It was, therefore, a major undertaking for *Hong Kong Connection* and RTHK, and of some potential political consequence, and problem. The first episode, *A Promise is a Promise*, not only carries on the approach adopted in *Four Years On* of interviewing a relatively narrow range of interviewees, but also re-interviews three of these: the physician, the lawyer and the academic. And the sense of being at greater ease that comes out here is palpable. Whilst, for example, in 1993, the academic felt considerable disquiet about the approaching 1997 handover, he, like the other two interviewees in 2007, now feels much more relaxed about the prevailing situation. In fact, all three are in consensus now that they are 'no longer scared' and that the 'promise' of one country two systems 'has been kept'. The physician, who selflessly carries out free medical treatment in poor areas of the mainland, and whose sense of Chinese identity has been augmented since the handover, also claims that 'China has won over Hong Kong'; whilst the lawyer, who now benefits financially from working on the mainland, and was the closest of the three in accommodating a pro-Beijing position in 1993, argues that 'you can't help jumping on the Chinese bandwagon'. The physician and the lawyer also profess to have greater faith in the Chinese government, and believe both that the communist state can be reformed and that direct elections will take place in Hong Kong in 2012. However, the academic begs to differ on these points, believing that the dictatorship will not change and elections are not likely to happen. Despite this, though, in general, criticism of the mainland regime is very tepid indeed in *A Promise is a Promise*. RTHK also seems not to have learned the lessons of *Four Years On* here. The main problem with *Four Years On* was, as argued, the contracted range of people interviewed; that problem is exacerbated in *A Promise is a Promise* because that range has now narrowed further. These individuals are even more comfortable and self-satisfied than they were in 1993, further tapering down the possible spectrum of opinion which could be solicited, and this clearly begs the question as to why the views of the uncomfortable and dissatisfied were not also solicited?

Despite this less than riveting beginning, though, the second episode of *Ten Years On: Under Two Flags*, is, arguably, the best in the series, and this is largely so not only by virtue of the filmic approach adopted but also because of the intrinsically interesting subject-matter dealt with: the complex matter of how the process of government administration had changed since the handover; and how the new hybrid form of capitalist-authoritarian government is actually constituted, and evolving. As argued, a common practice of *Hong Kong Connection* is to interview ordinary people. However, this approach, though laudable in its egalitarianism, does carry with it the potential difficulty that such people are not experts, are not used to public speaking, and, as in *A Promise is a Promise*, may also not be particularly engaging. *Under Two Flags* does, though, break with this practice in that it interviews some major political players of the time, including the former colonial-period Chief Secretary, Anson Chan. *Under Two Flags* paints a clear picture of gradual and insistent political intrusion into the civil service, and of a government which is becoming increasingly authoritarian, hierarchical, and disconnected from the people. The various points made in *Under Two Flags* are, therefore, radical ones, and perhaps the most far-reaching of these are the statements to the effect that there is a growing consciousness within civil society that the Chief Executive has no real legitimacy, because he was not elected; and that the lack of democracy in Hong Kong is making the city increasingly 'unstable' and 'divided'. The contrast between *A Promise is a Promise* and *Under Two Flags* also seems – perhaps unintentionally – to underscore this alleged 'division', and, whilst the participants in the former seem increasingly content with the new imperative, those in the latter are definitely not. When taken together, therefore, these two episodes reveal the existence of a growing separation within Hong Kong between those who are inclined to accept the authoritarian indenture and those who increasingly are not.

The third episode of *Ten Years On: And the Debate Continues* then carries the portrayal of this growing polarisation between pro and anti-establishment forces further. This episode is also structured around two interviews, each associated with one or other of these positions. The first interviewee, Vincent Lo, was involved in drafting the Basic Law, but left politics after the handover and is now a successful businessman. Lo puts the authoritarian case with apparently sincere conviction, asserting, for example, that democratic debate and argument are an impediment to economic progress and will lead to a divided society. Lo also believes that if universal franchise is introduced in Hong Kong, the city will lose its economic competitiveness. Lo seems to think only of money-related matters and does not address issues of rights, legitimacy or equality. Instead, he wants politics taken out of the picture altogether so that the existing political system will not be questioned. Lo is, however, balanced by the second interviewee, Martin Lee, probably the most important pro-democracy advocate at the time. Like Lo, Lee had also been a member of the committee which was tasked with drafting the Basic Law. However, unlike Lo, Lee was expelled from the committee following his condemnation of Tiananmen. Lee puts the case for democracy just as cogently as Lo did for authoritarianism, arguing that the people of Hong Kong want to elect their own leaders, and not have such leaders imposed upon them by Beijing. Lee also makes the point that, although the Basic Law provided for direct elections to take place in 2008, this will now not happen because 'the NPC [National People's Congress] said no to us in 2004'. Lee's point, in other words, is that the system which Lo holds up for praise cannot be trusted to carry out what it had stated it would carry out in terms of democratic reform for Hong Kong.

There is, however, a problem of balance with *And the Debate Continues* because the authoritarian position is not only put forward by Lo here but also by another prominent figure, Maria Tam, a member of the National People's Congress. Tam argues that if the people of Hong Kong were to elect a Chief Executive who was not to Beijing's liking, a 'constitutional crisis' could follow. Tam then goes on to argue that, in order to avert this, systems must be put in place that would make it impossible to elect somebody that Beijing could not sanction. The authoritarian position could hardly be put more clearly and is also put without any trace of irony. Tam then goes on to warn that it is the NPC and not the Basic Law which will ultimately decide whether or not Hong Kong will have democratic elections. Together, Lo and Tam outweigh Lee, and, though Anson Chan is once again referred to briefly towards the end of the film, as she puts forward proposals for elections to be held in 2008 and 2012 (proposals which were not adopted by the administration), this does not sufficiently compensate for Lee's diminution within the film as a whole. The effect here also appears to be to balance the previous episode of *Ten Years On*, which was predominantly critical of the system, with this episode, which imparts greater credence to the arguments that sustain that system. However, the 'balance' is not a real one, because this episode of *Ten Years On* also further reinforces the quietist and pro-establishment views expressed in the first episode of the series.

The fourth episode of *Ten Years On: Interfacing*, on the way that the Hong Kong media deal with reporting on the mainland, is, in many respects, the weakest in the series. Like *A Promise is a Promise* (and, perhaps, also, *And the Debate Continues*), this episode paints a generally optimistic picture of a mainland system that, according to the journalists interviewed, is loosening up in terms of censorship. According to one veteran Hong Kong journalist, 'things are better now'. Whilst, after Tiananmen, she had delayed having a child because she was worried about the future of Hong Kong, now she is no longer so worried, and the child has been born. Whilst, in addition, we do see one reporter arguing that the media is still subservient to the communist party in China, and also hear some comments about the continued prevalence of mainland censorship, the prevailing discourse in *Interfacing* is one of China gradually opening up, and allowing a greater degree of independent journalism to take place. Associated with this is also the idea that the Hong Kong media needs to 'understand how the mainland works' rather than constantly criticise or bemoan the degree of manipulation of the news – and of journalists – on the mainland. This episode of *Ten Years On* is also further weakened by the fact that these journalists are shown working in China, not Hong Kong; and, moreover, in a journalistic environment in which their questions to mainland officials seem to elicit only routine, inconsequential and pre-prepared responses. *Interfacing* was, perhaps, one episode too many for a series which, standing at six episodes, was itself probably too long for the constrained – or overstretched – capabilities of *Hong Kong Connection*. Unfortunately, the same may also be said for the final two episodes of the series: *Life under One Country Two Systems*, and *The First Generation of the SAR*.

The main problem with *Life under One Country Two Systems* is that the film is structured around an opinion poll and thus features a barrage of statistical findings, so many that it is difficult for the spectator to follow the threads of information compiled. This problem is compounded by the fact that the obligatory 'expert' consulted over the findings of the poll is an academic statistician, rather than a politician. This is hardly designed to set the pulse racing. To some extent, RTHK is taking cover behind these statistics, which provide the station with an 'objective' platform for any criticism of the government this film might mobilise. However, documentary films based largely on statistics rarely work, as the human element behind the statistics is concealed. Out of the mass of statistics does, however, come one finding that stands out: that 'people have shown an urgency for universal suffrage', and that if progress is not made on this 'more problems will occur'. *Life under One Country Two Systems* is also to be valued for turning to the condition of the poor, although it also has to be said that, in this series which targets a middle-class audience, this is *the only time* in six episodes that the poorer sections of society are covered. Nevertheless, we are given the alarming news that, since the handover, the gap between rich and poor has grown very much wider, and we are also given the example of a security guard who now earns *half* of what he was paid ten years ago, before the handover. Unfortunately, though, this startling and disquieting story is not dwelt on, and, instead, we head back to familiar middle-class territory, and to schoolteachers complaining about excessive workload. *Ten Years On* also ends with something of a whimper, rather than a roar, with *The First Generation of the SAR*, an episode which deals with youngsters who have spent their formative years within the SAR, after 1997. The episode focuses on the question of how these youngsters perceive their own sense of identity as Hongkongers and as Chinese nationals. Unfortunately, however, what comes out is entirely predictable. In an encounter with mainland students Hong Kong students affirm their own identity as Hongkongers, and criticise the mainland on various grounds. Startled mainland students who have been brought up under indoctrination then respond by affirming their own sense of Chinese identity. Though the film does showcase these divisions, little new knowledge is produced here, and it could be argued that closing the series by focusing on children was an error of judgment. Overall, *Ten Years On* attempts a balanced account of its subject, setting pro-establishment and pro-democracy voices against each other, and bringing in questions of Hong Kong versus mainland identity. To some extent, all these issues are left open within the series, presenting a picture of uncertainty within the territory which is thought-provoking. However, it could also be argued that, in terms of the issue of universal franchise, and as argued previously, the balance is weighted here slightly in favour of establishment positions.

TWENTY YEARS ON (2009)

Whilst *Ten Years On*, produced in 2007, concerns the handover, *Twenty Years On*, produced in 2009, returns to the subject of the 1993 *Four Years On*: the Tiananmen massacre. However, unlike *Four Years On*, which was made before the handover, *Twenty Years On* was made twelve years after the handover, and 'twenty years' after Tiananmen. *Twenty Years On* is also staged on a much larger scale than *Four Years On* and consists of four episodes: *The Exile*, *The Wound*, *The Patient Champions*, and *Hong Kong's Hopes*. These films largely follow the model of *Four Years On* and, to a large extent, *Ten Years On* also, in centering on middle-class people, though a far greater number of these are involved here than in *Four Years On*. *The Exile* begins with footage of the Tiananmen massacre but quickly moves on to narrate the stories of the various exiles it portrays. Around ten of these are involved, one in France, the rest in the United States. However, this extensive canvas has the effect of fragmenting the testimony of the exiles, as the film moves from one to the other without being able to go into sufficient depth over any one of them. The emphasis here is also very much on the personal experience of exile rather than on analysis of historical events and actions which led to exile, whilst the overall tone is one of nostalgia and regret over the severing of family ties consequent upon exile. As with *Four Years On* there is little commentary here (there is more commentary in *Ten Years On*), as the interviewees speak. There is also no doubt that, underlying *Twenty Years On*, there exists an acceptance on the part of the film-makers of the need to vindicate the Tiananmen protesters and finally call the Chinese government to account on the issue. However, this is never stated directly in the commentary as that would have risked strong criticism from pro-Beijing factions, both inside and outside Hong Kong. Instead, the film allows such sentiments to be expressed by the interviewees. *Twenty Years On* also shows one of the interviewees in *The Exile* using terminology which had been suppressed by those factions for decades. Zhang Jian, who was shot and wounded at Tiananmen, attests that the event was 'a real massacre', and, thus, the officially proscribed term, rather than the officially sanctioned nomenclature of 'incident', is uttered. *The Exile* is an effective film, which, despite its fragmented structure, movingly captures the experience of exile, and stresses the prevailing closeness of the family ties which had been corporeally sundered by forced expatriation. What is most notable though, are the exiles themselves, all motivated by the need to vindicate the protestors of 4 June, and all refusing to allow the memory of Tiananmen to fade.

The second episode of *Twenty Years On*: *The Wound* operates at an even more demonstrative level than the first, and covers eight people who have been acutely affected by Tiananmen in one way or another. However, again, the large number of people covered in a film that is only 22 minutes long tends to fragment and weaken the effect of the testimonies given. On the other hand, this fragmentation is countered by the fact that the testimonies buttress each other, as they are all from the point of view of the dissident. What is particularly striking here, though, is that these eight people remain in China, and are, presumably, taking part in this film at some risk to themselves. These are dissidents who did not, or could not, go into exile. But they are also, in most cases, prominent individuals, including Bao Tong, the former political secretary of Zhao Ziyang, the communist party General Secretary at the time of Tiananmen who interceded with the protesters and was then ousted by the ruling clique immediately after the massacre. Zhao was to spend the rest of his life under house arrest and, after his death in 2005, his Beijing home became the site of annual commemorative vigils by dissidents. Even today, the details of Zhou's life still remain under censorship within mainland China.[5] In defending Zhou's reputation in the way he did in *Twenty Years On*, therefore, Bao was confronting mainland authority and censorship law directly, and must have been placing himself in potential jeopardy. Bao was jailed for seven years after Tiananmen, and was then put under house arrest. He is still under house arrest today, and still refusing to be silenced. For example, writing in June 2013, on the twenty-fourth anniversary of Tiananmen, and just before the annual commemorative vigil in Hong Kong on 4 June, he unwaveringly insists that the 'massacre . . . must be completely repudiated'.[6]

The central premise of *The Wound* is that Tiananmen has created a 'wound' in China that will not heal until the truth of the matter is faced and resolved. Most of the interviewees in this film make this point as the film explores their memories of the massacre, and also records their differing accounts as to why it occurred. However, and as with the number of interviewees involved, there are also too many of these *accounts*, and this also means that *The Wound* cannot go into sufficient depth on any one. Because of this, the film is also unable to mobilise or examine any general *problematic*, although this is a common feature of the *Hong Kong Connection* approach, which aims to establish a number of interlacing testimonies instead. As mentioned earlier, however, this approach, though laudable, does not lend itself too easily to incisive in-depth analysis. Again, though, and as in *The Exile*, one is struck by the dignity and persever-ance of the people interviewed here, and, in this respect, the key figure to emerge, in addition to Bao Tong, might be Hao Jian, a professor at Beijing Film Academy. Hao speaks openly about Tiananmen and continues to mourn the cousin who was killed there. A key moment in the film shows Hao not only tending the grave of his cousin but also two other nearby graves which hold victims of the massacre – and this also raises the question as to how many such graves are in this particular cemetery? Hao then utters a Chinese idiom translated by the film-makers as 'under the dominance of great evil, where is goodness' to express the depth of his feelings. Working in a state institution as he did, one can only think that, like the incarcerated but still defiant Bao, Hao was taking risks here.

Like *The Exile*, *The Wound* makes no attempt to be impartial, and does not provide any testimony which supports the official communist view of Tiananmen, though that view is nonetheless referred to from time to time. The film also *satirises* the official account of Tiananmen in its opening credits, as those credits show the word 'massacre' being replaced by means of a fade by the word 'incident', and we are then told, through the credits, that, when this sort of obfuscation occurs, everything become 'absurd'. *The Wound* does show us people critical of the 1989 student movement, but only briefly, and their criticism is only that the students should not have confronted the state so openly. This is also similar to fraternal criticism made in 1989, within the student protest movement itself, and is not supportive of the official PRC position on Tiananmen. In addition, in one instance this criticism is subtly undermined by the film. Here, one of the interviewees, Chen Ziming, makes such remarks. But we then learn that he spent thirteen years in prison under the charge of 'incitement of anti-revolutionary sentiment and sedition' for his role in Tiananmen. We are, therefore, left with a conundrum: an activist who was severely punished by the authoritarian state and who has now become an – albeit reticent – critic of the critics of that state. The film leaves this paradox unresolved, and, in doing so, also applies a question mark to Chen's words, and to the quietist position that those words advance.

In the third episode of *Twenty Years On*, entitled *The Patient Champions*, we see reformists in China and Hong Kong who are 'championing' democratic, legal and human-rights reform on the mainland. However, unlike the partici-pants shown in the first two episodes of *Twenty Years On*, those shown in *The*

Patient Champions are working for change at the grass-roots level of society. They are, therefore, not radical voices calling for major change. Instead, they are persistently and 'patiently' trying to create a more rational, legal and fair civil society within China. As one of the interviewees says, though he was 'unable to take a big step' to reach his goal (as a dissident radical might attempt), he would carry on 'taking one small step every day'. Thus, what we see in *The Patient Champions* is a struggle for reform taking place through the creation of various rights groups, interest groups, think-tanks and advisory bodies. This is a politics of everyday life rather than grand politics, and is exercised by people who know that they cannot expect change to occur in China at the national-political level. For example, the interviewee Guo Yushan established a think-tank and discussion forums to 'exert the influence of the people over the government'. Another interviewee, Liang Xiaoyuan, says that she cannot expect 'anything big coming down from heaven' to change things in China fundamentally, but she can work to help build a society based on rules and regulations. Han Dongfan, a Tiananmen activist exiled to Hong Kong, also tries to resolve labour disputes in the mainland through providing legal advice to rural workers via the internet.

In some respects *The Patient Champions* is the most thought-provoking episode of *Twenty Years On* because it goes into depth over the way in which different and understated strategies are evolving to carry through a reformist process on the mainland, and, whilst the other episodes of *Twenty Years On* more or less tell us what we expected to hear, it could be argued that new – sometimes unexpected – knowledge is generated and expressed in *The Patient Champions*. Having said this, *The Patient Champions* does also, and for the first time in *Twenty Years On*, allow one interviewee to substantially criticise both the Tiananmen pro-democracy student movement and present-day dissidents. This comes through in the testimony of one Pu Zhi Qiang, who regrets that such a radical stance was adopted in 1989; and Pu also insists that now is also 'not the time to be a professional rebel or professional revolutionary'. However, and despite such sentiments, Pu's concrete activities are fully consonant with those carried out by the other individuals covered in *The Patient Champions*, and, whilst he may be the most vocal critic of the pro-democracy and dissident movement in the film, like those other individuals, his legal work seeks to create a more liberal society in China. Whilst *The Patient Champions* does provide an insight into the process of reform that is taking place in China, though, the pragmatic, cautious and gradualist tone which emerges in this film is in contrast with the powerful sentiments expressed in *The Wound*. The individuals shown in *The Patient Champions* have chosen to leave the national-political stage of high politics and concern themselves with quotidian interventions. Their choice is a valid and reasonable one. However, what they say will not put them in jeopardy, whilst the participants in *The Wound* took considerable risks. The contributors to *The Patient Champions* clearly feel that they are doing valuable work. However, *The Patient Champions* should, perhaps, have concluded with a commentary to the effect that the interventions it portrays would never become consequential on the larger stage in China. Continued reference to Tiananmen, on the other hand, might do.

The final episode of *Twenty Years On*, entitled *Hong Kong's Hopes*, explores some current attitudes towards Tiananmen in Hong Kong. Here, *Twenty Years On* allows more voices from the pro-Beijing side to be heard, but, in general, only in order to reaffirm the unstated but implicit position of the series on Tiananmen; and so these pro-Beijing voices are quickly passed over. For example, the film begins by showing us one of the most important pro-democracy figures in Hong Kong, the now late Szeto Wah, touring US universities to talk about Tiananmen. Wah had been one of the members of the committee tasked with drawing up the Basic Law, but, like Martin Lee, had been expelled from the committee following his denunciation of Tiananmen. During one talk he is berated by a mainland academic in the audience who demands that Wah stop talking 'accusatorily, hatefully and negatively' about Tiananmen. This critic also argues that the subject should not be discussed further, should be consigned to the past, and that 'enough is enough' on the matter. However, the haranguer appears over-emotional, fraught and discourteous to the elderly Wah, who, in contrast, seems composed and dignified, and, in response, asks his decrier whether he 'had seen the people bleeding' at Tiananmen. Echoing Wah's detractor, *Hong Kong's Hopes* then proceeds to show the first Chief Executive, Tung Chee-hwa, calling for Hong Kong citizens to 'let go of June 4th and look forward to better things'; and then the second Chief Executive, Donald Tsang, urging people to do the same, and instead focus on 'China's achievements'. However, the film does, then, also show Tsang making his controversial claim that 'my views [on the Tiananmen massacre] are representative of the general views in Hong Kong', a claim that provoked a walk-out at the time by the pro-democracy camp in the legislature. In the end, a sequence showing one pro-democracy legislator calling Tsang's statement 'repugnant' carries more weight within the film than Tsang's original declaration.

Whilst, however, *Hong Kong's Hopes* does, indirectly, undercut pro-Beijing positions on Tiananmen, it does, like *The Patient Champions*, also show individuals who have moved from a radical position on the issue to a more gradualist one of seeking some kind of future rapprochement with Beijing. So, we see Lau Chin-shek, who was once closely associated with Szeto Wah, arguing that Tiananmen was a 'knot' which existed between the democrats and Beijing, and that both parties should seek to untie the knot. Lau had been denied entry to China since Tiananmen, and had, therefore, been unable to visit his family. However, after distancing himself from a more radical pro-democracy position, he was granted an entry visa and we see him visiting his mother in

Guangdong for the first time in ten years. Here, *Twenty Years On* returns to the themes of nostalgia and exile with which the series began, though, here, we see a return from exile and a banishment of nostalgia, earned by the concession of a radical stance. In addition, we are not given any account of what Lau actually intends to do in order to 'untie the knot', and are left with the impression that nothing much is likely to happen on that front. And neither does *Hong Kong's Hopes* and, therefore, *Twenty Years On*, end with the likes of Lau, but with youthful activists determined to carry on the struggle to vindicate the 4 June protesters.

What is revealing about *Twenty Years On* is how *careful* the film-makers obviously felt they were obliged to be. There is no visceral footage (apart from the few sequences of the Tiananmen events which appear) or trenchant analysis here, no in-depth account of personal suffering in prison, or under torture. Senior Chinese leaders are rarely strongly criticised, and the overall tone of the series is one of regretful acceptance of an unremitting situation to which there seems no end in sight. This is, of course, partly because *Twenty Years On* is about China, and, in particular, about Tiananmen. If the series had been about an entirely Hong Kong matter, it might have been able to be more critical and analytical, as was the case with the two RTHK films on Article 23 which will be discussed shortly. However, whilst the film-makers of *Twenty Years On* may have been forced to tread carefully when making the series, this should not gainsay the considerable achievement here. It took nerve for RTHK to mount a four-part series tackling the virtually prohibited subject of Tiananmen on the twentieth anniversary of the massacre, and also featuring major dissidents. However, the film-makers knew that they had to tread carefully and their caution is understandable.

Twenty Years On also succeeds in bringing to our attention a number of individuals who, though enduring considerable hardship and reprisal, refuse to give up the struggle for what they take to be a just cause. As already mentioned, some of these interviewees may have taken considerable risks in agreeing to appear in the series, and in saying what they did. The fact that *Twenty Years On* made no real attempt to be balanced, but clearly, though implicitly, sides with the pro-democratic side, is another demonstration of the film-makers' commitment and resolution. However, *Twenty Years On* was made at a time of relative calm in Hong Kong, and this is reflected in the tone and pace of the film. This is also reinforced by the fact that much of the film is made up of interview-testimonies. Testimonies can often be sombre affairs by virtue of the deleterious and trenchant nature of the subject under discussion. *Twenty Years On* respects this. The interviews presented are often conducted in confined, almost claustrophobic spaces, with the camera close to the interviewee, an approach which emphasises the gravity of the moment. The result of all of this is a rather toned-down atmosphere and feel, though this should not be seen as a criticism of the series, but, rather, an imprint of its context.

ARTICLE 23 OF THE BASIC LAW: FEAR NOT, ONLY BELIEVE; AND ARTICLE 23 OF THE BASIC LAW: THE LAWYER'S LAST-DITCH BATTLE (2003)

Twenty Years On can be contrasted in a number of respects with two RTHK films which appeared in 2003, and which are about a Hong Kong, rather than China matter. As mentioned in the previous chapter of this book, Article 23, which covers the issue of 'national security' and anti-'sedition' legislation, was inserted into the Basic Law in the aftermath of Tiananmen as a direct PRC response to the flair-up of pro-democracy sentiment and sense of outrage over Tiananmen in Hong Kong. It was, therefore, specifically promulgated as a means for controlling pro-democracy opposition to the authoritarian state in Hong Kong; and that is why it was so controversial within a Hong Kong civil society which was both attempting to democratise and to keep that authoritarian state at bay. However, though Article 23 was inserted into the Basic Law in 1989, and promulgated within the Basic Law in 1990, it was not until 2003 that the Tung administration decided to implement the article.

In response to this, RTHK produced, amongst others, the two *Hong Kong Connection* films which will be discussed here: *Article 23 of the Basic Law: Fear Not, Only Believe*; and *Article 23 of the Basic Law: The Lawyer's Last-ditch Battle*. These two films carry out an incisive journalistic analysis of the case for and against Article 23, and also incorporate a wide range of characters, visual material and footage, all of which add to the overall dynamism of the film. *The Lawyer's Last Ditch Battle*, in particular, is of note because it analyses the written formulation of Article 23 term-by-term, and in great detail, exploring, for example, the meaning and potential consequence of terms in the Article such as 'subversion' and 'sedition'. As it ends with the voices of the pro-democrats, *The Lawyer's Last Ditch Battle* clearly aligns itself against Article 23; and both this film and *Fear Not, Only Believe* are a long way removed from the more guarded approach which had necessarily to be adopted in *Twenty Years On*. In addition, whereas Article 23 may have been highly controversial in Hong Kong, it was less so in China in 2003, and this allowed the producers of these two films a degree of latitude unavailable to the makers of *Twenty Years On*.

Like *Twenty Years On*, these two films on Article 23 were influenced and affected by their historical loci, in this case the febrile atmosphere of 2003, the year not only of the government's attempt to implement Article 23 but also of SARS, an infectious disease which created a climate of fear within the city.

In similar fashion, the next film to be discussed here, *Fifteen Years of 'One Country Two Systems'*, was also made against a heightened background of social and political tension, in 2012. The then Chief Executive, Donald Tsang, was the kind of politician who would always try to steer away from controversy. However, the low-key, bow-tied Tsang's watch was to end in ignominy in 2012 as he was seen to be colluding with mainland tycoons, and also accepting gifts from them. Tsang was forced to apologise to the Legislative Council, and ended his political career under threat of impeachment. These events ratcheted up pro-democracy sentiment in Hong Kong, and this process was then taken a step further when the third Chief Executive of Hong Kong, Leung Chun-ying, was appointed the same year. Given the nature of the political system imposed on Hong Kong by the Central Government in China, it was impossible for any Chief Executive to be appointed who was not favoured by Beijing. However, whilst Tsang had been seen as a pro-Beijing 'Hongkonger', Leung was viewed as closer to mainland power groupings, and to the Central Government. Leung's contentious appointment amidst an election process which was mired in indecorous scandal led to the appearance of further fractures within Hong Kong society, and it is this turbulent political context which is portrayed in *Fifteen Years of 'One Country Two Systems'*.

FIFTEEN YEARS OF 'ONE COUNTRY TWO SYSTEMS' (2012)

Unlike the slower-paced *Twenty Years On*, but like the two films on Article 23 just discussed, *Fifteen Years of 'One Country Two Systems'* is fast-paced, and also paints a picture of Hong Kong as divided, emotionally fraught and riven with protest. The predominant image in the film is of the protesters, and the predominant style of the film is in tune with this activism: *Fifteen Years* is an *agitated*, sharply edited film. *Fifteen Years* begins with a brief account of the signing of the Sino-British Joint Declaration in 1984 and then proceeds quickly to the handover ceremony of 1997. In this fast-proceeding introductory section we then see the swearing in of Tung Chee-hwa, and, later, Donald Tsang tearfully apologising before the Legislative Council. The music track in this section is plaintive in tone, evoking forfeiture and concern. The main section of the film then begins with an interview with a pro-Beijing Hong Kong unionist politician who surprisingly admits that 'one country two systems' is a contradiction in terms and a recipe for future conflict. The point being made here by this individual is that, in his view, the 'one country' must always supersede the 'two systems'; and this for him means that full democracy cannot take place in Hong Kong if it does not take place in China first. *Fifteen Years* then leaps upon this unexpected admission from a Beijing loyalist to expand further on the idea that the authoritarian state is in fact encroaching into Hong Kong in order to reduce the scope of 'two systems', before proceeding to a substantial interview with the pro-democratic legislator Alan Leong, whose main point, speaking as a barrister, is that the rule of law in Hong Kong has been under threat over the past fifteen years, and, like 'two systems', has been weakened. We are then shown more images of a Hong Kong seemingly in a state of permanent protest, as a pro-democracy activist lists the various problems the SAR is facing: growing intrusion from the mainland, growing gap between rich and poor, and so on. The camerawork and editing echoes the febrile atmosphere here, with lots of shaky hand-held camera-work and rapid, jumpy editing. We then go back to Alan Leong, who utters perhaps the most memorable individual statement in the film when asserting that, although he feels disappointed at what has happened to Hong Kong over the past fifteen years, he also feels he has no right to give up the struggle against authoritarianism when mainland dissidents are risking their lives every day in order to carry that struggle forward. The other main thesis to arise repeatedly in this section of *Fifteen Years of 'One Country Two Systems'* is that Hong Kong is now a divided society, with a centre that is increasingly failing to hold these divisions in place. As the film comes to an end, we see sequences showing an embattled-looking Leung Chun-ying, and then an escalating number of sequences of protests, and physical conflicts between protesters and police. One of the final sequences in the film, for example, shows an agitated protester being pepper-sprayed at close range by a policeman. *Fifteen Years* reflects the fevered state of Hong Kong society in 2012. However fevered that condition was, though, it was as nothing compared to the levels of emotion generated in 1989, after Tiananmen; levels portrayed in one of the most significant – though still unfortunately little known – documentary films to be produced in Hong Kong: *The Hong Kong Case*.

THE HONG KONG CASE (1989)

The Hong Kong Case makes its intent and tone clear from the outset as the film opens with a brief commentary-free sequence of footage of the Tiananmen massacre, and then proclaims that 'the unthinkable has happened'. This trenchant opening is then followed by further sequences showing wounded protesters in Tiananmen Square and elsewhere in Beijing: the 'bleeding people' referred to by Szeto Wah in *Fifteen Years of 'One Country Two Systems'*. The commentary then informs us that the massacre of 4 June 1989 was met with 'horror and revulsion by civilized people around the world' but that nowhere was that felt more acutely than in Hong Kong, and, here, the film links China, Hong Kong and the rest of the world together around the egregious pivot of Tiananmen, thus establishing the enormity and consequence of the event. This is an incendiary opening, and must have had a considerable impact on those watching the film in Hong Kong when it was first broadcast in September 1989. In fact, the *South China Morning Post* described it as having a 'shock effect', 'evoking intense emotions'.[7] Normally, in a conventional television documentary film, an introductory sequence would be tasked with setting out the general parameters of the issues and debates to be explored later in the main body of the film. However, and in contrast, *The Hong Kong Case* opens with a visceral, emotion-laden piece which over-rides any distanced, rational stance that might be adopted by the spectator. The 'unthinkable', the film-makers seem to be saying, cannot and should not be encountered through any spirit of spectatorial ratiocinative disinterestedness.

However, and despite this passionate opening call to attention, *The Hong Kong Case* remains in many respects a conventional television documentary film, tasked, indeed, with setting out the issues and debates involved, and it must, therefore, drop away from the portrayal of barbarous mercilessness set out in its opening sequences in order to carry out that task. The consequent shift from the diabolical-callous to the documentary-prosaic thus necessarily takes place, and filmic matter-of-factness takes the form of a brief historical account of colonial Hong Kong from the founding of the colony to the present day. Of course, though, this is an account mounted from a British-colonial Hong Kong, rather than mainland Chinese historiographical perspective, as is made clear when the commentary mentions – rather unfortunately – that, following the First Opium War, China 'gave' Hong Kong to Britain. We then see a hurried succession of archival sequences showing, for example, the Japanese invasion of Hong Kong, and post-war economic development in the city during the 1950s and 1960s, and up to the 1980s. Here, British Hong Kong is depicted as a success story in which local Hong Kong people led by a 'benign government' currently enjoy 'one of the highest degrees of personal freedom in the world' (the fact that those same 'people' enjoy very little political freedom – at least in terms of political representation – is not mentioned). However, the commentary goes on to tell us that this personal freedom is increasingly threatened by the looming threat, returning like a 'bad dream', of the coming 1997 handover. We then see a large graphic map of colonial Hong Kong fading into a bright red one dominated by the PRC flag. At one level just a statement of fact – that the territory will one day soon come under China sovereignty again – this blood-red chart also takes on a Mephistophelean dimension here, and is meant to scare.

We then see Prime Minister Margaret Thatcher in Beijing in 1982. Thatcher had gone to seek concessions over the future of Hong Kong but had been told by the Chinese leader, Deng Xiaoping, that neither the date of 1997 nor any question of sovereignty, was negotiable. We then see Thatcher's famous 'fall' as she stumbles to the ground shortly after leaving the meeting with Deng. This collapse, of course, received great publicity at the time as presaging the inevitable miscarriage of the British attempt to retain Hong Kong, and also carries a similar connotation within this film. This section of *The Hong Kong Case* moves on to the signing of the Joint Declaration in 1984, and what is striking here is that Thatcher appears to be genuinely sincere about what she is engaged with. Close-ups of her face reveal her apparently believing that the deal which had been brokered, premised as it was on Deng's promise that the Hong Kong way of life would remained unchanged for at least fifty years after the handover, was, as she put it, 'a good one', which would ensure that 'the people of Hong Kong could face the future with confidence'. However, *The Hong Kong Case* immediately gainsays such precipitate sanguinity by showing long columns of would-be emigrants forming outside foreign consulates in Hong Kong, and by informing the viewer that 43,000 people left Hong Kong in 1988, whilst 60,000 more are now expected to leave in 1989 (these sequences were, of course, shot prior to Tiananmen, and so these figures cannot anticipate the substantial increase in such departures which occurred following the massacre). Scenes of people tearfully taking leave of relatives at Hong Kong airport then further accentuate the sense of hopelessness and anxiety involved here. Few of these people really want to leave Hong Kong, which, as the film tells us, is their 'home'. However, they feel that they have no choice but to do so. We then focus in on an example of one of these unenthusiastic emigrants. Here, *Hong Kong Connection* also resorts to the series' common practice of interviewing ordinary and, as we have seen, often middle class-individuals. We briefly meet a Mr Cheung, a businessman who had left for Canada together with his family in 1986. He now has a Canadian passport but must continue to live in Hong Kong in order to maintain his business, whilst his family remains far away in North America. The film stresses his sense of isolation now as he speaks tearfully to camera, and, in emphasising this state of sequestration, *The Hong Kong Case* also makes implied reference to the more general sense of separation prevailing at the time, and felt by the many other 'Mr Cheungs' whose families had felt a similarly pressing need to leave under the looming threat of 1997. The tears shed here by Mr Cheung will not be the only ones shed in *The Hong Kong Case*, a film which abounds with such tears.

After this brief familial interlude, *The Hong Kong Case* introduces us to the two local political figures and one local family who will reappear a number of times in the film, and whose arguments will serve to provide different perspectives on Tiananmen. The two political figures are Martin Lee and Leung Chun-ying (the latter of whom, as we have seen, when discussing *Fifteen Years of 'One Country Two System'*, was to become the third Chief Executive of Hong Kong in 2012). Lee seems to be given more status than Leung here, as the commentary attests that, with his frequent calls for democratic change, he is seen as 'a hero for many Hong Kong people'. At that time, Lee was the most important pro-democrat in Hong Kong, and (until Tiananmen) also a member of the Basic Law Drafting Committee, whilst Leung was Secretary-General of the Basic Law Consultative Committee. In the film we see archival footage of Lee pressing the case for the democratisation of Hong Kong, whilst, and in contrast, the pro–Beijing Leung follows the official PRC line that any political change that takes place in Hong Kong must be 'gradual'. Having been introduced to Lee and Leung, we now meet the working-class Au family. Unlike Lee and Leung, they are defined as 'non-political: just an 'ordinary' family who want to see a stable future after 1997. Although they may be 'non-political', though, Mr and Mrs Au, like the other Hong Kong citizens whom they are meant to represent in this film, are worried about what the future may hold for them after 1997. *The Hong Kong Case* then shifts its focus to China, and to the then talismanic figure of Deng Xiaoping, 'one of the most remarkable figures in recent Chinese history'. There is then reference to a 'new spirit of liberalism' abroad in China in the late 1980s, for which Deng is said to deserve credit. This view of Deng as singularly important is then reinforced when we return to Hong Kong to see Lee, Leung and Mrs Au united in their shared conviction that Deng was not only crucial to the reform movement in China, but was also an irreplaceable guarantor that Chinese communist promises over Hong Kong would be fulfilled. Martin Lee, for example, goes as far as to assert that the ageing Deng 'must not die'; whilst Mrs Au remarks that she hoped Deng would live 'beyond his hundred'. Later, though, *The Hong Kong Case* will go on to show that such a perception of Deng was fallacious, and that Martin Lee and Mrs Au had been led astray. It is not exactly clear when these sequences featuring Lee and Mrs Au were shot, but it seems likely that they were filmed prior to the expansion of the student protest movement in Beijing after April 1989. Certainly, Lee and Au do not seem to be aware that the Beijing protesters had a view of Deng very different to theirs leading up to 4 June, and that, as a film from May 1989 such as *Spring of Discontent* shows, those protesters were actually mocking Deng, and branding him as 'senile'.[8]

Following this, *The Hong Kong Case* then looks further back to before Tiananmen in order to point to signs that appear to show, in retrospect, how Beijing was insidiously seeking to exert greater control over Hong Kong than it had originally promised to do. We see various forms of growing Beijing intrusion into Hong Kong, and are told that 'something funny was happening to the Basic Law'. The charge is, essentially, that PRC negotiators were surreptitiously attempting to turn the evolving draft of the Basic Law (it was not promulgated until 1990, a year after *The Hong Kong Case* was made) 'into something more like the existing PRC constitution'; and were, through this means, intent on instilling within the Basic Law the same kind of authoritarian control mechanisms characteristic of that constitution (it should be remembered that the Basic Law Drafting Committee was dominated by Beijing functionaries, and concern over this at the time in Hong Kong is clearly exposed in this part of *The Hong Kong Case*). This section of the film, which leads directly up to the events of Tiananmen, then turns towards the troubled situation in Tibet, where a revolt, so the film's commentary tells us, was 'bloodily put down' by PRC troops in 1988. More tellingly, though, and in premonition of events which would soon take place in China, we hear that martial law was declared in Tibet in March 1989, and see more images of Chinese troops firing upon Tibetan protestors. The film then asks whether this is what could eventually happen in Hong Kong after the handover. Then *The Hong Kong Case* links Lee, Leung, the Au family, the people of Hong Kong, and the protest movement in China together by counter-posing the protesters in Beijing with huge shows of support for their demonstration then taking place in Hong Kong; and also by proclaiming sombrely that, 'in Hong Kong the response to the protest was simply the most massive ever witnessed in the territory'.

It has been argued by one historian that this moment of mass response, one in which local Hong Kong people came fully and fervently to support the China reform movement, was almost the first time that a sense of Hong Kong Chinese identity had become linked affirmatively, and on a mass scale, with affairs on the mainland.[9] This had not, for example, occurred during the Chinese Cultural Revolution, or during the associated Hong Kong riots of 1967. However, and in stark contrast with those events, the Hong Kong protestors of 1989 felt an acute sense of identity with the protesters in Tiananmen and elsewhere in China; and this was, in large part, because, if the reform movement in China succeeded, 1997 would not bring dictatorship to Hong Kong. This sense of identity with and placement of hope in the demonstrators is put very clearly by Martin Lee when he says that 'if China was democratic, if China was free, then Hong Kong would be fine'; and also by Mr Au, when he asserts that 'we thought that these students could save us'. *The Hong Kong Case* also manages to capture this transitory moment of a coalescence between Hong Kong and mainland Chinese reformist identities particularly well through its striking visual and aural counter-position of the protests in China and Hong Kong, and, through an edited cross-cutting which shows the two protests divided by topography becoming one within the diegetic realm of the film. Despite such cross-cutting, however, in terms of visuality, the two protests remain strikingly different. In Hong Kong the filming is vibrant and colourful whilst the camera is able to get intimately close to the spectators by mingling with them. In Tiananmen, on the other hand, the film sequences appear greyish and indistinct, whilst the protesters are largely seen from a distance, as though they are already in somebody's firing line.

The technique of cross-cutting between protesters in Hong Kong and Beijing used in these sequences also acts as a bridgehead into the next and most powerful section of *The Hong Kong Case*. As martial law is declared in late May, this cross-cutting first becomes more restless and fretful and then appears to come to a staying climax as the film, literally, *stops*; as though a metaphorical pause button has been pressed. An unnaturally stationary march of protesters in Hong Kong then fades to black, and the film restarts in the crucible of Tiananmen on the morning of 4 June. We see again some of the archival footage of the massacre previously shown at the beginning of *The Hong Kong Case*, and then reaction in Hong Kong to the massacre. The producers of *The Hong Kong Case* pull no punches in terms of the choice of language captured here, as is evidenced by the profusion of terms such as 'inhuman', 'slaughter', 'ashamed', 'barbaric' and 'murderers'. Mr Au now feels only 'hatred' for the regime, and Martin Lee, who, before Tiananmen, had placed his hopes in Deng, now claims that Deng was no 'saviour' but a 'traitor' to the Chinese people. Lee now says that 'if Mr Deng should die now, I don't think the people of Hong Kong would weep'. It is with these intense expressions of anger and demoralisation, in the immediate aftermath of 4 June, that what might be termed the 'first half' of *The Hong Kong Case* then comes to a conclusion.

The 'second half' of *The Hong Kong Case* then looks at the more extensive repercussions of Tiananmen in Hong Kong over the 100 days which followed the massacre (the broadcast of the film was timed to appear 100 days after 4 June). We are told that forty-eight hours after the massacre took place, 40 per cent of value was wiped off the Hong Kong Stock Exchange. Then we see evidence of a huge rise in the number of people attempting to leave Hong Kong, with consulates experiencing 'business like it has never been before', and panic-stricken people seeking access to the Singapore Consulate, in particular. Singapore was the preferred choice for many locals because of the shared ethnicity. Irrespective of where they might wish to go, though, Mrs Au, for one, now tells 'everyone to go if they can'. But although many people wish to go to Britain because of shared citizenship, they are unable to do so because of recent changes to British immigration law, changes which have resulted in the right of abode in the UK being retracted from over 3 million Hongkongers. On 13 June, a mere nine days after the massacre at Tiananmen, a hastily produced British television BBC *Panorama* programme, which was co-produced by RTHK, was broadcast in both Britain and Hong Kong. The programme, entitled *Hong Kong: A Matter of Honour?*, dealt directly with the right of abode issue, and whether, following Tiananmen, right of abode should now be granted to all Hong Kong people who might wish to emigrate to Britain. The programme also had a live link to Hong Kong, and to guests such as Martin Lee.

Hong Kong: A Matter of Honour? turned out to be a considerable ordeal for Sir Geoffrey Howe, the then British Foreign Secretary, who represented the Thatcher government position on this programme. From the outset, the programme's presenter, a visibly disapproving Jonathon Dimbleby, tore into Howe, suggesting that the Thatcher government's position on the retraction of the right of abode for Hong Kong people was morally indefensible given the events at Tiananmen, and questioning Howe's claim that the British people and Parliament would never accept a scenario in which over 3 million immigrants arrived in the country at more or less the same time. At one point Howe implies that part of the reason such an arrival would be unacceptable was that the people of Hong Kong were ethnically different to the majority of British people; and he then goes on to assert that the Chinese Hongkongers are 'strange to us'. A startled Dimbleby then asks Howe pointedly whether he is referring to race and goes on to ask whether 3 million white immigrants would be more acceptable than 3 million Chinese ones. Howe then stumbles lamely and unconvincingly away from the hole he has made for himself. However, the implication of his words is clear: Howe does not believe that his government, or British society, would be prepared to tolerate the arrival of such a large-scale ethnically Chinese arrival.

Hong Kong: A Matter of Honour? then crosses to the Hong Kong link where Martin Lee condemns Howe's comments as 'racialist'. Other Chinese speakers then insist that the Thatcher government's policy on the right of abode amounts to a dereliction of responsibility. One speaker claims that 'this is a matter of life and death for us', whilst another, expatriate speaker, angrily unfurls the actual British flag that was hoisted upon the liberation of Hong Kong from Japan in 1945, and asserts that the position adopted by the present British government represents a betrayal of the people of Hong Kong, and, therefore, of the flag. The camera cuts to Howe, who gazes fixedly at the floor, head lowered. Dimbleby then asks for comments from the studio audience in London. To his evident surprise, and apparent dismay, the majority of speakers back Howe, and are opposed to the right of abode being given back to Hong Kong people. Unlike Howe, however, none of these speakers brings up the matter of race; they instead point to the impracticality of receiving 3 million plus arrivals. Nonetheless, when the final vote is taken, one which Dimbleby finds 'surprising' given the comments that preceded it, there is, as Dimbleby puts it, a 'clear majority' in favour of the right of abode being granted once again to the people of Hong Kong. As Howe again reiterates his claim that 3 million new people could not be accommodated within the UK, the programme goes back to Martin Lee in Hong Kong, who announces that the vote illustrates that which was already well known to him: 'that the people of Great Britain are honourable, their government not'. Dimbleby then ends the programme by solemnly declaring that the fate of Hong Kong is now 'a grave matter'.

In its own way, and coming so soon after Tiananmen, *Hong Kong: A Matter of Honour?* is as intense and emotional as *The Hong Kong Case*. What is also particularly striking about *Hong Kong: A Matter of Honour?* is that the participants in the programme can hardly bring themselves to refer to the massacre at Tiananmen directly. There are frequent references to 'the event', 'the incident', to 'what happened in Peking', but no utterance along the lines of 'the massacre in Beijing by the Chinese government'. It is almost as though these people are still in a state of shock, and are unable to name the un-nameable, or face the un-faceable. Or maybe it is just because such a naming and facing would undercut the argument that the right of abode should not be granted in this case: the 'Hong Kong case'. Throughout, Dimbleby, in particular, in a driven demonstration of the political-interviewer's art, exudes an air of barely suppressed ire and indignation, and this also adds an imperative dimension to the programme. *The Hong Kong Case* also includes the excerpt from *Hong Kong: A Matter of Honour?* in which the studio-audience vote is taken, and in which Lee accuses the British government of lacking honour. However, and for reasons that remain unclear, *The Hong Kong Case* does not show Dimbleby's relentless pursuit of the chastened Howe, nor any of the other episodes from the *Panorama* programme in which Howe was made to squirm particularly badly. Perhaps re-screening the televised embarrassment of a British Foreign Secretary was still one step too far for RTHK, or for the colonial government of Hong Kong, which, of course, was directly subordinate to that Foreign Secretary. But there is no evidence of any form of political interference from the colonial government in the making of *The Hong Kong Case*, and the likelihood is that what we see at work here is the sort of considerate self-censorship that the *Panorama* programme, and Dimbleby, did not feel obliged to partake of so soon after the massacre.

Following this sequence, the most powerful emotion to emerge in *The Hong Kong Case* is anger, and that anger is no longer directed at the 'barbaric' regime in China but at Britain, and a real sense of outrage comes through here as the British government is accused of shirking its 'moral responsibility' towards Hong Kong, and of abandoning the people of the colony to their uncertain fate. The film now focuses on this sense of betrayal, showing close-ups of protesters venting their wrath at the British government and crying 'shame on you'! Then *The Hong Kong Case* turns to various surreal arguments mounted by a number of well-known British pundits of the day concerning how up to 6 million people could be moved out of the colony before 1997, and deposited in countries such as Britain, Australia and Canada; and we see graphic and animated maps, complete with directional arrows, showing how the imagined mega-diaspora could be organised. But such a transmigration would, of course, have been impossible, and, anyway, not all Hong Kong people wanted to leave. We see interviews with some self-confessed 'small potatoes' including labourers and taxi drivers, who will stay because they feel that, precisely as 'small potatoes', they will probably not be overly affected by 1997. We then meet Vincent Lo, who will later reappear in 2007 as a pro-Beijing businessman in *Ten Years On* (see the earlier discussion on this RTHK series). Although Tiananmen has modified his pro-business stance to the extent that he now admits to having some inkling of a 'political consciousness', Lo nonetheless still thinks that 'democratisation' should come only gradually to Hong Kong, so that business interests are not unduly disturbed. Lo believes that 'we have to learn to walk before we can run'. Like the 'small potatoes', Lo also intends to remain in Hong Kong after 1997. Indeed, he has already forged business links with the mainland and is doing rather well. Lo puts the authoritarian position here in arguing that what matters most is the creation of wealth, and that democracy is not only of secondary importance but may also even hinder such creation. At this stage *The Hong Kong Case* also posits a growing division in Hong Kong, one much aggravated by Tiananmen, between a business elite intent on establishing further ties with economic and political power groupings on the mainland, and 'the ordinary people of Hong Kong', who are demanding democracy. Finally, *The Hong Kong Case* comes to an end by looking back to 1986, and to the visit of Queen Elizabeth to Hong Kong. The film concludes with her final salutation that 'our thoughts will always be with you'. But the expression on the face of the Queen is the giveaway here. She does not smile.

According to the *South China Morning Post*, the Director of RTHK, Cheung Man-yee, was 'rightly proud' of *The Hong Kong Case* because 'it provided a balanced coverage which explained the changes in the Hongkong public, the local Government, as well as Sino-British ties since June 4'.[10] Presumably Cheung was trying to fend off expected pro-Beijing criticism here because no objective viewing of *The Hong Kong Case* could possibly arrive at the conclusion that the film was 'balanced'. To their credit, these film-makers made no attempt to show genuine balance in the face of atrocity and the intolerable, and what 'balance' there may be in the film is also not central to its underpinning project, which is to condemn the massacre. On the other hand, and as previously mentioned, *The Hong Kong Case* does not contain the sort of incisive interrogation of a major political figure that is carried out by Jonathon Dimbleby in *Hong Kong: A Matter of Honour?*, and it may be to just such an absence of – presumably 'unbalanced' – stridency of attack that Cheung was referring when she argued that *The Hong Kong Case* was 'balanced'. Cheung might also have had in mind the fact that *The Hong Kong Case* provides the testimony of some individuals (Lo, the 'small potatoes', the business elite, and so on) who do not feel that Tiananmen has rendered the idea of 'one country two systems' unworkable. However, none of these compensations affects the raw power and intent of this film. As a documentary film, *The Hong Kong Case* remains of genuine international and historical importance, and deserves to be better known than it is.

CONCLUSIONS

The Hong Kong Case works at the macro-level of the national-political narrative. However, the main RTHK vehicle, *Hong Kong Connection*, cannot do this on a regular basis. As a more-or-less weekly programme, the series is limited in what it can achieve, and how in-depth it can be. In addition, it is not shown at peak viewing time. As things stand, the series cannot be compared to a British series like the one mentioned in this chapter, *Panorama*, which sometimes makes films which shake the British establishment. *Panorama* is not a weekly series, and the remorseless schedule of *Hong Kong Connection* must impair the ability of the film-makers to make more affective films. Yet RTHK is clearly *able* to make ground-shaking films, as *The Hong Kong Case* amply demonstrates. As far as the production of authoritative television documentary film in Hong Kong is concerned, the future also lies with RTHK to a large extent, as the commercial broadcasters cannot be relied upon *as institutions*, despite the best endeavours of committed film-makers working within them. Both *The Hong Kong Case* and the more recent *Fifteen Years of 'One Country Two Systems'* demonstrate that the way forward is through the production of 'specials' which have the scope and finance to go into a subject in depth.

NOTES

1. Interview with Dominica Siu, Hong Kong, 2010.
2. Ibid.
3. Ibid.
4. CB (C8) 4/9/3 (92) pt. 22, Government Secretariat, letter to RTHK Programme Staff Union, 18 January 1992.
5. Tsang, Steve, *A Modern History of Hong Kong* (Hong Kong: Hong Kong University Press, 2009), p. 251.
6. Bao is quoted in the *South China Morning Post*, 3 June 2013.
7. Fong, Bernard, 'Compulsive Viewing from RTHK Team', *South China Morning Post*, 13 September 1989.
8. See Chapter 4 of this book, on the documentary films of TVB and the *Pearl Report*.
9. Tsang, *A Modern History*, p. 246.
10. Fong, 'Compulsive Viewing'.

CHAPTER 6

Aesthetics and Radicalism: An Overview of Independent Documentary Film in Hong Kong, 1973–2013

SCOPE AND BACKGROUND

This chapter provides a general overview of the independent documentary films produced in Hong Kong from the early 1970s up to and including the early years of the second decade of the new millennium. It is intended both as a background to and a comprehensive perspective of the field of independent, non-broadcast documentary practice in the contemporary era, enabling the reader to form a clear picture of the various strands of development over a vibrant and often turbulent forty-year period in the city's history; this includes, of course, the 1997 transfer of sovereignty to China and the relatively short but fertile period of post-colonial non-fiction film creativity.

By sharp contrast with the government-sponsored and television company-driven initiatives of previous decades, the independent sector that emerged in the late twentieth and early twenty-first centuries, while being very much preoccupied with Hong Kong's present and future state and status, was somewhat reminiscent of the early Hong Kong independent film work of Lai Man-wai in its relative freedom from institutional control. This factor has been of crucial importance in the emergence of a small but expanding and lively documentary film practice in the city, which, to judge by the work of both established practitioners and newer voices, has impinged on the critical attentions of both local and global audiences and commentators. The overview offered in the present chapter will provide a platform for exploring a number of specific and significant films by major contemporary practitioners in the final chapter.

During the 1960s and 1970s Hong Kong began to emerge as one of the more economically resilient cities of Asia. Two decades after the traumatic events of the Japanese occupation and the deprivations of war, the colony was already making a spirited recovery. The increase in economic stability enhanced the emergence of a new middle class, and the baby boom in the post-war recovery contributed to a new kind of society, in which residents would start to identify themselves as 'Hongkongers' rather than refugees and temporary residents, as had been the tendency in the late 1940s and 1950s. This distinct growth in local cultural recognition, largely influenced by discrete elements of westernisation and modernity, succeeded in creating a unique identity for the new Hong Kong population, distinguishing them sharply, at least in their own minds, from their China mainland counterparts. During these decades Hong Kong residents necessarily became more aware of impending political change and of the issues surrounding decolonisation, with the city's cinema playing its part in this socio-political awakening following its nervous isolationism of the Cultural Revolution years. The vicissitudes of the city's fortunes over the past forty years certainly have provided fertile ground for independent documentary perspectives, as the present chapter will elucidate.

THE RE-EMERGENCE OF LOCAL INDEPENDENT DOCUMENTARY IN THE 1970s AND 1980s AND THE BIRTH OF THE ACTIVIST DOCUMENTARY

By the 1960s and 1970s Hong Kong's old left-wing patriotic cinema and social-realist school of the pre-war years and the 1950s had fallen into decline as a result of institutional restructuring, accompanying the rapid development of large-scale capitalist enterprise in the city. In consequence, many of the local independent Cantonese film companies were superseded by better-financed and more technologically advanced Mandarin-language film studios, notably the Shaw Brothers from Shanghai and the Cathay Company from South-East Asia. Inspired by the commercialism of Hollywood, these companies produced entertaining films on a lavish budget, mixing martial arts with historical or contemporary romance and generally eschewing sensitive social image issues. Instead of portraying sentimental or tragic scenes of social hardship, as in previous decades, they conveyed modern energy, glamour and excitement in their films.

One of the first western academics to write on Hong Kong cinema, I. C. Jarvie, described this as a period of 'Mandarinisation of Hong Kong cinema'; for him it represented a crossover phenomenon that succeeded in creating a robust market among both the traditional audience and the younger generation.[1] This new cinema became enormously popular and successful at the box office, eclipsing the old independent Cantonese film companies. In 1970 former Shaw Brothers executive Raymond Chow formed his own company Golden Harvest, producing the internationally popular Bruce Lee Kung Fu films, the Hui Brothers comedies, and later the films of local Kung Fu star Jackie Chan. Bruce Lee's iconic status as Kung Fu superstar, and his own widely publicised 'Jeet Kune Do' martial arts school, transformed the local film industry into the major worldwide exporter of Kung Fu movies. Lee rose to international prominence after the release of *The Big Boss* (1971), *Fist of Fury* (1972) and *Enter the Dragon* (1973). Despite the untimely death of the martial artist at the height of his fame, his films continued to boost his reputation and spawn imitators, many of them paying tribute to Lee's acting and philosophy alike. Furthermore, as a consequence of the enormous popularity of Hong Kong-born martial arts stars and also the local taste for comedy movies, the pendulum began to swing back towards Cantonese language after a period of Mandarin-language domination.

The first major international documentary to explore Lee's work and short life was *The Real Bruce Lee*, directed and edited by Jim Markovic in 1973. Interesting as the film may be for the Bruce Lee fan on account of its inclusion of rare archival footage of the young Lee acting with his father in *Kid Cheung* (1947) and as a small child in San Francisco and Hong Kong, it cannot be described as a genuine Hong Kong documentary. Indeed, its principal motivation seems to have been related to attempts to launch the careers of now long-forgotten Bruce Lee imitators. Four Hong Kong biopics of uneven quality were also released over the following few years to exploit the insatiable interest in Lee's sadly abbreviated career. These were *Bruce Lee: A Dragon Story*, directed by Shut Dik, and *Bruce Lee: The Man, the Myth*, directed by Ng See-yuen, both made in 1976; Leonard Ho's more balanced, in-depth retrospective, *Bruce Lee, the Legend* (1977), which incorporated extensive footage of Lee's life and even rare shots taken at his funeral; and Wong Sing-lui's 1978 documentary, *He's a Legend, He's a Hero*, which concentrates on investigating lesser-known details of the star's life and enigmatic death.

During this period conventional film distribution channels, and thus access to public screening, were not open to independent film-makers, and independent documentary-makers were conspicuous by their absence. As Stephen Teo has pointed out, the movie business and local productions were largely influenced by the decisions of film distributors and exhibitors, and not by movie producers.[2] Producers and directors generally found it hard to secure finance for film-making unless the projects had the backing of major studios. Close integration between the Cantonese film companies and the distributors was lacking, and the result was a lack of adventurous or genuinely alternative films in this era, since such films stood very little chance of getting a mainstream release. Thus, as regards the documentary mode, travel documentaries designed to promote tourism in China remained dominant in terms of cinema exhibition, although the production of these had stalled during the upheaval caused by the Cultural Revolution.

Independent local film-making during this period can, therefore, be regarded as a niche activity, and most keen amateur interest was focused on European art cinema, particularly on French film-makers from the *Nouvelle Vague* such as Godard. While most films were made in 16 mm format, a relatively portable and inexpensive alternative to 35 mm film, filming was still considered an expensive project for those who had little or no financial backing. Another result of this lack of finance was that films were shot and then were often discarded or remained undeveloped. In most cases, film-makers simply did not value what they had shot as sufficiently important to keep. However, film-friendly new publications targeting a younger generation of film aficionados, such as *Chinese Student Weekly* and *College Life*, began to provide Hong Kong-born intellectuals with new insights into art films, and encouraged the creation of alternative and more diversified cultural products. While documentary productions were still very uncommon in this era, the increasing awareness of film criticism and appreciation of European art films helped to forge an alternative film culture, and consequently stirred interest in engaging in a contemporary realist social discourse. The ideological positions adopted and expressed in these and other publications became important in the thematic study of independent film-makers' ideas and cinematic practices in Hong Kong.

Law Kar and Tang Shuxuan were among the most critically respected writers who emerged from this period, involving themselves in numerous independent film projects. Tang's films of the 1960s and early 1970s were the focus of Law's critical analysis, while in 1976 Tang founded *Close Up*, an intellectual periodical devoted to film and television criticism. The inter-relations between literary products and films, for instance, and the relationship between Tang, Law and the critic Lau Shing-hon, have been explored by Hector Rodriguez, in whose estimation these very diverse film-related cultural activities fed into the discourses that led to the 'New Wave' in Hong Kong's late 1970s and early 1980s film culture.[3]

As a vigorous advocate of the independent film-making scene, Law Kar demonstrated that the act of engaging in independent projects could be regarded as a declaration of creative independence from the mainstream film industry. Law Kar's films include works that set him apart from those involved in the old-fashioned, mainstream film companies. His contribution to film criticism was followed by his participation in a milestone short activist documentary in 1971, both as cameraman and editor. Law, along with two other cameramen, was invited by political activist Mok Chiu-yu to film the Diaoyu Islands protest organised by the Hong Kong Federation of Students. The purpose of the demonstration was to urge the Chinese government to take action in reclaiming the islands that were historically claimed as Chinese territory, yet ceded to Japan in 1895 under the treaty of Shimonoseki. The islands were officially 'handed over' to Japan by the United States in 1970 when it was thought they could be of strategic importance to a now pro-western government.

The documentary footage appears to have been intended as no more than a record of popular protest by young Hongkongers, expressing solidarity with what they saw as China's legitimate claims to sovereignty. Indeed, this issue has never been satisfactorily resolved, and grievances over the Diaoyu Islands continue to affect China–Japan relations. The eventual moving-image document, funded by the Student Union of Hong Kong University, was entitled *Protect Diaoyutai* [Diaoyu Islands] *Movement*, a black and white silent film shot in 16 mm. It recorded the details of the protest on 10 April 1971, the conflicts between students and policemen, the dispersal by police officers using tear gas, and eventually the arrests of some of the protestors. The 15–minute film was screened under the title *Changes in Hong Kong Society Through Cinema*, and was included in the 12th Hong Kong International Film Festival in 1988. In the programme catalogue critic Stephen Teo comments on the qualities of this piece of activist film-making:

> Seen today, the footage constitutes celluloid evidence of a students' movement in Hong Kong which directly parallels those popularly seen in the West. Although the movement was largely inspired by the nationalistic features of Mao Zedong-thought (which reflected the dominance of Maoist-inclined students in the movement), the political thrust of Diaoyutai was also a filtrated mixture of radical sentiments which expressed solidarity with student movements in the Western world opposing the Vietnam War and the Russian invasion of Czechoslovakia, for example.[4]

The latter-day independent documentary film genre re-emerged in Hong Kong in the aftermath of these activist initiatives. Typically these films were necessarily rudimentary, but they shared common approaches with the direct cinema of Frederick Wiseman, and were also influenced by 'situationist' film-makers active in the west in the 1960s and 1970s, especially those who employed a sense of immediacy and spontaneity in their treatment of anarchic individuals and large-scale anti-establishment actions. More film-makers participated in various kinds of film-making with the more affordable super 8 format, and more cinephiles could afford to buy equipment for production, post-production and exhibition, including a camera, editor, splicer, viewer and projector.[5] Active film-makers and cameramen of this period include Cheung Kwok-ming, Cheung Kin and George Chang. The first-named of these created a studio with his own money and that of a few friends, and directed eight documentary shorts during 1972–5, but unfortunately most of his films were lost.

Documentary enthusiast Lau Fung-kut was one of the few that consistently filmed short documentaries, later preserved in VHS format by the Hong Kong Film Archive, with titles such as *Hong Kong's Housing* (1973), *Protest* (date not available), *Eighty Seven Gods on the Wall* (1973) and *Diaries of Five Men* (1973).

The 1970s, therefore, saw a considerable expansion in the number of would-be documentary film-makers from the younger generation, including many who had received a westernised education and aspired to express modern political ideas. The influence of local literary and cinematic institutions and the increasing number of events provided by such organisations proved both practical and theoretical. Starting from 1973 the Phoenix Cine Club offered competitions, regular screenings, equipment rental services, and small-scale film-making training. In the late 1970s, Law Kar, Tsui Hark and Clifford Choi Kai-kwong formed the Hong Kong Film Cultural Centre, which offered film appreciation and production classes, with 'New Wave' directors Ann Hui, Tsui Hark and Allen Fong as their associate speakers.[6]

Perhaps the most significant development of this period was the founding of the Hong Kong International Film Festival (HKIFF) in 1976, which has since blossomed into one of the key film festivals in Asia, and has, from the very beginning, represented an important showcase for local independent film-makers. This festival has established a reputation for programming important international films as well as showcasing local Hong Kong films. Since its inception, the festival was organised under the umbrella of various governmental departments up until 2004 when the Hong Kong International Film Festival Society was officially established as an independent, charitable organisation to manage the development of the HKIFF. Crucially for the longer-term development of Hong Kong documentary cinema, the HKIFF among its various categories for international awards now includes a Best Documentary Category.

For the most part, though, independent documentary film during this decade, with the exception of very limited exercises in independent newsreel activity, represented more of a potential genre, predicated on the efforts of amateur film buffs and activists, than a real presence in cinemas. Prominent film-makers of the period produced significant work in fictional forms, but nothing of note in the documentary mode. At the same time, the social and political issues of the period fostered an activist and strongly independent spirit that, in hindsight, came to define the documentary style of succeeding decades. Thus, a small number of critical and experimental talents emerged at this time, some of whom adopted socially and politically radical positions; the amateur documentary documented this radical spirit in a complete departure from the more politically responsible positions adopted by institutional documentary producers – specifically the by-now-defunct Hong Kong Film Unit and its successors, RTHK and the commercial television stations.

HONG KONG INDEPENDENT DOCUMENTARY CINEMA IN THE 1980s AND 1990s; THE ROLE OF NEW TECHNOLOGY, ORGANISATIONS AND FILM FESTIVALS

As we have seen in the previous chapter, television documentaries began to reach larger audiences in the 1980s, with different stations featuring social issues with a greater emphasis on criticism and analysis than had been evident hitherto. In many ways the period could be regarded as the golden age of television documentaries, a context in which a number of unexplored social and cultural topics in Hong Kong could be investigated in half- or one-hour programmes. As regards theatrical releases, a handful of alternatives to the predominant travel and festival recording documentaries made by left-wing mainland-oriented film companies, keen to promote the People's Republic of China, began to be screened more widely. Also, forty years after the Japanese occupation of Hong Kong, the critical historical documentary had become a topic of interest both in mainland China and in Hong Kong. One film in particular, produced at the beginning of the decade in 1980, epitomised this sudden trend: Hong Kong-born but educated in the United States, Edwin Kong made his 1980 film *Rising Sun* entirely from archival footage resourced in the National Archive in Washington, DC while he was studying in the United States.

The film, which will be discussed in greater detail in the following chapter, dealt with Japan's imperialist expansion and decline in the Second World War. Inspired by the British Thames Television documentary series, *The World at War* (1973), Kong searched for material among obscure war archives and obtained film prints primarily from the National Archive in Washington, DC to assemble a historically-based piece covering the Japanese invasion of East and South-East Asia and its eventual surrender following the dropping of atom bombs on Hiroshima and Nagasaki respectively. Clearly, *Rising Sun* – a remarkable success at the box office, running for six continuous weeks – resonated with local audiences, and picked up on growing public sentiment related to the Diaoyu Islands affair. Significantly, what had hitherto been a small-circle activist and film club topic of interest to limited sections of the community was now capable of engaging a wider population. The film's success was due to the fact that it resonated widely with the Hong Kong population at large, rather than solely with the activist and left-wing patriotic segments of it. Its timing was also a relevant factor, both in terms of Japan's past and present involvement in geo-politically sensitive contexts. Following this success, Kong produced and directed *Wonders of Life* in 1983, again using archival footage from the United States for a nature documentary film, an unusual cinema release, and one that can now be regarded as ahead of its time. The Edko Group, as the company came to be known, taking its name from

Kong himself, can be regarded as the first to produce non-left-wing documentary films that gained a general release in Hong Kong cinemas.

While Edwin Kong was getting his films released commercially, other filmmakers were also creating documentary films independently. Stephen Teo, important both as a practitioner and critic and subsequently a film academic, was one of the most significant film-makers in Hong Kong during this period. He produced four documentary films in the course of the decade in Hong Kong and abroad with a number of them being selected for international film festivals. Teo collaborated with Lo King-wah, another major contributor to independent film-making. In his article, published in the special catalogue for the Hong Kong International Film Festival, *Changes in Hong Kong Society through Cinema*, Teo describes their collaboration on the super 8 local politics documentary, *War of Positions* (1983), thus:

> Hong Kong's first direct-cinema documentary . . . In *War of Positions*, the camera followed two social workers as they campaigned, and won the 1983 Urban Council elections, the first time that such direct elections had been held on a wide-spread franchise in the territory. The film shows a political process at work and two people participating in the system.[7]

After their collaboration on *War of Positions*, Teo and Lo made *My Filipina* (1984), a 50-minute film shot in super 8 about the conditions of Filipina domestic helpers in Hong Kong. This film was selected as a part of the Hawaii International Film Festival in 1985.

As the Sino-British negotiations related to Hong Kong's future status took place in the first half of the 1980s, a strong local identity on the part of the educated middle class began to emerge in the contemporary art scene in areas such as installation, performance and video art. The broad idea of an art collective took concrete shape when Videotage, a non-profit organisation focusing on the development of video and new media art in the city, was founded in 1986 by Ellen Pau and May Fung. Dedicated to activities such as cultural exchange, visual education, publication, distribution, screenings and film/media festivals, Videotage (a portmanteau term conflating the words 'video' and 'montage') had a consciousness-raising purpose, promoting the use of film and video for self-expression and artistic creation, and generally making visual creativity less inaccessible and more viable for local cultural expression. Even today, the organisation remains one of the most important promoters of independent videos in the city.

Meanwhile, another theatrical release, *Warlords of the Golden Triangle* (1987), garnered box-office receipts of HK$1.9 million, an impressive achievement for this time. The film was produced by the political democracy activist John Sham through his company D&B Films. The narrative background relates how units of the Kuomintang army escaped to a remote forest area of present-day Myanmar, in Shan State, after their defeat by the Chinese communists, and how the KMT and the communists integrated with the ethnic insurgent groups. Directed by Adrian Cowell and shot by Chris Menges, a cinematographer who worked closely with Cowell, Lindsay Anderson and Ken Loach in the 1960s, the film was a sister product of the documentary *The Heroin Wars* for which Cowell and Menges spent sixteen months in a remote region of eastern Burma, investigating how the small-scale domesticated opium business had created powerful warlords such as Law Sit-han and Khun Sha. The second part of the three-part film depicting Hong Kong's thirty years anti-drug campaign is entitled 'Smack City', and focuses on the illegal drug trade via Hong Kong as well as in the notorious Walled City in Kowloon, a lawless area of Kowloon that remained an anomaly in the colonial period prior to its eventual demolition, not being subject to British rule and nominally still part of mainland China

By sharp contrast, legal trade and business also continued to flourish in Hong Kong from the 1960s onwards, and by the 1980s the city had started to become affluent. Cultural life was also enriched by a renaissance in film, music and visual art. However, the mood of nascent optimism that had developed regarding Hong Kong's future under Chinese sovereignty, prompted by the more pragmatic and reformist political climate of the mainland, was rudely dispelled by the defining event of the immediate pre-handover period, the Tiananmen crackdown in Beijing. Despite the obvious potential of this material for full-length documentary coverage, and despite Hong Kong people being actively involved in escape lines and support networks, very little independent film directly on the subject of the events came out of Hong Kong. Numerous videos were shots during the protests, rallies and demonstrations, but they tended to be small-scale and not widely distributed.

The best-known feature-length film on the Tiananmen events was the critically lauded three-hour *The Gate of Heavenly Peace* by the American documentary-makers Carma Hinton and Richard Gordon, which was five years in the making and appeared in 1995. Mainstream distribution of the film was belatedly suppressed in Hong Kong following shrill complaints from across the border, but not before its initial release in commercial cinemas. However, one independent Hong Kong film on the subject does stand out. Kenneth Ip (also known by his artistic pseudonym, Shu Kei), a film lecturer at the Academy for Performing Arts, ventured a personal response with his full-length documentary *Sunless Days* (1990). The film, based mostly on his own voice-over interviews with friends and family together with selected news footage of the events, explores the pertinent subject of the post-1989 Hong Kong diaspora. *Sunless Days* reveals the fear and insecurity of the interviewees and, like the RTHK documentary *The Hong Kong Case*, opened with arresting shots of street violence and bloodied students and workers fleeing the bullets and clubs of the military. It conveys the helpless feeling of Hong Kong residents, mainly people known to the film-maker, with the handover to mainland Chinese rule now a mere six years away. Shu Kei's interest in the interface between local and national politics had been demonstrated by his script for TVB's 1977 film under the direction of Yim Ho, entitled simply '1977' in which, to quote Teo, he attempted to 'pose a dialectic of politics as a purely ideological process and as a process in which practice makes perfect'.[8] *Sunless Days*, financed and broadcast by the Hong Kong branch of Japanese Television and generally shunned by major distributors on account of its subject-matter as well as its technical format, was produced as a 16 mm print and only shown in one or two venues such as the Hong Kong Arts Centre.

One major reason for this phenomenon is that the film, with its contemplative voice-over complementing the interviews, constitutes more of a personal essay partly on the events and on Hong Kong people's future than an analytical exegesis. Its narrative thread is provided by the situation of a family in transition, as the mother is left behind by sons who have migrated overseas in response to the mood of pessimism that prevailed in Hong Kong as a result of the 4 June events. The narrator's disembodied voice-over reminds us that the injunction to forget such an atrocity is in itself a further act of violence against the memory of the dead. Over the opening shots the director himself reads an anonymous poem found posted on a wall near the square, recounting an old father who kills his sons and rapes his daughter, another apt and haunting image, albeit non-visual. He wonders whether the writer is now in prison, in hiding, in exile or dead. This strategy of emotional response and eloquent commentary is what drives the film, rather than any measured analysis of what happened and why. Since then, Shu Kei has been a tireless advocate of film as a medium for self-expression and has worked in a number of advisory and pedagogical capacities. *Sunless Days* is an important film in spite of its somewhat rambling, discursive style. More than anything else, it encapsulates a general feeling or *zeitgeist*.

One of the independent film-makers from this period, Jimmy Choi, subsequently founded the independent collective 'Videopower', with the aim of gathering socially committed video-makers to share resources and ideas, and use video as a tool in the struggle for democracy. Moreover, the era of digital video in the 1990s led to increasing numbers of film-makers participating in a wider range of genres in documentary film-making. Professional film-makers, ones that were active in commercial film-making, also participated in making personal documentaries in the low-budget format. In addition, some had the opportunity to have their films distributed in VCD (Video Compact Disc) format, even if they were not screened in art-house cinemas.

Meanwhile, the government began to offer more financial subventions for alternative media and arts. The creation of the Independent Film and Video Awards (IFVA) by the Hong Kong Art Centre in 1995 provided an encouraging platform for amateurs, academics and professionals alike to create an alternative voice distinct from the media-policy-makers from the television broadcasting industry. In order to stimulate greater creative imagination among film-makers, the IFVA rewarded experimental stylistic features in the works of both established film-makers and newly emerging talents. Short documentaries have won the top prizes, including the Grand Prize in 1995 awarded to *A Tragedy Ahead* by Cheng Chi-hung, and subsequently the following year for *Neon Goddesses* by Yu Lik-wai. In 1998 there was a special mention for Joanne Shen's and Martin Egan's half-hour biopic of the life of local rebel and graffiti artist Tsang Tsou-choi, entitled *King of Kowloon*. Their film was the first documentary about the self-dubbed 'King of Kowloon', who defied both colonial and post-colonial authority to share his caustic views in the form of calligraphic inscriptions on walls, postboxes and other public utilities. The latter gave frank interviews about his unusual life's work to the film-makers in this whimsical and insightful piece.

During the 1990s independent collectives such as Videopower produced a number of independent activist documentaries, sometimes with financial help from the Hong Kong Arts Development Council and other agencies. The government-run Arts Development Council, founded in 1995 with the aim of promoting creativity and innovation in a wide range of art forms, became a consistent source of subventions for film art, including documentaries. Other non-profit-making collectives were formed around this time; these included Ying e Chi – meaning literally 'the will to create cinema' – an independent group formed by enterprising independent filmmaker Vincent Chui Wan-shun and friends in 1996. The financial and logistical backing from entrepreneur Alan Zeman's Media Centre was a decisive factor, and, as David Bordwell has noted, 'By the spring of 1999 Ying e Chi was distributing several 35mm shorts and features, and Hong Kong seemed to have laid the foundations for a lively sector of independent film-making'.[9] Over time this film-maker alliance has also provided new distribution channels for independent film-makers, and helped to disseminate the works of local film-makers. In 1997, Ying e Chi organised the first of its annual screenings at the Hong Kong Arts Centre, and, two years later, it collaborated with the Hong Kong International Film Festival. Another important contribution to independent film in the city has been the Ying e Chi series of independent releases on VCD and DVD.

This period also saw the emergence of a new media platform enabling the direct uploading and web-streaming of videos on free web-broadcasters such as Youtube. As a consequence, television documentary no longer enjoyed the dominance it had formerly possessed in the documentary field, and independent creativity on a modest, home-grown scale began to flourish. A further creative initiative was introduced by a group of film-makers of more experimental and abstract documentaries, such as those produced by film and local culture academics Kenneth Ip (Shu Kei), Makin Fung and Yau Ching. The last-named's 1997 work *Diasporama: Dead Air*, one of the first documentaries to be funded by the Hong Kong Arts Development Council, is a composite video-shot, semi-experimental documentary comprising several interviews with people who have left Hong Kong (hence the 'diaspora' part of 'diasporama'), including a former Legislative Councillor, Christine Loh, who has British citizenship. During Loh's long interview, she talks about how she came to be involved in politics and why she became an ardent supporter of democracy in Hong Kong. Visually, the interviews themselves are intriguingly framed, never placing the interviewees in the centre of the frame, and starting out with a wide shot to emphasise their environment. At the same time, previously discouraged subjects, such as sexuality, feminism and homosexuality, were also further explored in films such as *Yang and Yin: Gender in Chinese Cinema* (Stanley Kwan, 1996), which presented a survey of 100 years of Chinese cinema, focusing on issues of sexuality, including the homoerotic imagery in films made since the 1930s, and forms of 'male bonding' observable in the Hong Kong action cinema of today.

INDEPENDENT DOCUMENTARY FILM-MAKERS AND FILMS OF THE NEW MILLENNIUM

In the mid-to-late 1990s two independent documentary directors, whose impact as full-length, non-fiction film-makers was to be significant, emerged on the scene. Their respective bodies of work would help to raise the profile of Hong Kong independent documentaries in the new millennium in both the regional and the international context, even if the genre remains a minority choice. These were Hong Kong-based and Canadian-educated Tammy Cheung and Hong Kong and Macao-educated and New York-based Evans Chan. Both flourished as documentary film-makers, although the latter showed a propensity for mixing fictional and factual elements in some, though not all, of his films.

Chan was born in 1953 in Guangdong, China, and grew up in Hong Kong and Macau. In 1990 he formed Riverdrive Productions to produce his own films, and also served as line producer for the Hong Kong sequences of Peter Greenaway's fiction film *The Pillow Book*. He came to prominence for his semi-factual, semi-fictive Hong Kong-set film *To Liv(e)* in 1991, inspired by actress and UNICEF goodwill ambassador Liv Ullmann's criticism of Hong Kong's forced deportation of Vietnamese refugees. This mixed-mode drama-documentary was related to two then current concerns in the city, the one arising out of post-Tiananmen anxiety and consequent emigration, and the other related to the controversial matter of Hong Kong's obligations to the UN agency for refugees, the UNHCR, to receive Vietnamese 'boat-people' refugees. Chan's film, though on the surface a fictional work, dealt with many real-life issues and skewered the hypocrisy of the official American and British stances on the refugees, as well as exploring real-life artistic interpretations of recent events in China. *To Liv(e)*, which featured bilingual Hong Kong actress Lindzay Chan, who would go on to act in most of his films, won the Special Jury Prize at the Singapore Film Festival.

As a director and creative artist, Chan is influenced by Bertolt Brecht's epic theatre ideas as well as by Jean-Luc Godard's counter-cinema methods. Many of his films feature dramatic sub-plots, theatrical performances, interviews with political figures, and archive footage of the city of Hong Kong and elsewhere. *Journey to Beijing* (1998) – which will feature in the next chapter of this book – deals with, among other things, the transfer of sovereignty of Hong Kong to China in 1997, whilst *Adeus Macau* (1999) similarly addresses the handover of Macau to China in 1999. This filmic diptych is also sometimes referred to as 'China Decolonised'. Moving into the first decade of the new century, Chan's films evince a considerable degree of diversity in terms of theme and subject-matter, but all of them exhibit his trademark episodic style. *The Life and Times of Wu Zhong Xian* (2002) is a documentary based on veteran activist Mok Chiu-yu's play about the Hong Kong-born democracy activist Ng Chung-yin (the titular Wu Zhong Xian is the mandarin Chinese version of his name), which Chan was involved in producing in its New York run; the archival material employed for this screen adaptation included grainy extracts from Law Kar's previously referred to 1971 *Protect Diaoyutai Movement* film.

Sorceress of the New Piano (2004) celebrates the transcultural career of Singapore-born, New York-based professional pianist, Margaret Leng Tan. Incorporating vintage footage of Merce Cunningham's dance, Jasper Johns' art-work, and extracts from Marcel Duchamp's 1926 work *Anemic Cinema*, the latter film is a meditation upon the role and importance of an independent-minded Asian-American woman in the western musical avant-garde. Chan's latest film, the critically praised *Datong: The Great Society* (2011), is both a portrait of the early twentieth-century political thinker and reformist Kang Youwei and his exile in Sweden and an exploration of the 1911 revolution that overthrew the Manchu Qing dynasty, the last Chinese imperial dynasty.

Chan's interest in philosophy and social issues, especially those concerning human rights, as well as his arts journalism background, combine to make him a relentlessly questioning and challenging film-maker. He is just as critical of the political actions and lack of principled behaviour he finds in his adopted homeland of the United States as he is when exploring China and Hong Kong-related subjects. As Chan observes at the opening of his film about Hong Kong radical activist Ng Chung-ying (Wu Zhong Xian), the Latin word 'radix', from which 'radical' is derived, has a primary meaning of 'root', and thus for Chan the connection between Hong Kong roots and Hong Kong radicalism is essential. However, rather than adopting a polemically confrontational or satirical approach in the manner of a Michael Moore, Chan prefers to employ more dialectical and discursive methods of exploration and critique. This methodology is clearly reflected in his episodic, apparently dislocated, style, which juxtaposes seemingly disconnected or loosely connected material often to extremely thought-provoking effect. The results are essayistic, nuanced, intellectually stimulating and aesthetically profuse, but inasmuch as he rejects the unified strategies of the more traditional documentary, Chan's hallmark dialectics, together with his tendency to suspend typically documentarian authoritative judgment, runs the risk of misinterpretation by film audiences unused to the technique.

In many ways, Chan's films exemplify Brecht's dramatic method through which a work of art can encourage audiences to conceive of 'making things work out differently', to quote Stanley Mitchell in his 'Introduction' to Walter Benjamin's *Understanding Brecht*, a worthy enterprise in the new-age documentary mode.[10] Despite his strong links to Hong Kong, it would be accurate to see Chan as an internationalist figure in the documentary-making world. Bearing in mind his translation and editing work on Susan Sontag's essays and his occasional stage drama writing, Chan evidently tends to follow his own instincts and interests as an independent artist in every sense of the word. Michael Berry's interview chapter on Chan in his *Speaking in Images: Interviews with Contemporary Chinese Film-makers* refers to him intriguingly as 'The Last of the Chinese' – which is the title of Chan's own collection of written essays and stories published in 1999.[11]

Tammy Cheung (Cheung Hung) can be regarded as the first independent film-maker in Hong Kong to devote her career completely to the documentary film, whether producing her own films through her own independent company, Visible Record, or curating ground-breaking documentary festivals. Cheung was born in Shanghai, China in 1958, moving to Hong Kong not long afterwards, where she grew up and was educated. Her interest in the combination of social responsibility and film was apparent in Hong Kong where she studied sociology, and later at Concordia University in Montreal, Canada, where she specialised in film studies. While in Montreal, she established the Chinese International Film Festival to showcase films by Chinese film-makers and films with Chinese content. She served as the director of the festival from 1986 to 1992, and returned to Hong Kong in 1994, where she worked in film criticism, commercial film production, teaching and translation, while also contemplating the feasibility of making her own documentary films.

Now, without doubt, the leading Hong Kong-resident documentary film-maker, Cheung's initial ideas came to fruition in 1999 when she made her directorial debut with a short documentary focusing on the Indian female population of Hong Kong and entitled *Invisible Women*. This film began her experiments with the observational approach of Direct Cinema, the same 'fly-on-the-wall' idea used by American documentary director Frederick Wiseman. The observational style aims to reduce the director's influence on the events that the camera is capturing while allowing the subjects to reveal themselves. It is clear to see from *Invisible Women* that while her technique was in its infancy in this film, which focuses on three Sindi Indian residents in Hong Kong, her ability to sympathise with her subjects without presenting them with excessive sentimentality was fully developed early on. Motivated by a passion to simply learn about her society and reflect what is actually happening on a daily basis, Cheung started working with photographer Augustine Lam on social documentaries that illuminate inadequate social structures in Hong Kong and bring her audience closer to her subjects: people struggling to make their lives better, often in difficult circumstances. Her laudable attempts at producing non-intrusive films document a Hong Kong that tends to contrast sharply with the image of the city held by the general public, or the 'official' imagination.

Cheung's other works to date include *Secondary School* (2002), which chronicles a typical day at a top Hong Kong boys' school and girls' school respectively; *July* (2004), which focuses upon the events of one single day on 1 July 2003, in which the citizens of Hong Kong took to the street to protest about the introduction of draconian security measures in the SAR; and *Moving* (2003), which, alongside *Rice Distribution* (2003), depicts the relentless problems of the poor and the elderly within the city. The latter will be discussed at greater length in the final chapter. *Moving* follows the stories of several elderly residents of Ngau Tau Kok Estate and two social workers helping the elderly residents adjust to their relocation out of the estate. Cheung and Lam shot the film in the months leading up to the demolition of the ageing and dilapidated estate compound and found their subjects through the two social workers. Since the announcement of the plan, Ngau Tau Kok Estate had become something of a living nostalgic attraction for Hongkongers. Cheung captures the atmosphere created by some of the media, photographers and tour groups that began to arrive to document the demolition.

By contrast, *Election* and *July* both deal with more overt political events in the SAR, but employ a direct, fly-on-the-wall cinematography unmediated by spoken narrative or voice-over commentary. Cheung sees her role as documentarian in these two films as one of documenting events and expecting the viewer to judge the resultant images for herself. The film captured vehement street demonstrations critiquing the performance of Tung Chee-hwa's compliantly pro-Beijing government and calling on the government to drop planned Article 23 subversion-related legislation (as the controversial proposed bill is known). By incorporating footage of the speeches, songs, chants and banners that enlivened the proceedings, always without external commentary, she contributed to the construction of an anti-establishment discourse. As the newspaper *Ming Pao* pointed out in reviewing the premiere screening of the film in December of that year, 'the film gave Hong Kong people a memento of what happened to us all in July 2003'.[12]

Election, which was a featured presentation in the 2009 Hong Kong International Film Festival, is based on footage of the hotly contested 2004 Legislative Council elections in Hong Kong. To a considerable extent the film can be seen as something of a sequel to *July*, inasmuch as it portrays the reputedly apathetic Hong Kong citizens participating in the political process. It captures the animated and intense process of canvassing in the weeks leading up to what were seen as watershed elections in the SAR. Despite the limited nature of the elections, keen public interest in the views and positions of the various parties is evident in the film. Cheung's roving, independent camerawork and tight editing is extremely revealing. It creates a distanced framing of party canvassers, public and media, frequently finding angles and shots that speak volumes about candidates' diverse political stances, without any need for verbal intervention. This defamiliarising vérité effect enhances the documentary's external viewpoint, allowing the film to stand outside the often heated debates and amusing publicity stunts portrayed in the documentary.

However, her most simple, stripped-down work can be seen in the pair of films entitled *Speaking Up* (2005) and *Speaking Up II* (2007). In this diptych Cheung departs from her usual direct film-making style to adopt a talking-heads driven interview format, in which ordinary people in Hong Kong and China discuss a range of questions related to politics, society, personal growth, and the role of education. Her spare methodology in the two films involved keeping her subject in an identical lighting and camera set-up, asking her questions off camera and recording the responses, as the interviewees look directly into the camera. This represented a definite shift in style for Cheung, as well as in content, since some of her questions also dealt with the thorny topic of relations with mainland China. Perhaps the most fascinating footage of all in these films is the sequence in *Speaking Up II* in which schoolchildren in a China mainland middle school offer their opinions on various adult topics with disarming ingenuousness. The youngster who dares to differ from his classmates and nominate early twentieth-century writer Lu Xun as the greatest ever Chinese celebrity, as opposed to Mao or other politically correct and propagandised figures, stands out from the rest.

During the period from 1999 to 2009, Cheung contributed eight films to the catalogue of Hong Kong documentaries, and provided an improvement in the standard of quality. She shaped a distinctive path by incorporating existing forms of direct cinema and vox-pops and exploring mixed-mode strategies within her and Lam's range of techniques. She has worked assiduously to promote documentary film-making, education in film art and documentary festivals, more recently enabling banned mainland documentaries to be shown in Hong Kong, and always confronting in her work the indifference that many people show toward social problems.

Eventually a third significant independent film-maker emerged after Evans Chan and Tammy Cheung had established their strong respective bodies of work. Around the beginning of the 2000s Cheung King-wai, who had originally trained as a classical cellist, started to make short films in New York as an alternative to a career in music, which seemed to be going nowhere. Back in Hong Kong he initially came to attention as an important documentary film-maker through the help of the China-Hong Kong-Taiwan documentary film promotion organisation CNEX, which supported his debut film *All's Right With the World* (2007), documenting the lives and struggles of five families living in poverty during the Lunar New Year in Hong Kong. It was, however, with his second film, *KJ: Music and Life* (2008) – one of the featured films in the final chapter of this book – that he earned hitherto unparalleled box-office success and local recognition for a Hong Kong-made documentary film. Drawing on his expertise in classical music, the film is a portrayal of a precocious middle-class child pianist prodigy, set within the heavily middle-class and privileged environment of one of Hong Kong's elite schools.

Cheung gained recognition as a screenwriter, winning an award for his script for Ann Hui's social realist film *Night and Fog*, before he made his feature documentary debut in 2007 with *All's Right with the World*. While Hui was seeking funding to make the film, she also served as a consultant on Cheung's documentary. Shot before and after Lunar New Year 2007 at five different locations, the film follows five families living in poverty. Mostly made in 'talking-heads' interview format, *All's Right with the World* is composed mainly of static shots. While this established a stylistic feature for Cheung as a film-maker, it was also a choice resulting from technical constraints; the Panasonic P2 camera Cheung uses does not generate stable moving shots, hence the decision to keep most of the film static (only panning slowly or occasionally tilting). The result is nevertheless an aesthetically harmonious, almost serene look at some of Hong Kong's poorest areas. The final sequence – a montage of the characters watching the New Year fireworks either from afar or on TV – remains a bittersweet ending to the film. Cheung does not quite make these characters emotionally engaging, because he spends too little time with them for there to be any narrative, but he makes them memorable in that we do not get lost in his broad canvas. Cheung's portrait of the poverty he reveals is gentle and balanced and marks him out as one of the most significant relative newcomers on the independent documentary scene.

Gradually other resourceful and imaginative documentarians have been gaining prominence in the last ten years; full-time academics and dedicated film-makers Louisa Wei Shiyu and Anson Mak are two of the most stimulating and productive of these. The work of both has been featured in festivals and subsequently screened in alternative local arts venues such as the Hong Kong Arts Centre, the City University, the Lee Shau Kee School of Creativity, and the Jockey Club Creative Arts Centre. Both film-makers are progressive and critical in outlook, like Evans Chan and Tammy Cheung, although Wei, who was born in Shandong province in the mainland and studied creative media in Canada before joining Hong Kong's City University, has more ties to China than the Hong Kong-born Mak, who focuses entirely on the Hong Kong context in her work.

Starting her career in RTHK and then TVB, Mak wrote music and scripts, and developed her own independent and necessarily mobile film-making skills in video, super 8 and digital formats. An articulate Baptist University, RMIT Melbourne and Hong Kong University-educated creative artist, Mak's potential as a film-maker has started coming to fruition. Her shorter community-related videos and experimental work as a sound and video artist, as well as her involvement as an Arts Development Council advisor, keep her rooted in ethnographic film-making. However, she also has two important full-length documentaries to her name, both of which have made their mark locally and to an extent internationally.

Her highly original 2007 essayistic film *One Way Street on a Turntable*, which is one of the featured works under discussion in the next chapter, while hardly a box-office success in the mould of *KJ*, attracted admiration from film academics and critics such as Timothy Corrigan. In Corrigan's 2012 *The Essay Film: From Montaigne, after Marker*, the film is referenced in company with the essay films of Marker, Godard and others, and cited as a recent example of an innovative and exploratory documentary work. Mak's latest full-length work, *On the Edge of a Floating City We Sing* (2012), was featured in the 2012 Hong Kong International Film Festival and subsequently screened in London in a festival called 'Exposure: Contemporary Media Art from Hong Kong, Taiwan and mainland China'. The film celebrates Hong Kong's peripheral independent music scene, shot mainly in and around spaces in Kwun Tong, and is also a work in the reflexive documentary mode, inviting reflection, reminiscence and nostalgia, but also exuding a distinct critical spirit, challenging establishment discourses and policy on the use of public spaces.

Louisa Wei, like Mak, has concentrated on producing documentaries and reflecting on documentary methods. Her first 2006 film was a music documentary about China's rock-musician icon of free thinking, Cui Jian, entitled *Cui Jian: Rocking China*. Her second, later in 2006, was a full-length meta-documentary made in collaboration and discussion with her Beijing-based film teacher, Situ Zhaodun, entitled *A Piece of Heaven: Primary Documents*. However, the film that established her reputation in Hong Kong was her partnership with Shanghai director Peng Xiaolian in *Storm Under the Sun* (2009), a two-and-a-half hour epic study of the persecution of Hu Feng and other writers in Mao Zedong's China. The film was a critical success at the Hong Kong International Film Festival, and also met with considerable critical praise overseas. Like *One Way Street on a Turntable*, the film will be discussed at greater length in the following chapter.

Wei's most recent documentary feature, shown at the HKIFF in 2013, is *Golden Gate Girls*, in which she displays an imaginative and creative use of archival and previously neglected footage, and structures the film around a quest motif, employing quirkily amusing graphics to enable her to segue from one section to the next. Her film explores the careers of Chinese American producer and director Esther Eng (Ng) and American pioneer woman director Dorothy Arzner – both women unabashed lesbians. The former was a remarkable and high-profile feminist, patriot, film and drama enthusiast and latterly restaurateur, who threw herself into early talkie film-making in San Francisco and Hong Kong, but subsequently slipped into obscurity. As with Malik Bendjelloul's 2012 documentary hit *Searching for Sugarman*, the film is predicated on the film-maker's act of uncovering the subject's hidden past; however, her subject remains tantalisingly remote, unlike the figure of Sixto Rodriguez, the search for whom is dramatically rewarded. Wei does a highly accomplished job, nonetheless, in reconstucting both women's lives from archive material in a patriarchal – and racist – pre-war US cinema world. The documentary takes its title from Eng's 1941 romantic feature *Golden Gate Girl*, in which Bruce Lee made his screen debut – playing a baby girl!

The remaining independent films of note have not, so far, suggested the likelihood of a substantial body of Hong Kong-related and -produced work on the part of the film-makers. In many cases they represent the only theatrical release by the particular documentarian, and indicate that to date no further significant work has been produced, despite the manifest qualities of the films referenced in this section. Barbara Wong Chun-chun's provocatively conceived and titled *Women's Private Parts* (2000) was a full-length feature documentary employing an all-female film crew, which enjoyed a certain *succès de scandale*. The film consisted of frank and sometimes amusing interviews with Hong Kong females of a wide age range and from all walks of life, including sex workers, housewives, career women and even children on the subject of their bodies. In a completely different vein, veteran director Clifford Choi Kai-kwong's timely 2002 tribute to Hong Kong's first significant, but long-neglected film director, entitled *Lai Man-wai: Father of Hong Kong Cinema*, ran to 140 minutes and used archival footage to present a layered, insightful and nuanced filmic biography of the great movie pioneer. The five-part film, which premiered at the Hong Kong International Film Festival in 2001, made a strong case for seeing Lai as a figure of central importance to the development of Chinese cinema. Produced by Choi's erstwhile collaborator from the 1970s and 1980s, Law Kar, and written by Choi himself, the film and subsequent DVD package is a valuable resource and an important contribution to Hong Kong and China's cinematic history and culture. However, it represented a rare foray into the documentary genre for Choi, and one that he does not appear to have followed up.

Quentin Lee (Lee Mang-hei) is known for his independent feature film *Ethan Mao* (2004), but in 2007 he essayed his first documentary film entitled *0506HK*. The director's exploratory take on conceptions of Hong Kong culture in this film was apparently prompted in part by the lack of confidence Hongkongers seem to have in 'their own unique and distinct culture'. It is aptly described by the director as 'part autobiography, part travelogue, part cultural criticism'.[13] As do some of the directors referred to above (Yau Ching, Tammy Cheung, Evans Chan, and so on), Lee employs the technique of direct interview, but unusually he opts to question a number of Hong Kong independent film-makers and artists, including Tammy Cheung and Vincent Chui, as well as various lesser-known friends, on the way they perceive culture, politics and sense of place in Hong Kong. Indeed, the very notion of defining a Hong Kong culture becomes a defining theme in the film, suggesting that this is both the private and public cornerstone on which the work rests. Lee's curiosity was piqued by the fact that he immigrated to Canada from Hong Kong at the age of fifteen and his Hong Kong documentary, made in the course of two visits in 2005 and 2006 (hence the title), marked a sense of homecoming and belonging, as well as a certain nostalgic desire. His own voice-over provides the continuity and depth to the work, with his reflections and uncertainty on whether or not to return to his birth city or go home to his current city, Los Angeles, creating some tension as to the outcome. The film, distributed and promoted by Ying e Chi and shown at the Hong Kong Asian Film Festival in 2008, having premiered at the Vancouver Festival, deftly interweaves Lee's own thoughts, feelings and desires with those of his interview subjects to create a subtle and thought-provoking mosaic. The film is one of the best recent examples of a Hong Kong guided-tour documentary, albeit a very personal and idiosyncratic one, including footage of juvenile films by the teenage Lee.

Homeless FC, made by James Leong and Lynn Lee in 2006, is only in part a Hong Kong film, since the directors are Singaporean. This engaging documentary follows a group of eccentric and troubled homeless people who come together to form a football team – albeit a rather inept and fractious one – to participate in the Homeless World Cup Football Tournament. Thanks to funding from the Singaporean government, the directors were successful in getting their work screened via Tammy Cheung's Chinese Documentary Film

Festival, an annual event in Hong Kong. However, the film was not able to obtain a general release, in contrast to *KJ: Music and Life*, which achieved a remarkably long release, and another successful box-office documentary, *This Darling Life* (Angie Chen, 2008), which focuses on the trials and tribulations of dog owners, as their beloved pets become old, and sick.

Chen's most recent documentary work, whilst not as commercially successful as *This Darling Life*, was a critical success at both the Hong Kong International Film Festival and the Taiwan Film Festival, and was given special screenings at the Broadway Cinemathèque cinema. Entitled *One Tree, Three Lives*, this lovingly crafted, intimate portrait of China-born writer Hualing Nieh Engle (whose father was also a writer and poet) incorporates photos, documentary footage, interviews, visually poetic imagery and text extracts to tell the story of a remarkable woman and an uncommon life. Nieh escaped from war-torn China in a boat up the Yangtze River as a young woman, making her way, via a stay in Taipei, to the United States, where she met the young Paul Engle and co-founded the internationally famous Iowa Writers' Workshop as well as marrying him and putting down roots in Iowa City. Chen's sensitive and revealing biopic documentary works particularly well because it follows the subject exploring her old haunts in Taipei and Iowa, closing with shots of the presentation of her honorary doctorate at Baptist University in Hong Kong. 'I am a tree with roots in China, but the leaves bud in Iowa,' she explains to Chen's camera about her eclectic life experience and spiritual identification with places. Chen opts to let her subject and her reminiscences of a long life lead the documentary where it will, and this strategy is felicitous.

In contrast to these individually crafted works, a music documentary such as *Dare Ya!* (Louis Tan, 2002), or a mockumentary such as *Heavenly Kings* (Daniel Wu, 2006) – the latter drawing on the model of the celebrated American mockumentary *This is Spinal Tap* (Rob Reiner, 1984) – had of necessity to rely on the collaboration and participation of well-known popular artists, musicians, actors and producers in Hong Kong, such as actress Cecilia Yip and pop singer Daniel Wu. Even with such celebrity involvement, both films were able to gain only limited release, and consequently limited box-office revenue, although both films had their merits as tongue-in-cheek responses to Hong Kong's prevailing ethos of lightweight and derivative popular music and entertainment. Similar non-mainstream documentaries, which received exposure in a variety of art-house venues, include *Hong Kong UFO Documentary* (Prodip, 2008), which explores UFO sightings in Hong Kong; and *Decameron* (Denise Ho and Mak Yan-yan, 2009), which explores mental disorders. Both of these films employ a combination of interview format and striking stylisation, whilst *HK Style* (2006) by Mathias Woo, the Xuni Icosahedron Hong

Kong theatre director who trained as an architect, is more experimental in approach.

In Cheuk Cheung's compelling 2011 film *My Way*, on two contrasting young men whose lives revolve around Cantonese Opera, the deliberate choice of a more traditionally heuristic interview-based documentary style is a felicitous one. The film was seven years in the making and follows the two subjects Paris Wong and Alan Tam, both very talented young performers who are trying to make the once-popular genre their life's profession. Friends (despite the gap in their ages) and stage-partners on occasions, they complement each other in that Paris with his remarkably high-ranging voice and stylish gestures is a Daan (female) role, while Alan plays the Sang (male) role. Thus the film explores a cultural phenomenon that is often under-valued in Hong Kong, while implicitly questioning the convention that Daan roles have to be played by female actors not by cross-dressing male ones. Depicting their home, rehearsal and performance environments and portraying the stresses, sacrifices and challenges of embracing this career, the documentary, rather like *KJ: Music and Life*, adopts a longitudinal non-intrusive methodology which helps the subjects express their hopes, ambitions and frustrations and engage the viewer's empathy. Cheung's first documentary was an official selection for the Hong Kong Asian Film Festival 2012 and for the Beijing International Film Festival 2013, and was a good example of promising new work being supported by the CNEX Foundation.

FESTIVALS, FUNDING AND OUTREACH

In addition to the increased activities and initiatives of independent filmmakers and their small companies, the new millennium saw more opportunities provided by the expansion of existing film distribution and funding channels and the formation of new ones. The Hong Kong International Film Festival Society (HKIFFS), a non-profit and non-governmental organisation, was set up initially in 2004 to organise, manage development and run the Hong Kong International Film Festival, though their activities have expanded to other projects that serve to enhance the Festival and community. Through its year-round programmes, the mission of the Society is to strengthen the global appreciation of Chinese film culture and to promote good films from around the world, enriching the cultural life of Hong Kong in the process.

The Society organises three annual main events, the Hong Kong International Film Festival (HKIFF), the Hong Kong-Asia Film Financing Forum (HAF), and the Asian Film Awards (AFA). It also organises a scaled-back, annual summer edition, the Summer International Film Festival (SIFF), with a fresh schedule of films which are different from the main, spring event. The Festival has also assisted with the ten-day, twelve-film Macau International Film and Video Festival, and a European touring festival featuring a dozen Hong Kong films, and entitled the Hong Kong Film Panorama.

Further opportunities are offered by the 'I Shot Hong Kong' Film Festival, which was started in 2005 on a small scale by a group of three film-makers but has quickly grown in terms of both audience and submissions. One of the festival's stated goals is to foster the local market. As a consequence, the festival requires that all submissions feature one scene filmed in Hong Kong. Furthermore, the co-founders want the festival to help renew interest in Hong Kong as a filming location, and to attract help in raising the general quality of Hong Kong film productions. The festival has shown dedication in its recognition of documentary film, as evidenced by an individual award sponsored by the *South China Morning Post* in 2009 for documentary films. In 2009, the winner of the award was *Save the Human! Don't Eat the Planet*, directed by Will Senn Lau and Bobsy. In the same year, a documentary entry entitled *Fin* succeeded in raising awareness of the environmental impact and mindless cruelty involved in the hunting of sharks for shark's fin soup. This was a timely reminder, especially to the Hong Kong government, whose officials have consistently refused to eschew the cultural 'delicacy' at their banquets.

Another significant festival is the IFVA 'greenlab' which is organised by the Hong Kong Arts Centre. IFVA 'greenlab' is intended to act as an incubator for film and visual media, and the competition is designed to attract innovative exponents of creative media and to help them 'incubate' their projects. The greenlab matches new media talents together to produce new media projects with an emphasis on creativity and innovation. In 2010 the 'greenlab' matched Jessey Tsang and Heiward Mak to work with music star Justin Lo, and in another group, IFVA veterans Vincent Chui, Rita Hui and Sham Ka-ki, along with the renowned visual artist, Chow Chun-fai, collaborated to create a programme entitled *A Creative Journey with Lung Kong*, thus paying tribute to this prolific *auteur* actor and director. Exciting new directors such as Tsang Tsui-shan – whose 2013 documentary on her native village in Hong Kong's New Territories, Ho Chung Village, entitled *Flowing Stories*, has been supported and promoted – benefit considerably from IFVA. Finally, continuing its efforts to broaden the scope of the festival and its initiatives beyond its international panorama of screenings, the organisers have brought in international visual artists for demonstration, interaction and classes.

With the aim of fostering a dynamic and creative film community, the IFVA have also managed to implement several outreach programmes. Aside from the creation of a 'Youth' category, they have conducted community tours of selected films together with free computer hardware and software workshops. However, the recent decision of the body to dissolve its separate award category for documentaries and include them in the 'Open' category has been somewhat contentious. On the one hand, having no designated category or award for documentaries has probably reduced the number of documentaries submitted; on the other hand, the decision tends to reflect a wider acceptance of documentaries and the corollary that the form is now capable of competing in the Festival alongside fiction films and music videos.

In addition, the annual Chinese Documentary Film Festival, held at the Agnès B. cinema in the Arts Centre in Wan Chai and organised by Tammy Cheung's Visible Record company from 2008 onwards, offers a very important platform to mainland and Taiwanese directors to have their documentaries screened in Hong Kong and then overseas. The independent mainland documentaries are often banned works or considered too controversial to be submitted to the censors in the Mainland. The festival includes a section for short films by newcomers and also films by local artists. However, the selection of new documentaries by mainland film-makers is critically important for maintaining links and nurturing the documentary form. Critical investigative films and studies of individual families and wider communities – whose stories are normally submerged by positivistic and collectivistic mainland discourses – can be aired thanks to such festivals as well as documentary-promoting organisations such as CNEX. The quality of many of these clandestine contrarian documentaries is remarkably high in terms of the testimony they provide. Films like these are also socially valuable in the local context, inasmuch as they let Hongkongers know that not all mainland China people are brash big spenders and aggressive shopping tourists, such as those who frequent the fashionable boutiques in the city and incite the animosity of many disgruntled Hong Kong citizens.

Finally, Ying e Chi's independent film festival, run in Hong Kong since 2010, has also featured documentary films in its programming, such as Lo Chun-yip's *Days after N Coming*, making the case for saving small villages in the New Territories that are scheduled for demolition to pave the way for the new high-speed train connection between Hong Kong and Beijing. However, one of the most moving and powerful documentaries in the 2013 festival was also one of the starkest and simplest. Hu Lifu's *Rainy Dawn, Windy Dusk* is a moving portrait of the parents of Shandong-based Xia Junfeng, who was awaiting judicial review on a death-sentence verdict for defending himself against thuggish 'security officers', and is documentary at its most searing and direct. Other new mainland documentaries in this festival, including Wen Hui's *Listening to Third Grandmother's Story* and Zou Xueping's *Satiated Village*, help to correct the official version of China's dramatic economic progress which marginalises and neglects the rural poor and elderly.

It is only thanks to initiatives such as these that Hong Kong is able to nurture an alternative independent documentary culture. While funding has certainly been made increasingly available in recent times, whether from government sources, or from independent private sponsors, foundations and organisations, the general decline of Hong Kong's own mainstream cinema industry, coupled with film-makers' need to collaborate and compromise in cross-border co-productions, means that a genuine spirit of independence in local film-making and its concomitant infrastructure of festivals, workshops and seminars is a priceless asset in the community. It is also one that needs to be valued and nurtured by that same community, if it is to survive in the perennially challenging economic climate, representing the price paid for this vital spirit of independence.

NOTES

1. Jarvie, Ian, C., 'The Social and Cultural Significance of the Decline of the Cantonese Movie,' in *Journal of Asian Affairs*, vol. III, no. 2 (Fall 1979), p. 41.
2. Teo, Stephen, 'The 1970s: Movement and Transition' in Fu, Poshek and Desser, David (eds), *The Cinema of Hong Kong: History, Arts, Identity* (Cambridge: Cambridge University Press, 2000), p. 91.
3. Rodriguez, Hector, 'The Emergence of the Hong Kong New Wave', in Yau, E. (ed.), *At Full Speed: Hong Kong Cinema in a Borderless World* (Minneapolis: University of Minnesota Press, 2001), pp. 58.
4. Teo, Stephen, 'Politics and Social Issues in Hong Kong Cinema', in *Changes in Hong Kong Society through Cinema* (Hong Kong: Urban Council, 1988), p. 38.
5. Choi, K. C. 'A Brief History of Hong Kong Independent Film and Video Making', unpublished conference paper, 2003.
6. Ibid,
7. Teo, 'Politics and Social Issues', p. 39.
8. Ibid.
9. Bordwell, David, *Planet Hong Kong: Popular Cinema and the Art of Entertainment* (Cambridge, MA: Harvard University Press, 2000), p. 262.
10. Mitchell, Stanley, 'Introduction', in Benjamin, Walter, *Understanding Brecht* (London: Verso, New Left Books; 2003), p. xi.
11. Berry, Michael (ed.), *Speaking in Images: Interviews with Contemporary Chinese Film-makers* (New York: Columbia University Press, 2005), p. 509.
12. 'Witnessing the 1st July protest', Anonymous, *Ming Pao*, 22 December 2003.
13. Lee, Quentin, *0506HK* DVD notes, ying e chi, 2007.

CHAPTER 7

A Critical Analysis of Significant Independent Documentary Films of the Past Three Decades

PREAMBLE

The six documentaries selected in this chapter for closer discussion and analysis in relation to the development of the independent documentary genre in Hong Kong over the past thirty years have been chosen on the basis of their merits as films. They are: Ed Kong's *Rising Sun* (1980); Evans Chan's *Journey to Beijing* (1998); Tammy Cheung's *Rice Distribution* (2003); Anson Mak's *One Way Street on a Turntable* (2007); Cheung King-wai's *KJ: Music and Life* (2008); and Louisa Wei's *Storm under the Sun* (2011). The films also offer a cross-section of diverse directorial styles and documentary categories, covering most types according to Nichols's basic typology – expository, reflexive, interactive, observational, poetic and performative, with their varying implications with reference to truth claims.[1] At the same time, they correspond to a small spectrum of approaches, whether essayistic, detached, polemical, more conventionally quasi–objective or mixed–mode. All six films have earned critical plaudits in varying contexts, mainly in film festivals, but two of them – *Rising Sun* and *KJ: Music and Life* – were also commercially successful in Hong Kong, and gave cautious grounds for optimism regarding the future viability of the documentary genre in the city.

RISING SUN (ED KONG, 1980)

At a time when very few documentaries were being made in Hong Kong, the success of *Rising Sun* surprised even the director, Edwin Kong, who was born and raised in Hong Kong, but made the film while living in the United States. Kong constructed his first film entirely from archival footage, having combed through obscure and forgotten film prints, primarily from the National

Archive in Washington, DC, to assemble a historically-based piece covering Japan's invasion of East and South-East Asia and its eventual surrender at the end of the Second World War.

As a film buyer for his father while also a tertiary student, Kong conceived of the idea of making a documentary about the Second World War. While most films or television series produced in the west, most famously the British Thames Television series *The World at War* (1973), focused primarily on the events in the west, Kong decided to examine the war from the point of view of the east, dealing specifically with the topic of how Japan developed as a military power prior to the Second World War, the Japanese wartime occupations and the massacres in parts of China over a period of five years. The title *Rising Sun* derives from the depiction of imperialist aggression designed to create the so-called 'Greater East Asia Co-Prosperity Sphere', forming the first half of Kong's 'rise and fall' film. It aptly suggested the sudden ascendancy of the Imperial Japanese Army, and at the same time ironically connoted the old British imperialist motto 'the sun never sets on the British Empire'. The film was also intended to resonate with the Hong Kong population's experience of occupation, depicting Chinese immigrants fleeing from both the civil war and then the Japanese occupation of Hong Kong, which lasted for forty-four months from Christmas Day 1941.

By presenting a clear history with a distinct historical angle on power relations, unlike most of the other Chinese productions that focused solely on the trauma of the war, *Rising Sun* became a big box-office success. It grossed $9.4 million in its continuous forty-three-day release, marking a historical record as the top-grossing film of the year. Stylistically, *Rising Sun* echoes the American newsreel serial *News on the March*, and other newsreels of the period it covers, despite being made four decades later. It makes use of an authoritative voice-over narrator[2] to tell the story and provide context for the images purveyed. The film focuses on military movements with additional reference to internal politics, but Kong chooses not to follow any specific persona or participant. As he states in an interview,[3] despite his intent to make the film image-driven, such extensive information exists for this vast and complex subject that the narration rarely pauses. Relying on juxtaposition and skilful montage of archival footage, his compilation documentary – to categorise it more precisely – builds an intense pace and rhythm thanks to the strategy adopted by Kong of maintaining a rapid succession of images.

The film opens with a proleptic epilogue showing images of the atom bombs dropping on Hiroshima and Nagasaki. Then the narrative backtracks to convey the historical development of the rise of militarism in Japan in the context of rapid industrialisation and modernisation with shots of tanks, planes and ships being fitted out for combat. This footage is mainly derived from contemporary Japanese propaganda films. Images of Japanese troops in China during their occupation of the country in the 1930s are included, showing Kuomintang and communist resistance armies led by Chiang Kai-shek and Mao Zedong respectively. Various shots of Shanghai and the concession areas under the control of western imperialist powers and of Japanese spies and collaborators, fomenting unrest in order to pave the way for the Japanese invasion, add to this measured and captivating historical filmic narrative. The assassination of a succession of inconvenient prime ministers in Japan by the militarist hard-liners in order to incite the population to support military aggression, which the film includes, is a salutary reminder, that – as in Hitler's Germany in the same decade – there were some citizens who opposed totalitarian policies and paid for their resistance with their lives.

The major events from this period are portrayed: the Marco Polo Bridge Incident in Beijing in 1937 (the skirmish serving as a fabricated 'provocation' for the full-scale invasion of China by Japanese forces); the Chinese retreat from the Forbidden City; the Japanese take-over of Nanking (Nanjing, as it is now known), followed by harrowing and graphic shots of the subsequent atrocities committed there; and the spirited but costly eight-day battle for the defence of Hankow (Hangkou) and Guangzhou. The Chinese collaborationist Wang Jingwei is featured being received officially by the Japanese Government. Hitler is also depicted meeting the Japanese puppet prime minister of the time, and there is breathtaking aerial footage of the attack on Pearl Harbour, culled from Japanese propaganda archives. The Hong Kong invasion sequence included lasts only about five minutes, but it features footage of the relentless bombing of Hong Kong Island prior to the assault, leading to Hong Kong's inevitable capitulation. Likewise, the fall of Bangkok, Malaysia and Singapore to the Japanese equivalent of Hitler's *Blitzkrieg* of 1939–40 is emphasised by a contemporary Japanese map showing much of Asia under the control of its forces.

As the film progresses, more footage is taken from Library of Congress archive material, presenting the gradual ascendancy of British and American forces from 1944 onwards, including the invasion of Okinawa and the battle for Iwojima. This is offset with striking late-war footage from Japan depicting kamikaze fighter planes attacking Allied ships. The appalling suffering of Japanese citizens in the final stages of Japan's capitulation is then represented in shots of endless corpses laid out, and the film ends where it began with shots of the 'mushroom' clouds from the atomic bombs that effectively ended resistance.

The rhythm of *Rising Sun* is fast-paced, and flows in accordance with the narration, delivering a stream of information which coincides with the visuals as well as supplying background information not visually available. The music, comprising primarily horns and drums, provides militaristic associations with war, alternating with orchestral string sections at strategic moments in the narrative. Kong also employs animated maps at times to give clear indications of troop movements and the spatial relationships of the armies. In the same way that he chooses particular moments for making a shift in the music, Kong breaks away from the normal conservative visual style for moments of emphasis, and employs temporal manipulation. These come especially as the narrative deals with the emotive subject of 'the rape of Nanjing'. Leading into this section, Kong shows the Japanese Lieutenant-General Hisao Tani riding a horse towards the camera. As the horseman reaches the camera, Kong freezes the frame on his face, whereupon the narrator states gravely that 'he would later be hung by the Allies for what his troops were about to do'. All of the subsequent footage of the 'rape of Nanjing' is conveyed in slow-motion in an attempt to heighten further the emotions felt by the viewer.

While the film focuses on the Japanese political and military movement, *Rising Sun* is told from the viewpoint of a distanced Hong Kong perspective. Although it avoids making generalised statements about the Japanese, the film is clearly conceived from the position of a film-maker from an invaded and violated land. The director, Kong, and the other writers, Leslie Steinberg and Robert Endelson, actually employed a Japanese script consultant on the project. Nevertheless, recognising the subtle slant is important. The film clearly shows the Japanese forces as the aggressors, and is sympathetic to the peoples victimised by the imperialist aggression.

Early in the film, referring to the Japanese army occupation of the Korean peninsula, the narrator states: 'The Japanese army in Korea was infested with nationalist fanatics.' He then highlights the spies and the web of twisted plots to manipulate the local population. Kong thus makes the point of clarifying that the Japanese aggression originally stemmed from a faction of militarists that took over the civilian government, and fanned the flames of nationalism, in a similar way to the rise of totalitarianism in Nazi Germany. When showing the war atrocities perpetrated by the Japanese army occupying north-eastern China, the narration observes with understandable partiality, 'these barbaric acts only strengthened the will of the Chinese to fight'.

Historical records confirm the events described in *Rising Sun* and the terrible suffering endured by the populations of the countries that they attacked, especially the atrocities inflicted upon Nanjing, as well as the Japanese army's use of so-called 'comfort women'. To omit these events would be to ignore some of the worst crimes of the entire war. Thus the use of hyperbolic language is understandable from the standpoint of heightening the drama for audiences of *Rising Sun*. But the point of perspective, veiled or not, is also of interest in determining the reasons behind the enormous popularity of *Rising Sun* in 1980s Hong Kong. A new generation had grown up in the city, leaving only older people with concrete memories of the Japanese occupation of the 1940s. By this time, Hong Kong had resumed its colonial status under British rule and was enjoying the fruits of economic regeneration during the 1970s. The film needed to walk a thin line in terms of balancing historical accuracy with retrospective selection and judgment of events, but achieved this impressively, resonating with Hong Kong audiences as a result of the city's unique circumstances and, perhaps also, the perception of vulnerability during the recently ended Cultural Revolution. *Rising Sun*'s long run was also partly due to the fact that many primary and secondary schools organised trips for students to view and discuss the events that the film depicts, representing unprecedented sucess for a Hong Kong documentary that would remain unparalleled until 2008's *KJ: Music and Life*.

JOURNEY TO BEIJING (EVANS CHAN, 1998)

Evans Chan's pair of documentaries made between 1997 and 1999, the ambiguously titled *Journey to Beijing* and the more nostalgic *Adeus Macao*, cover the transfer of sovereignty of Hong Kong in 1997 and Macau in 1999 to China. Both films explore the mood and feelings of individuals and, to an extent, of more marginalised groups and public figures on the cultural and political scene. Although neither film adopts an alarmist or negative perspective on the respective handovers, each expresses the aspiration for autonomy of the individual and mutual respect for cultural-historical differences, some of which represent the inevitable legacy of a long period of colonial influence. The two films can be appreciated singly, and, of the two, *Journey to Beijing* is the more ambitious in scope.

The work brought Chan's documentary-making to international critical attention at international festivals in 1998, and is a layered and skillfully edited work. Tony Rayns, in *Sight and Sound* magazine, described it as 'a set of mini-essays of life in Hong Kong' and 'the best corrective to the self-important and seriously off-beam international coverage of the 1997 Handover'.[4] It follows the trail of an assorted, group of Hong Kong 'pilgrims' on a charity walkathon from Hong Kong to Beijing under the auspices of the Christian Sowers' Action Group. The broad-based Project Hope collects funds through sponsorship and other activities to develop schooling facilities in poorer regions of China.

At the literal level the film charts the progress of the miscellaneous band of walkers toward their destination, with their arrival timed to coincide with the handover of Hong Kong, thus ensuring maximum publicity. At the metaphorical and symbolic level, however, the journey is presented as a microcosm of the complex process of reunification and reciprocal understanding or even reconciliation between Hong Kong people and mainland Chinese, between two radically different cultural and political systems, and even between seemingly incompatible sets of values. The scene which begins the film is set in

Hong Kong at the opening ceremony for the walk. Here, Chan introduces the various characters using 'talking-head' interviews, in which various walkers explain their motivation for joining the walk. Stylistically, Chan chooses to use onscreen text to explain the set-up and plunge the viewer straight in to the narrative. He also uses other cinematic conventions such as slow-motion, non-diegetic atmospheric music and stylised transitions such as screen-wipe and onscreen maps to get the viewers more involved with the walk from the start.

However, immediately after the film's commencement, Chan shifts the focus to the Mai Po Nature Reserve in the northern New Territories bordering mainland China, a seemingly digressive topic, only marginally related because these wetlands provide the habitat for a bird sanctuary lying along the path of the walk. During this section, Chan interviews nature experts about the state of the area, and learns how the rapid development of the busy city of Shenzhen is driving the birds away from China into Mai Po, sitting as it does just across Deep Bay from Shenzhen. As we come to realise, these interviews serve implicitly to highlight important issues of environmental policy and sustainable development, and are thus tangentially related to the central concept.

Following this digression, the film returns to the progress of the walkers as they arrive in Guangdong province across the Chinese border. Chan uses onscreen text here, as elsewhere, to inform the viewer how many walkers have joined the walk *en route*. He focuses on the personae he has established in the Hong Kong-set prelude, cutting back to their interviews in which they continue explaining their differing motivations for joining the walk. Chan also continues to introduce new subjects, and, in the course of these interviews, he questions walkers about how they see Hong Kong and the impending handover, thus drawing some general political implications regarding Sino-British-Hong Kong relationships. The interviews offer a spectrum of sincerely held views, some diametrically opposed, for example in the figures of veteran Second World War pilot Charles Shu, who expresses patriotic pleasure at the prospects of reunification with the motherland, and busineswoman Circle Yuen, who articulates scepticism about the Communist Party's intentions. The interviews also hint at internal conflicts within the group, regarding excessive hospitalitity by their hosts, for instance. However, Chan never shows these people airing grievances as a group, and there are relatively few interactions between walkers that portray a group dynamic. Essentially, the filmmaker appears to be more interested in relating to the walkers as individuals than as a collective.

The first half of the film switches back and forth between the walk and the various issues and perspectives Chan wishes to foreground. Most of these interludes – such as on Hong Kong director Stanley Kwan making a documentary entitled *Yang or Yin* about his coming out as a homosexual film-maker, and Hong Kong choreographer Helen Lai's post-modern dance adapting

Peking opera on the subject of the Chinese revolution – are only remotely connected with the theme on the surface, until one begins to appreciate the common thread of individual freedom and personal aspirations for the future, of necessary ambivalence and alterity in interpretation, and, above all, of the importance of respecting differences.

Shot as it is on DV, the film lacks the technology to do full justice to the landscape. This is, perhaps, due to the fact that Chan seems to prioritise essayistic association rather than a visual aesthetic, and is more interested in the themes and ideas than the basic composition. Some interviews are achieved standing up, with the speaker's head in the centre of a wobbly moving frame. A similarly simple framing method applies equally to the more static, 'talking-head' interviews. Chan's use of evocative and lyrical, albeit sparing (a strategy that tends to foreground it for the audience), musical accompaniment to the varied imagery of the film, its judiciously selected insets, superimposed images and slow-motion sequences are placed in the broader context of the film's respect for the walkers' generosity of spirit and their emergent awareness of spiritual and cultural-historical ties with mainland people. His often wittily succinct 'chapter' titles, such as 'In the Land of Mickey Mao' – an ironic nod to China's growing predilection for consumer capitalism – for the stop-over in Shaoshan, the town of Mao's birth in Henan province, and 'Threatened Haven' for the Mai Po footage, accentuates the discursive, episodic quality of the film.

Filmed excerpts from stage performances, including a play about Hong Kong's relationship with China, entitled *Crown Ourselves with Roses*, by one of Chan's New York-based collaborators, Joanna Chan, make the point about Hong Kong's situation more eloquently than any voice-over: 'Our only survival tactic is to be of use to Britain and now China', reflects one character in the carefully selected play extract, 'We're programmed to prove our usefulness'.[5] This use of stage material to communicate a quasi-Brechtian dialectic is even more directly evident in his later 2003 documentary *The Life and Times of Wu Zhong Xian*, and from the beginning has represented a signature device in his documentary work.

The film then cuts to the final days of the walk, showing the walkers arriving in Beijing after several short segments filmed at destinations reached along the way. Chan interposes segments on the uncertainties of the Hong Kong-China relationship, such as ideological differences on the issue of 4 June, with pro-democracy figure-head Martin Lee arguing the urgent need for democracy in the future Hong Kong. Footage of the Tiananmen Square candlelight vigil on 4 June in Hong Kong's Victoria Park is rendered all the more effective by poetically powerful editing and the image of the Hong Kong-constructed copy of the original statue built by protestors in Tiananmen and known as 'The Goddess of Democracy' superimposed on the candle-waving throng.

The film closes with commentary-free official footage of the handover ceremony between Britain and China. Thus, the parallel journeys to Beijing are brought to their conclusion, which is, however, only the beginning for Hong Kong people and for beneficiaries of the charity action alike. Chan's end-titles inform us that US$2.6 million was raised by the walkers. The film can thus be seen to function partly as a tribute to the spirit of ordinary Hong Kong people, reminding us that they are not a passive element in the political process. The closing dedication of the film is to Chan's mother, 'who died the year before the homeland she left behind finally caught up with her', precisely the sort of gently ironic reflection that is the normal prerogative of the printed essay.

According to Tony Williams, who cites the important thematic music composed by Milos Raikovich used by Chan and entitled *Dream Quartet*, to support his argument, the film 'intuitively evokes a dream journey for the positive aspects of a common unity between the Mainland and Hong Kong, in which all barriers may eventually be removed by a process of historical contact'.[6] This tends to underline Chan's intellectually critical idealist creative impulses *à la* Brecht. At the same time Chan himself is clearly aware of the way the film's dualism reflects his own ambivalence about the actual process of decolonisation and reunification:

> *Journey to Beijing* is very interesting in terms of its reception. When it played in Hong Kong, some audiences were saying it was very negative about the Handover. But when it played overseas in Vancouver, Berlin, and elsewhere, people said, 'Oh, you are so positive about the Handover . . . The mission of the march was to raise funds for basic education in China. It's a good deed, one beyond reproach. Yet even within the walkers themselves, there is this nagging ambivalence. The state ended up spending tons of money on celebratory events, leading to an implicit feeling that they were being exploited as a show of the people of Hong Kong embracing China.[7]

As Chan goes on to point out, the march itself would have made for a fairly straightforward documentary. However, his aim in hybridising the work, and 'punctuating it with other voices',[8] results in what might be termed a multi-accented documentary style, exploring divergent views, attitudes and beliefs. Aesthetically, perhaps, these elements do not always appear to be tightly integrated, but the intentional looseness of structure in the film makes a lot of sense in the context of the world-cinema essayistic documentary form, which Chan clearly had in mind in embarking on his own distinctive *Journey to Beijing*.

RICE DISTRIBUTION (TAMMY CHEUNG, 2003)

By sharp contrast with *Journey to Beijing*, Tammy Cheung's short but visually eloquent documentary *Rice Distribution* eschews the discursive, episodic documentary form in favour of a concentration and unity of time, place and theme that is almost Aristotelian in structure and concept. It was her third documentary made in the observational mode, and one of two films made in 2003 to mark the founding of her and cinematographer Augustine Lam's company Reality Film Production, created for the purpose of making a socially conscious intervention in Hong Kong via documentary film. Cheung employs a clear structure and climax predicated on the organisation of a specific, temporally circumscribed philanthropic event to make it one of her most accessible and technically accomplished films to date. Her unadorned direct cinema method relies on the single, hand-held camera of Lam to record a Taoist organisation in Hong Kong donating rice to thousands of elderly people as part of a religious ceremony to mark the Hungry Ghost Festival in August 2002. The distribution is scheduled to begin in the afternoon of an initially hot and subsequently rainy summer's day. Elderly people are seen making their way into an open park area in Wong Tai Sin – a traditionally working-class district of Kowloon – in the morning, with some queuing well before dawn to make sure they are able to receive tickets from the organisers which will entitle them to free bags of rice.

The relatively fast editing rhythm of the film contrasts with the apparently static conceptual content of waiting for something to happen. Also, thanks to Lam's perceptive and revealing camera-work and Cheung's and Lam's astute editing choices, the viewer is able to adopt an initially neutral view of the proceedings. It is only as the film progresses and the events of the day unfold that the reflective viewer begins to see problems with the way the organisers have planned and managed their philanthropy. In the process one is likely to arrive at the conclusion – although the direct cinema style of presentation does not impose this interpretation, even if the selection and editing clearly suggest it – that the representatives of the Taoist organisation are more concerned with performing the ceremony and meeting their charitable religious obligations, than with the well-being of the elderly. Ultimately, the images tend to speak for themselves and represent a powerful challenge to, and even indictment of, their motives and methods.

Cheung begins the documentary as fresh arrivals are being corralled like cattle into holding sections marked by steel barriers intended for crowd control. One of the first images is of an elderly woman swearing at a policeman and accusing another man of jumping his place in the queue, much to the amusement of the others sitting on the ground nearby. The police officer is calm and ignores her vituperative comments, while briefly attempting to calm her down and reason with her. Placing this scene at the start of the documentary is crucial, as it establishes the two most visible of the three parties involved in the event, namely the police officers and the elderly recipients of the charitable offerings. Cheung patently refrains from portraying her elderly subjects in a blanket sentimental or condescending fashion. The shots and edits reveal that while some are self-controlled and reasonable, others are cantankerous and pushy, and, as we see from the shots of the first aid tent, they are in variable states of physical and mental health. When one organiser tries to explain the dangers of pushing and shoving, a woman is heard muttering, 'It's like he's talking to children'. In many ways the implicit criticism contained in this comment applies both to the old people theselves and to the organisers, and perhaps also more generally to Hong Kong society's lack of respect for the rights and agency of the elderly as a social group.

A dominant theme in the documentary is the inadequacy of planning and facilities for the elderly, despite the organisers' experience in running the event on an annual basis. It is telling that one helper (not an official organiser) makes an effort to apologise to the hard-pressed superintendent of police with the tacit acknowledgement of justifiable but unspoken criticism of the organisation he works for: 'We've done this for years and given the Police so much trouble'. The Temple's established and outdated system means that people who want to collect a free bag of rice must wait in line for hours just to receive a numbered ticket on a first-come-first-served basis.. When the tickets have all gone, those without them are expected to leave empty-handed. Those with numbers must leave and return in the afternoon to prove their eligibility to claim their rice. The flaws in this system are played out in front of the camera as, after all tickets have been claimed, most of the elderly remain in the area, reluctant to leave in case they miss out, while the police make strenuous but unavailing attempts to get them to leave. The police officers' appeals are met with the reasonable explanation that it is difficult to leave because they are old, not very mobile and the venue is inconveniently located. With nowhere to go, the people with numbers start to queue again to be among the first to receive their rice in the afternoon, which causes further problems for the harrassed but endlessly patient police officers.

One particular shot is emblematic of the apparent detachment of the Taoist temple organisers: it occurs during the performance of the ceremony when a Taoist priest watches dispassionately as a police officer physically removes an unco-operative elderly person from the area. There seems to be little interest in or concern for the well-being of the woman, and the ceremony continues, as the film shows, almost as a separate, unrelated event. As for those arriving too late to receive a number, there is little consolation, but many still remain in line, leaning on the barriers hoping for better luck in the afternoon. At one point an officer walks over to a group of people without tickets to ask them to leave, but simply ends up hearing appeals to stay. Overall, there is considerable variation in the use of close-up, medium and wide shots, but Cheung and Lam avoid lingering on close-ups to portray individuals or create framed 'talking heads'. Occasionally, medium close-ups on subjects are selected, giving the audience a sense of the relationship that this subject has with the group, or there is a cut to an already framed close-up which is held relatively briefly. Lam and Cheung are at pains to ensure that the fly-on-the-wall method prevails throughout, with the result that conventional empathy with interview subjects and specific individuals is not a relevant consideration. In a very different way from Evans Chan's work but in a similarly investigative spirit, *Rice Distribution* keeps the viewer at a distance, with the purpose of inviting them to question the motivation behind this act of philanthropy through an inductive approach to the material. In the light of the damning evidence presented by Cheung and Lam, that motivation is seen to be suspect.

The climax – but also an anti-climax – is inevitably reached when the organisers finally distribute the bags of rice. Although there is no particular drama at the point of distribution, it indicates a defining moment in the pre-ordained sequence of events, promoting anxiety, tension and either satisfaction or disappointment on the part of the elderly. However, the lack of consideration for those receiving rice at the hands of the Temple authorities is still in evidence: at this point the recipients must now deal with the problem of struggling up steep steps with their eight-kilogram bags of rice to the nearest bus stop. The on-duty police officers help some of the less able-bodied in this operation, again, underlining the positive way the police generally manage to conduct themselves throughout the proceedings. Lam's restless camera returns to those who have lingered behind in the vague hope of still receiving free rice. Cheung then cuts to the temple volunteers who were responsible for distributing the rice, and we see them closing the stalls and chatting, and then hear an announcement that there are considerable quantities of rice remaining. A senior figure is heard informing these volunteers they can take one or two bags home with them, ignoring the disappointed latecomers, who wander disconsolately over the now-twilight, litter-strewn public space. This is one of the lasting images that remain with the viewer after watching *Rice Distribution*.

As with other direct cinema works, notably the films of Frederick Wiseman, expository, reflexive, performative and interactive modes play no part in the film's conceptualisation or aesthetics. The hand-held camera adds an immediacy and raw aesthetic that fits with both the subject-matter and theme, and since the participants are presumably not accustomed to the film-camera, there is a certain direct sincerity in the way they are represented. Moreover, its mobility allows Lam and Cheung to come upon a scene and shoot it with little disruption to the subjects. Naturally, a degree of intervention is inevitable, since subjects may 'act up' for the benefit of the camera. On this question of intervention, Wiseman has argued that even if subjects exaggerate their reaction because of the camera, this is still an accurate and ontologically real shot, because it represents their natural reaction to the situation, though a somewhat exaggerated one.[9]

Cheung's and Lam's cinematic motivation appears to be to reveal some intrinsic truth about the situation the elderly face in this particular instance. One can only speculate about the motivation of the organisers, while those of the police appeared to be based on bona fide goodwill and the desire to avoid mishap and negative publicity. As for the elderly subjects, the viewer is left impressed by their resilience, resourcefulness and sheer persistence in a society that is portrayed here as only superficially caring and benevolent toward them. One may also speculate that a severe case of bad social conscience may have prompted the awards of Grand Prize and Open Category Gold Award for the film at the Hong Kong Independent Short Film and Video Awards for that year. Clearly, however, *Rice Distribution* won both awards entirely on its own merits as a documentary.

ONE-WAY STREET ON A TURNTABLE (ANSON MAK, 2007)

One-Way Street on a Turntable is the first feature-length documentary by documentarian and visual culture academic Anson Mak. Following its premiere at the 31st Hong Kong International Film Festival and a showing at the 2007 Singapore Film Festival, it was nominated for a Grand Jury Award for best feature-length documentary in the latter, and also featured at the Vancouver and Barcelona festivals, garnering critical attention and recognition in the process. Categorising it as an experimental essay film, Timothy Corrigan points out: 'Anson Hoi-shan Mak's *One Way Street on a Turntable* works to locate a self in Hong Kong between movement and rootedness permeated by reflections on Walter Benjamin'.[10]

Inspired by Benjamin's meditations on the interaction of the individual consciousness and the city in his aphoristic essayettes in the 1928 collection, *One-Way Street*, the film quotes his text liberally in both onscreen text and voice-overs. This strategy is very much part of Mak's imaginative intertextual method, employing classic suggestive techniques of juxtaposition and montage to create a multi-layered impressionist mosaic of city life and a work that is, like Benjamin's mini-masterpiece, idiosyncratic and capricious, but, equally, evocative of a mood of both melancholy and celebration of life in the teeming city existence. From the use of Hong Kong Film Unit footage culled from the Hong Kong Public Record Office to contrast the colourfully positivist depictions of Hong Kong in the 1960s and 1970s and her own gray-toned portrait of modern Hong Kong to the voice-overs of Mak and the life stories of her 'actress' subject, *One-Way Street on a Turntable* is clearly intended both as a personal and a broad portrait of how Mak sees Hong Kong. The film is styled as 'an interactive moving image book' with its 'chapters' or 'essays' lending themselves to being 'read' in random, non-linear sequence.

In distinctly post-modernist style Mak deconstructs the notion of authoritative voice one can find in the more traditional documentaries she mischievously 'quotes' from earlier in the film. By contrast, her quirky essay film valorises the role of the observer-*flaneur* in the spirit of nineteenth-century French poet Charles Baudelaire, and early twentieth-century German critic Benjamin. Indeed, Mak's cinematic reflections on Hong Kong life apply the German critic's precepts and aphorisms shrewdly to Hong Kong's literal and metaphorical one-way streets. As Izod and Kilborn have discussed in relation to the reflexive mode of this type of documentary, such non-normative documentaries pose questions 'by refusing the visible or epistemological bases in which certainty is found'.[11]

The notion of going out there to find life on the street is evident in the film, which follows the principal human camera subject, Yvonne Leung, in her exploration of aspects of a real, if fractured and incoherent, Hong Kong everyday life, with its ubiquitous injunction to 'post no bills' on its walls taken directly from a quotation from Benjamin's work. Benjamin's polemically engaged critical style underpins the work and informs its mood, which is redolent of dissidence, even if the dissidence and disenchantment of that Hong Kong so-called 'post-80s generation' (the local term for youth activism) are qualities that often communicate to the viewer by implication rather than through explicit statement. The disembodied voice on the record turntable reading from Benjamin's work is curiously evocative of the smooth-talking 'voice of god' authoritative voice-over in the colonial-era documentaries which Mak's mixed discourse reframes to parodic effect. Imitating the discourse of Government Information Services' Hong Kong Film Unit documentaries of the 1960s, Mak invites us to 'take a place like this', meaning Hong Kong as a place. Whereas the source film text was inviting the entrepreneur and visitor to 'take the place', here it is more a question of Mak using artistic licence to 'take it back' on behalf of Hongkongers. Employing a post-modern palimpsest technique, she cheekily superimposes her own titles and texts over the original footage. Taking two personal histories – that of the director herself as a native Hongkonger, and that of the actress (or 'talent' as Mak's credits designate the *flâneur* figure) who came to Hong Kong as an immigrant from China in the 1980s – Mak, the film-making critic, explores and subverts conventional ideas of identity currently heard in many Hong Kong and mainland discourses.

Significantly Benjamin's criticism of the 'imperialists' and the 'greed of the ruling class'[12] echoes with, and to an extent inspires, Mak's own cultural intervention on super 8. Three of the most telling of Benjamin's aphorisms heard in the 'Post No Bills' section of the film in the context of the Hong Kong socio–political predicament, and possibly in relation to the very idea of documentary objectivity, are as follows: 'He who cannot take sides should keep silent', 'Objectivity must always be sacrificed to partisanship, if the cause fought for merits this', and 'The public must always be proved wrong, yet always feel represented by the critic' (all taken from 'The critic's technique in thirteen propositions' from Benjamin's own 'Post No Bills' section). They underline the correspondences between Benjamin's critical stance and Mak's more oblique critical voice in this film. Indeed it is in the process of making this first documentary that she finds the critical edge as a documentarian that is evident in her second, *On the Edge of a Floating City We Sing* (2012).

The 'chapter headings' of the thirteen sections of the 'moving image book' follow those of Benjamin's mini-essays quite closely, and each deals with a parallel Hong Kong aspect of the famous German critic's sometimes cryptic and allusive observations. For example, over the section title 'Antiques', also the title of one of Benjamin's meditations on beloved objects and time, Mak constructs a powerful tribute to the passing of the Hong Kong Island Star Ferry terminal at Queen's Pier on 9 August 2006, its last day of operation prior to its demolition and reconstruction as 'pseudo-historical' kitsch close to the outlying island ferry piers in Central. With more than a hint of trademark irony, Mak juxtaposes the hyperbolic line from the colonial-era narrative of 'Made in Hong Kong' – 'Hong Kong has everything' – with her melancholy footage of the Star Ferry clock tower and concourse area.

In other important respects, the film is also in part a homage to women's resilience and empowerment, with the opening titles expressing a dialectic of movement and settlement, of escape and rootedness. 'Movement can be the legacy of heroic women who step beyond their own history', asserts Mak. Foot-binding, a necessary case of stasis and rootedness, persisted in China from the Southern Tang dynasty of the ninth century all the way to the end of the Qing dynasty in the early twentieth century, and even beyond. 'Hakka women' (from whom many Hong Kong natives descend), she reminds the viewer, 'did not engage in the practice, [i.e. footbinding] having to earn a living in the fields; they had to earn money in order to survive and have a room of their own'.

The feminist focus is accentuated in the second half of the film as Mak develops the narrative of her 'talent's' life experience. Again the dialectical approach is evident: Mak was born and raised in Hong Kong growing up and living in the middle-class Kowloon Tong district and working in the more plebeian, light-industrial Kwun Tong district in East Kowloon; Yvonne, the 'talent', moved to Hong Kong with her parents in 1980 and grew up as an unwelcome mainlander in the midst of Hong Kong 'belongers' – those who had moved to the city much earlier or the second generation who had been born in Hong Kong – in Mei Foo Sun Chuen (Mei Foo Housing Estate in West Kowloon). Yvonne's voice-over is rendered in Mandarin Chinese while Mak's own is in Cantonese, as the local ethos of the Mei Foo and Kwun Tong spaces are affirmed in stark contrast to the expatriate-oriented, more affluent parts of Hong Kong.

As if to emphasise the dichotomy of Chinese and British forms of imperialism, parallels with the Urban Renewal Authority's 'alterations' to contemporary Kwun Tong are presented to the viewer in the onscreen narrative. The reference to the forced relocation of Hong Kong inhabitants in 1662, in the early Qing dynasty, to 50 miles away from the coast, and away from their livelihood in the local salt fields is a critique of the other imperialist narrative found in the Film Unit's work, which suggest that Hong Kong's history depends on its colonial legacy. As the film informs us, the etymology of the name Kwun Tong refers to its status as official salt-fields. However, once the place was reclaimed for renovation as an industrial area in 1953, the Chinese characters were altered by use of a homonym to obscure their original reference. Mak's sly critique comments on this deliberate erasure of the local. Her caption 'Our sense of history begins with British rule' is steeped in irony, not just about the colonial narrative, but about all of the grand narratives, including those of the new corporate developers with their ties to Beijing.

In some ways Mak's deliberately worked grainy black and white footage recalls what remains in the Hong Kong Film Archive of the great Hong Kong documentary pioneer Lai Man-wai, whose films recorded turbulent times in impressionistic but intellectually engaging style. The effect of this roughly hewn authentic look is to underline a sense of genuine, as opposed to artificially grafted, cultural heritage in the city and to convey a palpable spirit of place. Although the editing alternates between the deliberately inert and the kaleidoscopic, the film conveys a softer melancholic quality to complement its hard edges as connoted by angular, linear contours of the urban architecture, shot from deliberately disorientating angles. Strangely, Mak's editing appears both calculated and loose at the same time. She allows scenes in the second half of the documentary to extend way beyond conventional shot-timings – a scene of a child on a swing in a park is of inordinate length – but still manages to keep the viewer engaged thanks to the feel of slow fade-out. This use of visual metaphor creates an unconscious association between the documentary images of the city and the city itself as organic entity. The film's unsettling and slightly melancholy ending chimes with the needle stuck in the groove on the still-revolving turntable, implying a sense of random recurrence in its elegiac and existential conclusion.

KJ: MUSIC AND LIFE (CHEUNG KING-WAI, 2008)

KJ: Music and Life is the second feature-length documentary by Cheung King-wai, who made his documentary debut with *All's Well with the World* the previous year. Unlike his first film, which features a broad canvas of people from the lower socio-economic class, *KJ* follows one central subject from an upper-middle class family – the son of a competitive doctor besotted with classical music and determined to inculcate his three children into the fierce competitiveness of the music world. The film presents a kind of six-part diary of two periods in the life of the prodigiously talented younger brother, Wong Ka-jeng, referred to habitually only by his initials KJ. Shot in 2002 and 2007–8, the film is structured by KJ and his interaction with his surrounding people – his teacher, his father, his siblings and schoolmates. The film also jumps back and forth between two time periods: Cheung captures KJ in 2002, when at the age of eleven, he goes to Prague with his father to play Beethoven's Piano Concerto No. 1 in a concert followed by a studio recording, and then as a seventeen-year old student in the Diocesan Boys' School six years later, instructing and conducting a school string orchestra, where his passion is ignited not by the general school ethos of achievement and honour, but exclusively by music for its own sake.

Director Cheung, as a former music student himself, started out with the modest goal of focusing on young local musical talents when the project first came to him in 2002. That project metamorphosed into a study of one particular boy, whom Cheung found fascinating as a subject on account of not just his precociousness, but also his restless, questioning attitude to life and music, and his aspiration for perfection in all he did. 'He asked questions that went far beyond music, questions about the meaning of life, about why he had fingers that could play like his . . . I couldn't believe I was hearing stuff like that from an eleven-year old', reminisces Cheung in a recent newspaper interview.[13]

The film, alternating as required between interactive interview and observational direct cinema modes, contrasts the stable and relatively happy pre-adolescent life of KJ with the more troubled later footage of the talented youngster as an upper-form student at Hong Kong's prestigious and competitive Diocesan Boys' School in located in Kowloon. His demanding musical rehearsals showcase not only his flair as a conductor and interpreter, but also his critical response to those who settle for anything less than their best. Implicitly his individualist thinking challenges Confucian traditions of 'filial piety' as well as such hallowed concepts as team spirit and uncritical collectivism, which Cheung's camera-work and editing elicits with great skill and obvious intention. The extent to which Cheung has a thesis in this film is disguised by the observational element, but, given his own life experience of the pressure-cooker atmosphere in which young middle-class people grow up in Hong Kong, we may deduce a certain degree of societal critique in the work.

KJ opens with the 2002 footage, showing the boy arriving in the Czech Republic with his father. The visual quality of this part is a little uneven, featuring many hand-held shots due to the nature of the trip and the limited space of several of the main locations, including the room where KJ talks with adult musicians. The film then engages with one of its main themes, his relationship with his inspiring piano teacher, Nancy Loo. In the next section, we immediately see why KJ is such a compelling character; in the 'talking-head' interviews which Cheung conducts, we hear her periodically asking questions, and also see KJ's interactions with Ms Loo in piano lessons. In the process he is encouraged to immerse himself in the music with his whole body and use his imagination to conceive of certain passages as ribbons waving and so on. In other words the music should be experienced as organic – as both physical and spiritual – not merely technical or mechanical. When Nancy Loo visits his school rehearsal, we also see him trying to impress her, and when the orchestra lacks sparkle, he chides the musicians for embarrassing him in front of his teacher and urges them to respect the music that they are playing.

Cheung cuts effectively between rehearsal footage from the 2002 concert in Prague and the 2007–8 school orchestra and piano quintet rehearsals and performances, including extracts from prize-winning performances of Brahms and Schumann piano quintets (the latter deliberately transgressing competition rules) and a rousing ending of Rachmaninov's Piano Concerto No. 2. Other scenes look at KJ's relationship with his older brother, Lap, and his younger sister, Yiu. Even as a small boy in the 2002 section, KJ confides to the cameraman that Lap's talent is limited. By contrast, his sister, Yiu, who is being tutored by her brother for competitions, seems more responsive to his advice.

In the fourth part of the film Cheung focuses on KJ's relationship with his best friend, Samuel. Even though Samuel is the student representative of the school's music department, he plays second fiddle to KJ in the school orchestra rehearsals. Samuel is receptive to KJ's desire for musical perfectionism, even though he is irritated by his arrogant personality, as he declares in front of KJ in the lobby of Sai Wan Ho Civic Centre, where they are rehearsing for the competition. Samuel's religious background also prompts KJ to express his rejection of organised religion and to expound his own philosophical humanism. In numerous personal interviews, KJ attempts to answer several philosophically challenging questions about music. In addition at the tender age of eleven, KJ hypothesises that the ultimate beauty in life can only emerge if everyone dies together at the same time. This statement is followed by a remarkably precocious discussion on the subject of suicide.

As a seventeen-year-old KJ still continues to seek his ideas regarding 'the truth', and as a film-maker Cheung appears inclined to explore this relation-ship between ontology and music, presumably motivated by his own musical background and philosophical interests. Nevertheless his treatment of this subject tends to exaggerate his subject's insights: the problem is that KJ is still a teenager with little real-life experience. Not surprisingly, KJ's virtuoso per-formances and exceptionally mature musical talent and intellect tend to make him seem detached from his classmates and emphasise the anti-establishment thinking that is reflected in the film's underlying ideological connotations.

KJ explains his dislike of competition, saying that performances should not be about winning but participating. This is dramatically illustrated when he deliberately chooses a movement from the Schumann quintet which is a minute longer than the allowed length, knowing full well it might lead to disqualification. He convinces the other four musicians to play the piece nonetheless, even though they are bemused about his reasoning. After hearing the sound of the Schumann piece in a brief blackout, we see the quintet being awarded first prize in the competition, earning lavish praise from the adjudicators despite the breach of rules. KJ's solipsism borders on vanity and self-righteousness, as he explains to Cheung, 'I don't care about the flag, I'll use it to wipe my ass'. Intriguingly, as far as the validity of the would-be non-interventionist documentary mode is concerned, at this point he may well be telling Cheung what he believes the latter wants to hear.

Without doubt, the musically and intellectually gifted subject of the film radiates personality and presence on-screen despite his angst and scepticism. The seventeen-year-old KJ evinces a critically independent spirit and deter-mination to seek his own truths in preference to the values inculcated by his elite school. He displays a growing self-awareness and self-confidence in both his solo piano performance capabilities and his musical leadership of school chamber groups and orchestras, as well as a quiet contempt towards competi-tion for its own sake, in opposition to the prevailing school culture.

In the latter part of the film we also witness his sense of betrayal and bitter-ness at the break-up of his parents' marriage and his anger towards his father. Director Cheung King-wai compellingly contrasts this with footage shot much earlier of a precocious but essentially trusting eleven-year-old, who exhibits amazing talent as well as curiosity about such topics as death, the future and the possibility of a world without humans. His assertive – and, for middle-class young Hongkongers, unusual – individualism is inevitably contrasted with the predominantly collectivist ideology of the Hong Kong education system. Not surprisingly, the viewer is encouraged to empathise with the individual as a result of this admittedly slanted technique. One of the most remarkable com-ments made by the young prodigy is that he aspires to simply be 'a human being with conscience and humanity' with all that implies. Sadly, by the time of the film's completion, KJ had become virtually a drop-out in reaction to his problems on both the domestic and school fronts. His subsequent departure for the fresh pastures of Bloomington to study music at Indiana University is not referred to at the end of the film, which leaves the subject and the viewer in limbo. However, it seems that he has consistently maintained his resistance to competitive performance during his studies at Indiana University.[14]

As in *All's Right with the World*, the cinematography of *KJ* is a strong aspect of the work. Shot on HD and featuring controlled interior settings, Cheung's composition uses the superior clarity of the HD format, which allows for some beautiful shots to be produced. Having said that, the 2002 footage, probably shot on regular DV, appears somewhat rougher by comparison. Even the static framing can be distracting, and this includes the shot of KJ playing the piano solo with the rapt audience seen clearly in the background. The film ran continuously in cinemas in Hong Kong between July 2009 and February 2010 with an average of more than 90 per cent ticket sales (many of them young people of KJ's own age), and it subsequently won three Golden Horse Awards at the Hong Kong Film Awards in 2010 for best documentary, best editing and best sound. In box-office terms, it was the longest-running and most successful film of the year – truly a remarkable achievement for a documentary film in the Hong Kong context.

STORM UNDER THE SUN (LOUISA WEI/PENG XIAOLIAN, 2011)

Another strongly independent voice and vision in the documentary mode is that of Louisa Wei, a Hong Kong-based documentarian and teacher of film, who originates from mainland China but studied film and comparative literature in Canada. In *Storm under the Sun*, a film featured in the 33rd HK International Film Festival, Wei collaborates with mainland China film-maker Peng Xiaolian on a thoroughly absorbing and also moving documentary which deals with an under-explored historical subject – as with Ed Kong's *Rising Sun* – but in a very different filmic treatment. The narrative concerns Peng Xiaolian's father, Peng Boshan, and his circle of friends and fellow-writers in the Hu Feng group of leftist writers who were protégés of the great Chinese modernist and reformist writer, Lu Xun. The project began as a book, researched by Peng herself who had met the surviving members of the ostracised and now neglected group. She could not distribute the film in the mainland due to the sensitivity of it critiquing 'the Great Helmsman', Mao Zedong. Even today the Chinese leadership makes it amply clear that Mao's dubious legacy is still not up for re-evaluation in the way that Stalin's was when Nikita Khrushchev succeeded him in the 1950s.[15]

The film takes its name from references to Mao as 'the Sun' in propagandistic songs of the period, such as 'The East is Red'. The storms were also a metaphorical – and thus safer, because more oblique – reference to the various purges he instituted to consolidate his power. Initially appointed Minister of Propaganda for the new 1949 Communist government, Peng was arrested and imprisoned in 1955 and subsequently beaten to death by Red Guards in 1968. His crime was to have been supportive of what the authorities called 'the Hu Feng clique', which advanced subjectivist literary theories and techniques following the path of Lu Xun.

The film's well-structured narrative of the persecution of a group of sincere and steadfast intellectuals at the personal instigation of Mao Zedong, who considered their manifesto an unacceptable challenge to his 1942 Yan'an doctrines on literary ideology, is eclectic in style and wide-ranging in literary-historical scope. Unlike other so-called 'rightists', including Deng Xiaoping himself, who had been fully vindicated by the 'glasnost' of the post-Cultural Revolution era, the verdict on these earlier literati, rather like the verdict on the 4 June students and workers, has never been reversed, although they were freed from prison after the fall of the Gang of Four. Wei's and Peng's film functions, thus, as a tribute to the intellectual honesty and courage of these purged writers and intellectuals and also as a piece of activist advocacy. The film's obvious partiality, therefore, is offset by its investigative ethos and its scrupulous approach to damning documentary evidence. Its truth claims would be difficult for any putative future documentary on the subject to refute.

Employing witty original cartoon sequences to deconstruct the crude political hate cartoons propagated by Mao's acolytes to repress intellectuals, the film is a multi-accented, mixed-mode work based on rigorous and intelligent research. Naturally it is also a *pièce à thèse*, putting a clear case for the long-awaited and overdue apology and vindication. Over and above its visual style and effects and its virtuosic mosaic of documentary detail, the real value of *Storm under the Sun* lies in its affirmation of decency and the human spirit, in its admittedly pyrrhic victory over those who sought for various motives – whether jealousy or personal advancement on the part of the group's acquaintances and rivals, or paranoia and intolerance of autonomy on the part of Mao Zedong – to suppress their creative intellects. As Zhu Zeng, Lu Xun's best-known biographer, asserts in respect of Mao's appropriation of Lu Xun's memory, his praise for Lu Xun was 'merely strategic'.[16]

In a carefully composed five-part work Wei and Peng reconstruct the past lives of Hu Feng and his associates. Their aim is clear simply from the semiotic content of the poster still for the film – taken from the latter part of the documentary – and subsequent DVD cover image: a black and white Hu Feng confronts Mao, clad in customary blue jacket and cap, superimposed against a background of the Long March, in a stark challenge to the official version of history and values. Hu Feng, as the documentary makes clear, never swerved from his communist beliefs, and, far from being the 'rightist' that Mao's campaign and 1965 show trial claimed him to be, was a great admirer of the Chinese leader, writing one of the best laudatory poems ever written about him, 'Time Begins', which was published in the *People's Daily*. His indefatigable literary work in the two journals he founded, *Hope* and *July*, is evidenced by a collage of covers of surviving issues of the magazine. Ironically, today's literary professors in China study these journals and his theories freely. Equally ironically, Hu Feng always believed Mao had a good impression of his work and that his persecution resulted purely from the envy of lesser figures, such as his former mentee, Shu Wu, who turned 'informer'. In fact, as junior prosecutors in the case, whom Peng interviewed for her book, affirmed, 'there were no official documents on the matter – everything came from the top'.[17]

The first part of the documentary is entitled 'Heart of the Storm' and starts the narrative effectively *in medias res*. It deals with the campaign of vilification against Hu Feng and his literary group and their wider circle of friends in 1955, deploying posters, cartoons and newspaper articles of the period. Among the 'cast of characters' introduced are Peng Baoshan, Lu Xun, Hu Feng, both poet and literary theorist, and his wife Mei Zhi, the poets Ah Long and Lu Ling, and interview subjects such as latter-day academic and former Hu Feng associate, Jia Zhifang, and Hu Feng's elder son Zhang Xiaogu. Interestingly, Wei and Peng include a filmed phone conversation by another associate, the still spry Lü Yuan, attempting to persuade Shu Wu to open up on the subject, but he declines to be interviewed for the film. The 'talking-head' interviewees offer detailed testimony of events, but Wei and Peng inter-cut the interviews judiciously with archive footage of the broader events and still photos of the group members.

One technique used to enliven the narrative – a device also employed by Wei in her latest documentary, *Golden Gate Girls* – is the animation of contemporary political cartoons and posters of the anti-Hu Feng campaign. This device – one might describe it as semiotic modification – satirically undercuts their message, serving to highlight their absurdity and crudeness. Naturally the film's credibility in traditional 'objective' documentary terms may be considered to be adversely affected by this artistic decision, but so exhaustive is the documentation and use of primary material elsewhere, the whimsicality serves to enhance rather than trivialise the film-makers' aim, precisely because latter-day animation technology is used to trump the graphic animation of the 1950s.

The next four parts extend the weather metaphor of the film's title – 'Early Drizzles', 'Rolling Thunder' 'Rainy Season' and 'After Sunset' – each introduced by a painting, together with Robert Ellis-Geiger's atmospheric weather-inspired music sound-track. They contextualise the narrative by providing the pre-war background as well as the relationship between Hu Feng, Lu Xun and others in the literary circle and Mao and the Party. Several now-middle-aged players come into the story at this point: among them are Zhang Xiaoshen, Hu Feng's younger son, who still remembers the sense of shame he felt at school when he learned of his father's 'crimes' from other children who dubbed him "Little Hu Feng', and Peng Xiaolian herself, who recalls the confusion and unhappiness caused to her as a child by the loss of her father and the cloud that hung over his name. Peng also visits a former left-wing associate of Hu Feng in Japan, now an academic, who continues to specialise in Hu Feng's work and reminisces about the synergy they felt as well as the personal dangers they faced both in Japan and in China in this period. However, perhaps the most moving testimonies come in the last part of the film in which we see the psychological and physical damage caused to many members of the group. A few, such as Hu's doughty wife, Mei Zhi, and the sprightly Jia Zhifang (who recalls the day in 1975 when 'the Sun set', referring judiciously to Mao's death) have come to terms with their experiences. Other interviewees such as Wang Rong, who died shortly after the interview, and the gifted poet Lu Ling, who ended up as an impoverished street-sweeper, mentally traumatised and spiritually numbed, never managed to do so. The latter had even forgotten that he had ever been a writer. On hearing about Lu's state from his son who was asked to visit him in Beijing, Hu wrote back, 'Now you see how the system can destroy a person'.[18]

Kirk Denton, another researcher and specialist on the period, who was also consulted during the film, points out that 'politics and history were always personal and the personal always political in Mao's China',[19] which is why Peng and Wei cannot adopt an impersonal and distanced tone. The film can be interpreted as a personal, if posthumous, reckoning with Mao and a personal vindication of those who suffered. As Peng Xiaolian points out, when she met the group individually and collectively it was like a family gathering: 'most of them didn't know my father, but they are all like family to me. They call each other brothers and naturally I have become their niece'.[20] To reinforce this concept of family, Wei manipulates the individual snapshots of Peng photographed with the surviving group members as a series of captioned family images spread across the screen.

Although Wei's voice is heard for Peng in the English-language version of the sound-track, the viewer is never in doubt about the personal orientation of the documentary. The poetic ending, a starburst image that metamorphoses into a white flower, accompanied by a simple Ah Long poem on innocence, underlines the film's *parti pris* position as well as its admittedly emotionally manipulative, but factually rigorous use of source material. No rebuttal of Peng's and Wei's version of this 'page of history' is likely to be heard in any case, since the case was officially long closed. Re-opening the wounds via the medium of documentary film is unwelcome to those who prefer to let them suppurate. This is why a film like *Storm under the Sun* represents the Hong Kong independent documentary at its most valuable, and why in the final analysis, despite the subject-matter, it is nevertheless a genuine Hong Kong documentary.

POSTSCRIPT

The sample of independent documentaries presented in the foregoing discussion illustrates the extraordinary diversity of styles, themes and approaches that are discernible in this often neglected sector of Hong Kong film culture. None of the above films closely resembles any other in conceptualisation or execution, and the directors have widely divergent backgrounds, although many of them have trained overseas in western academies or lived part of their lives in other countries. This particular selection should certainly not be construed as representing a 'top six' league table of Hong Kong documentary films, since there are no valid criteria for making such arbitrary choices. For the sake of variety and breadth of selection, only one film each by the relatively prolific Tammy Cheung and Evans Chan is included. Both directors have impressive filmographies and both merit dedicated books on the subject of their *oeuvre* (one on Chan as an *auteur* director is forthcoming).

Essentially, what the above films have in common is their independence and freedom to explore subjects and issues in whatever way the directors deem appropriate, as well as their accomplished exploitation of a broad range of devices available to the contemporary documentary-maker. Hong Kong remains the only place in China, apart from Taiwan, where this is possible. Unlike mainland China documentarians – who are increasingly pushing the boundaries of what they may or may not make films about – the directors are not *personae non gratae* in their home city and are free to work according to their own principles, not being subject to political censorship, thanks to Hong Kong's treasured rule of law. In the Introduction to her screenplay for *Storm under the Sun*, Louisa Wei asserts this sense of freedom which is integral to her work: 'what we have in mind is a work that is not dictated by the government and that constructs history through personal stories'.[21]

NOTES

1. Nichols, Bill, *Representing Reality: Issues and Concepts in Documentary* (Bloomington: Indiana University Press, 1991), pp. 32–75.
2. The copy of the film made available to the authors was only available in a Cantonese version, which was watched with the help of simultaneous interpretation. See acknowledgements.

3. Michael Ingham, interview with Ed Kong, May 2008.
4. Rayns, Tony, 'Hong Kong Notes: History in the Making', *Sight and Sound*, vol. 8, issue 7, July 1998, p. 5.
5. Chan, Joanna, 'Crown Ourselves with Roses', in Xiaomei Chan (ed.), *The Columbia Anthology of Modern Chinese Drama* (New York: Columbia University Press, 2010), p. 1096.
6. Williams, A., 'Issues of Decolonization: Two Essay Documentaries by Evans Chan', *Asian Cinema*, vol. 18, no.1 (Spring/Summer 2007), pp. 177–201.
7. Evans Chan, cited in Berry, Michael (ed.), *Speaking in Images: Interviews with Contemporary Chinese Film-makers* (New York: Columbia University Press, 2005), p. 521.
8. Ibid.
9. Wiseman, Frederick, cited in F. Spotnitz, 'Dialogue on Film', in *American Film*, vol. 16, no. 5 (1991), pp. 17–18.
10. Corrigan, Timothy, *The Essay Film: From Montaigne, After Marker* (New York: Oxford University Press, 2011), p. 105.
11. Izod, John, and Kilborn, Richard, 'The Documentary', in Hill, John and Church Gibson, Pamela (eds), *The Oxford Guide to Film Studies* (Oxford: Oxford University Press, 1998), p. 431.
12. Benjamin, Walter, *One Way Street and Other Writings* (London: Penguin, 2009), p. 114.
13. Lau Kit-wai, 'Entertainment Topics', *South China Morning Post*, 19 July 2012.
14. Conversation and personal email correspondence with university friend of Wong-Ka-jeng, May 2013.
15. Li, Raymond, 'Politburo Boss Urged to Stick to Party's Line on Socialism', *South China Morning Post*, 27 June 2013. In a speech in June 2013 the new Chinese leader Xi Jinping warned that discrediting late leader Mao Zedong would lead the country into turmoil. Quoted in Li, this reference.
16. Wei, Louisa, and Peng, Xiaolian, *Storm under the Sun* (screenplay) (Hong Kong: Blue Queen Communication, 2009), p. 148.
17. Ibid, p. 70.
18. Ibid, p. 204 (Hu Feng, cited in private correspondence).
19. Denton, K. A., 'Storm under the Sun: An Introduction', Blue Queen Communication website, Hong Kong, www.bqcc.com/storm_e.htm.
20. Peng, quoted in Wei and Peng, *Storm under the Sun*, p. 214.
21. Wei, 'The Making of Storm under the Sun', in Wei and Peng *Storm under the Sun*, p. 38.

Conclusions: The Future of Independent Documentary Film in Hong Kong, China and the Region

According to Michael Chanan:

> In short, despite appearances, so to speak, documentary has a power, if not directly to reveal the invisible, nonetheless to speak of things that orthodoxy and conservatism, power and authority, would rather we didn't know and didn't think about. And this is exactly why we need it.[1]

Chanan's timely reminder why a thriving documentary practice is important in any civilised society relates to his experience of documentary-making during the vicious civil war fuelled by the United States government during the 1980s in El Salvador. However, it also applies to the Hong Kong situation, even if the conditions for making documentaries in Hong Kong and around the region are not usually so hazardous. Bearing in mind the inevitable convergence between Hong Kong and China, culminating in the 2047 date for complete reintegration, it is essential for Hong Kong to build on the strong recent developments in independent film, as well as encouraging new digital online platforms for documentaries, which both democratise the form and contribute to a healthy and diverse public discourse on socio–political matters. As Chris Berry has observed in relation to independent film-makers in general and Tammy Cheung's documentaries in particular:

> If we apply a broader definition, including documentary, short films and animation, it may be more accurate to consider the cinema of Hong Kong as undergoing a transformation. The development of Tammy Cheung's career as an independent documentarian is a part of this glass half-full/half-empty situation.[2]

China's continuing practice of the persecution of intellectuals, artists and activists is a major obstacle to the growth of a genuine documentary film-making culture in the nation. For example, when Tibetan film-makers Dhondup Wangchen and Golog Jigme shot *Leaving Fear Behind* in the wake of the 2008 unrest in Tibet, the footage had to be smuggled out of their occupied homeland. Shortly after the film was completed, the two were arrested, and they have been missing since March 2009. There are many other such examples. However, in a country where censorship and surveillance are ubiquitous and documentary films are controlled by the state television company CCTV – which also has its own centrally managed documentary film-making branch (the Central Newsreel and Documentary Film Studio) – independent film-makers are still able to explore sensitive political, social and cultural issue, though often with considerable difficulty. These films are often made under cover, with little or no sources of funding, by dedicated bands of film-makers networking together. They also make their way into Hong Kong from time to time, and cross-border film-making alliances are now being formed. In 2011 and again in 2013 planned independent documentary film festivals in Beijing were cancelled at the last moment, such is the sensitivity of a whole gamut of documentary subjects to the Chinese government.

However, in recent years a growing number of independent organisations dedicated to the development of Chinese documentary film have appeared. CNEX, a good example of this trend, is a Taiwan-based organisation established in 2007 with the objective of supporting independent film-making exchange between China, Taiwan and Hong Kong. Providing that the present modest level of financial support continues to be available in Hong Kong, that externally imposed censorship, as well as self-censorship, can be avoided, and that exchange and exhibition of films are organised effectively, there are prospects for continued growth and interaction. These prospects are also helped by the distribution efforts of Tammy Cheung's Visible Record Company, and by the company's administration of the annual Chinese Documentary Festival, which continues to showcase documentary films from mainland China, Macao and Taiwan in Hong Kong. Recent Festival highlights have included *Let it Be* (Cecilia Ho and Hong Leng Hou, 2010), a study of ten indigenous Macanese women aged from ten to ninety, and Taiwanese director Kuo Shiao-yun's *Domestic Violence* trilogy (2008–12).

In addition to Visible Record's Chinese Documentary Festival, Chinese documentary films continue to be showcased in increasing numbers in Hong Kong in the Hong Kong International Film Festival, and award-winning examples of this phenomenon are *Last Train Home* (2009) by Lixin Fang, a Canadian-Chinese director, and Wang Libo's daring critique of China's Three Gorges Project's ecological damage in *Oh, the San Xia* (2013). The recent formation of CIFA (Chinese Independent Film-making Alliance) as a five-way co-operative venture between [Ying e Chi] from Hong Kong, South Taiwan Film Festival, Chongqing Independent Film and Video Festival, Art de Vivre from Shenzhen and Macao Film Festival is a further initiative that offers the chance of greater integration and synergy in regional independent film-making in general, which is beneficial to the documentary as well as to the fiction practice. The opportunities to develop this partnership have led to the Hong Kong Independent Film Festival (or *HKIndieFF* as it has come to be known), which [Ying e Chi] has coordinated, starting in 2011–12.

Beyond the China, Macao and Taiwan nexus, there are links now taking place between Hong Kong documentary film and independent film-makers in other countries in the region, such as Singapore, Indonesia, Malaysia, Thailand and the Philippines. These embryonic links have been reinforced by several conferences on Hong Kong and regional documentary film organised by Hong Kong Baptist University in 2009, 2012 and 2013. This South Asian connection is one that has considerable potential for development, both in terms of past commonalities related to colonial-era film-making and present and future prospects, with many Asian societies experiencing changes and internal and external pressures similar to those in Hong Kong. There is also a growing interest in university screenings of recent documentary films, such as those by Evans Chan, Tammy Cheung and Anson Mak. Research on documentary film infrastructure in China, India and Africa, as well as in other countries, in five of the universities – Hong Kong Baptist University, Chinese University of Hong Kong, the University of Hong Kong, City University and Lingnan University – continues to grow apace and attract funding, thus helping to remedy the previous neglect. Indeed, so bad was that neglect that in a 2001 article documentarian Philip Robertson was moved to describe Hong Kong documentary (with a degree of irony perhaps) as 'the genre that never was'.[3]

Hong Kong does not have a state-controlled media monopoly, and the two existing television stations and the public broadcaster RTHK benefit from a degree of editorial independence set out in the Broadcasting Ordinance. However, government interference and monopolistic cronyism have been causes of public concern, especially in the case of HKTV's application for a free-to-air licence being rejected without apparent justification. Thus, in practice, self-censorship and veiled managerial decisions by embedded elites to maintain the authority of the un-elected status quo have played a part since the colonial days and continue to do so. The possibility for reform of the broadcast institutions and television current-affairs documentary film remains, therefore, in considerable question, and rumours of managerial interference in presentation, selection and editing of material in organisations such as RTHK surface regularly in more independent local news media.

As Ackbar Abbas has pointed out in his assessment of Hong Kong's cinema in the international context, the reality for Hong Kong is that it has all that is required for a national cinema without actual nationhood:

It is a cinema that has emerged out of the impossibility of a nation-state: specifically, of nationhood understood as a search for independence, and for autonomy as its corollary. What we find in the Hong Kong case, both before and after 1997, is the paradox of autonomy without independence, where nationalism is bracketed by colonialism on one side and by globalization on the other; hence the need, among other things, for a politics of memory. On the other hand, the Hong Kong cinema can cast a cold eye on the aspirations typically associated with nationhood – precisely because they make no sense in a Hong Kong context.[4]

The future of documentary film, and the right to exercise that important option of casting a cold eye on events in Hong Kong and its environs, then, is one that is certain to be beset by struggles. A recent plea by Hong Kong's Film Development Council – responsible for nurturing local talent, creativity and initiatives – for the integration of film culture within a consistent cultural policy in the city on the lines of South Korea's more holistic model is likely to fall on deaf bureaucratic ears. In a recent *South China Morning Post* article,[5] Ma Fung-kwok, the Council's chairman, argues passionately for changing the remit of the film industry from its present incongruous position under the Commerce and Economic Development Bureau to a more appropriate context within a more dynamic cultural and creative industries set-up, in which its creative needs could be better addressed. According to Ma's comments, in spite of improved government funding in recent years, to the tune of nearly HK$400 million since 2007, there remain a plethora of problems for the film industry, including a severe lack of post-production facilities.

In view of the current development of the project known as West Kowloon Cultural District – a new state-of-the-art hub for arts and leisure in the city – attempts have been made to establish a Cultural Heritage and Cultural Identity Commission to explore the needs of cultural policy. However, so far, this proposed co-ordination of arts policy, which could potentially place fiction film and documentary under the umbrella of creative arts, as opposed to being considered a pure business enterprise, thus giving it a shot in the arm, has yet to occur. Without doubt, the creation of the West Kowloon complex offers exciting possibilities for Hong Kong documentary films to reach wider audiences within the city, and for more Hong Kong people to become aware of the power of the documentary form to reflect, and possibly even advance, their hopes for more enlightened social policy and their striving for genuine representation. Further critical investigation into the role and sustainability of the documentary genre in Hong Kong will certainly be needed in the coming years.

Michael Ingham, Hong Kong, June 2013

NOTES

1. Chanan, Michael, 'Filming the Invisible', in Austin, Thomas and de Jong, Wilma (eds), *Rethinking Documentary: New Perspectives, New Practices* (Maidenhead: McGraw-Hill Open University Press, 2008), p. 132.
2. Berry, Chris, 'Hong Kong Watcher: Tammy Cheung and the Hong Kong Documentary', in Kam, Louie (ed.), *Hong Kong Culture: Word and Image* (Hong Kong: Hong Kong University Press), p. 216.
3. Robertson, Phillip, 'Hong Kong Documentary: The Genre That Never Was', *Metro*, issue no. 126 (2001), p. 99.
4. Abbas, Ackbar, 'Hong Kong', in Hjört, Mette and Petrie, Duncan (eds), *The Cinema of Small Nations* (Edinburgh: Edinburgh University Press, 2007), pp. 125–6.
5. Chow, Vivienne. 'See the Bigger Picture on the Film Industry', *South China Morning Post*, 17 June 2013.

Bibliography

SECONDARY SOURCES CITED (ALPHABETICAL)

Abbas, Ackbar, *Hong Kong: Culture and the Politics of Disappearance* (Hong Kong: Hong Kong University Press, 1997).

Abbas, Ackbar, 'Hong Kong', in Hjört, Mette and Petrie, Duncan (eds), *The Cinema of Small Nations* (Edinburgh: Edinburgh University Press, 2007), pp. 113–26.

Aitken, Ian, 'The Development of the Official Film in Hong Kong', *Historical Journal of Film, Radio and Television*, vol. 32, no. 4 (December 2012), pp. 531–51.

Benjamin, Walter, *One Way Street and Other Writings* (London: Penguin, 2009).

Benjamin, Walter, *Understanding Brecht* (London: Verso, New Left Books, 2003).

Berry, Chris, 'Hong Kong Watcher: Tammy Cheung and the Hong Kong Documentary', in Kam, Louie (ed.), *Hong Kong Culture: Word and Image* (Hong Kong: Hong Kong University Press), pp. 213–28.

Berry, Michael, *Speaking in Images: Interviews with Contemporary Chinese Filmmakers* (New York: Columbia University Press, 2005).

Bordwell, David, *Planet Hong Kong: Popular Cinema and the Art of Entertainment* (Cambridge, MA: Harvard University Press, 2000).

Bordwell, David and Thompson, Kristin, *Film History: An Introduction* (New York: McGraw-Hill, Inc., 1994).

Carroll, John M., *A Concise History of Hong Kong* (Hong Kong: Hong Kong University Press, 2007).

Carroll, John M., *Edge of Empires: Chinese Elites and British Colonials in Hong Kong* (Hong Kong: Hong Kong University Press, 2007).

Chan, Evans, Interview, in Berry, Michael (ed.), *Speaking in Images: Interviews with Contemporary Chinese Film-makers*, (New York: Columbia University Press, 2005), pp. 509–42.

Chan, Joanna, 'Crown Ourselves with Roses', in Xiaomei Chan (ed.), *The Columbia Anthology of Modern Chinese Drama* (New York: Columbia University Press, 2010), pp. 1036–98.

Chanan, Michael, 'Filming the Invisible', in Austin, Thomas and de Jong, Wilma (eds), *Rethinking Documentary: New Perspectives, New Practices* (Maidenhead: McGraw-Hill Open University Press, 2008), pp. 121–32.

Cheung, Anthony, B. L., 'Reform in Search of Politics: The Case of Hong Kong's Aborted Attempt to Corporatise Public Broadcasting', *Asian Journal of Public Administration*, vol. 19, no. 2 (December 1997).

Childs, David, *Britain since 1945* (London: Routledge, 1986).

Christie, Ian, 'The Captains and the Kings Depart: Imperial Departure and Arrival in Early Cinema', in MacCabe, Colin and Grieveson, Lee (eds), *Empire and Film* (London: British Film Institute and Palgrave Macmillan, 2011).

Corrigan, Timothy, *The Essay Film: From Montaigne, After Marker* (New York; Oxford: Oxford University Press, 2011).

Chu, Tinchi, *Hong Kong Cinema: Coloniser, Motherland and Self* (New York: Routledge Curzon, 2003).

Fonoroff, Paul, *A Brief History of Hong Kong Cinema* (Hong Kong: Chinese University of Hong Kong, 1988).

Fox, Jo, 'John Grierson, His "Documentary Boys", and the British Ministry of Information, 1939–42', *Historical Journal of Film Radio and Television*, vol. 25, no. 3 (2005), pp. 345–69.

Fu, Poshek and Desser, David (eds), *The Cinema of Hong Kong: History, Arts, Identity* (Cambridge and New York: Cambridge University Press, 2000).

Graham, Gerald G., *Canadian Film Technology 1896–1986* (Newark: University of Delaware Press, 1989).

Fu, Winnie (ed.), *Hong Kong Filmography, Vol. II, 1942–1949* (Hong Kong: Hong Kong Film Archive, 1998).

Havinden, Michael and Meredith, David, *Colonialism and Development: Britain and its Tropical Colonies* (New York: Routledge, 1993).

Hong Kong Government, Committee for the Review of Public-Service Broadcasting, *Report on Review of Public-Service Broadcasting in Hong Kong* (Hong Kong: Hong Kong Government Printer, 2007).

Hong Kong Government, 'Status and Responsibilities of RTHK and Relationship with CEDB and the Secretary', *Charter of Radio Television Hong Kong* (Hong Kong: Hong Kong Government Printer, 2010).

Hong Kong Government, Broadcasting Review Board, *Report of the Broadcasting Review Board* (Hong Kong: Hong Kong Government Printer, August 1985).

Hong Kong Government, Water Supplies Department of the Government of the Hong Kong SAR, *Milestones of Hong Kong Water Supply* (Hong Kong: Hong Kong Government Printer, 2011).

Hong Kong Journalists' Association, *2006 Annual Report: RTHK under Siege – Hong Kong Government Takes on the Public Broadcaster* (Hong Kong: Hong Kong Journalists' Association, 2006).

Hyam, Ronald, *Britain's Declining Empire: The Road to Decolonialisation, 1918–1968* (Cambridge and New York: Cambridge University Press, 2006).

Ingham, Michael, *Hong Kong: A Cultural and Literary History* (Oxford: Signal Books, 2007).

Izod, John and Kilborn, Richard, 'The Documentary', in Hill, John and Church Gibson, Pamela (eds), *The Oxford Guide to Film Studies* (Oxford: Oxford University Press, 1998), pp. 426–33.

Jarvie, Ian, C., *Window on Hong Kong: a Sociological Study of the Hong Kong Film Industry and its Audience* (Hong Kong: Centre of Asian Studies University of Hong Kong, 1977).

Jarvie, Ian, C., 'The Social and Cultural Significance of the Decline of the Cantonese Movie,' in *Journal of Asian Affairs*, vol. 3, no. 2 (Fall 1979), pp. 40–50.

Jacobs, Lewis, 'Precursors and Prototypes (1894–1922)', in Jacobs, Lewis (ed.), *The Documentary Tradition* (New York and London: W. W. Norton and Company, 1979), pp. 2–11.

Kwok, Ching-ling (ed.), *Hong Kong Filmography, Vol. IV, 1953–1959* (Hong Kong: Kong Film Archive, 2003).

Kwok, Ching-ling (ed.), *Hong Kong Filmography, Vol. V, 1960–1964* (Hong Kong: Kong Film Archive, 2005).

Kwok, Ching-ling (ed.), *Hong Kong Filmography, Vol. VI, 1965–1969* (Hong Kong: Kong Film Archive, 2007).

Lai, Linda, 'Hong Kong Cinema in the 1930s: Docility, Social Hygiene, Pleasure-seeking and the Consolidation of the Film Industry', http://www.latrobe.edu.au/www/screeningthepast/firstrelease/fr1100/IIfr11h.htm.

Lai, Shek, *The Diary of Lai Man-wai* (Hong Kong: Hong Kong Film Archive, 2003).

Lam, Agnes (ed.), 'Oral History: Lai Man-wai', in *The Hong Kong-Guangdong Film Connection* (Hong Kong: Hong Kong Film Archive, 2005), pp. 130–9.

Law Wai-ming, 'Hong Kong's Cinematic Beginnings 1896–1908', in *The 19th Hong Kong International Film Festival: Early Images of Hong Kong and China* (Hong Kong: Hong Kong Government Printer, 1995).

Ma, Eric, Kit-wai, *Culture, Politics and Television in Hong Kong* (New York: Routledge, 1999).

MacCabe, Colin, 'To Take Ship to India and See a Naked Man Spearing Fish in Blue Water: Watching Films to Mourn the End of Empire', in Grieveson, Lee and MacCabe, Colin (eds), *Empire and Film* (London and New York: BFI and Palgrave Macmillan, 2011), pp. 1–7.

Mitchell, Stanley, 'Introduction', in Benjamin, Walter, *Understanding Brecht* (London: Verso; New Left Books, 2003), pp. vii–xix.

Moss, Peter, *GIS through the Years*, http://www.info.gov.hk/isd/40th/2.html.

Moss, Peter, *No Babylon: A Hong Kong Scrapbook* (New York: iUniverse, 2006).

Nichols, Bill, *Representing Reality: Issues and Concepts in Documentary* (Bloomington: Indiana University Press, 1991).

Pepper, Suzanne, *Keeping Democracy at Bay: Hong Kong and the Challenge of Chinese Political Reform* (New York: Rowman and Littlefield Publishers, 2008).

Porter, Bernard, *The Lion's Share: A Short History of British Imperialism, 1850–1995* (London and New York: Longman, 1996).

Pronay, Nicholas and Croft, Jeremy, 'British Film Censorship and Propaganda Policy during the Second World War', in Curran, James and Porter, Vincent (eds), *British Cinema History* (London: Weidenfeld and Nicolson, 1983), pp. 144–63.

Rayns, Tony, 'Hong Kong Notes: History in the Making', *Sight and Sound*, vol. 8, issue 7, July 1998, p. 5.

Reinhard, Wolfgang, *A Short History of Colonialism* (Manchester: Manchester University Press, 2011).

Robertson, Phillip, 'Hong Kong Documentary: The Genre that Never Was', *Metro*, issue 126 (2001), pp. 99–103.

Rodriguez, Hector, 'The Emergence of the Hong Kong New Wave', in Yau, Esther (ed.), *At Full Speed: Hong Kong Cinema in a Borderless World* (Minneapolis: University of Minnesota Press, 2001), pp. 53–69.

RTHK, 'Historical Background', *RTHK – History and Development* (Hong Kong: RTHK/Hong Kong Government Printer, 1984).

RTHK, 'Things about RTHK', http://rthk.hk/about/80book.htm.

Spotnitz, F., 'Dialogue on Film', *American Film*, vol. 16, no. 5 (1991), pp. 16–21.

Stokes, Lisa Odham and Hoover, Michael, *City on Fire: Hong Kong Cinema* (London: Verso, 1999).

Teo, Stephen, *Hong Kong Cinema: The Extra Dimensions* (London: British Film Institute, 1997).

Teo, Stephen, 'Politics and Social Issues in Hong Kong Cinema', in *Changes in Hong Kong Society through Cinema* (Hong Kong: Urban Council, 1988), pp. 38–41.

Teo, Stephen, 'The 1970s: Movement and Transition', in Fu, Poshek and Desser, David (eds), *The Cinema of Hong Kong: History, Arts, Identity* (Cambridge: Cambridge University Press, 2000), pp. 90–110.

Tsang, Steve, *A Modern History of Hong Kong* (Hong Kong: Hong Kong University Press, 2009).

Wei, Louisa and Peng Xiaolian, *Storm under the Sun* (screenplay) (Hong Kong: Blue Queen Communication, 2009).

Wei, Louisa, 'The Making of Thunder under the Sun', in Wei, Louisa and Peng Xiaolian, *Storm under the Sun* (screenplay) (Hong Kong: Blue Queen Communication, 2009), pp. 32–47.

Williams, Anthony, 'Issues of Decolonization: Two Essay Documentaries by Evans Chan', *Asian Cinema*, vol. 18, no. 1 (Spring/Summer 2007), pp. 177–201.

Wong, Mary (ed.), *Hong Kong Filmography, Vol. 1, 1913–1941* (Hong Kong: Hong Kong Film Archive, 1997).

Yan Mei Ning, 'The Role of Academic Research in the Making of Broadcasting Policy: The Case Study of Hong Kong', *International Journal of Communication*, vol. 2 (2008), pp. 396–405.

Yang, Jeff, *Once Upon a Time in China: A Guide to Hong Kong, Taiwanese and Mainland Chinese Cinema* (New York: Atria Books, 2003).

Yau, Esther (ed.), *At Full Speed: Hong Kong Cinema in a Borderless World* (Minneapolis: University of Minnesota Press, 2001).

Yu, Mo-wan, 'History of the Development of Hong Kong Newsreel Documentary Film', in *Changes in Hong Kong Society through Cinema* (Hong Kong: Urban Council, 1988), pp. 96–7.

NEWSPAPER ARTICLES CITED (CHRONOLOGICAL)

'Top Critics Praised Malayan Film Unit Productions', *The Straits Times*, 3 October 1954.

'This is Hong Kong Receives Oscar Award for Best Film', *South China Morning Post*, 14 March 1961.

'Speed is the Watchword of G.I.S. Film Unit', *China Mail*, 8 May 1965.

'New G.I.S. Travel Film Should be a Winner', *South China Morning Post*, 10 April 1968.

'Film Unit Productions World Successes', *South China Morning Post*, 16 October 1968.

'Squeezing the $ out of the Magic Stone', *China Mail*, 28 April 1969.

'London Sees Film on Colony', *South China Morning Post*, 8 July 1971.

'Hong Kong Style the Best Film Yet on Colony', *South China Morning Post*, 30 August 1971.

'Government replies to Film Unit Queries', *South China Morning Post*, 14 January 1972.

'New Films Show a Changing Pattern', *South China Morning Post*, 10 August 1972.

Choi, Linda, and Yeung, Christopher, 'Tung Sparks RTKO Autonomy Fears', *South China Morning Post*, 3 May 1985.

Fong, Bernard, 'Compulsive Viewing from RTHK Team', *South China Morning Post*, 13 September 1989.

Li, Angela, Yeung, Jimmy and Ng Kang-chung, 'Qian Instructs Media Not to Back Calls for Taiwan Split', *South China Morning Post*, 20 August 1999.

Lo, Alex, 'Show Ends for Heavyweight Defender of Independence', *South China Morning Post*, 20 October 1999.

'Comments' section, 'Beijing's Stamp on Hong Kong', *South China Morning Post*, 27 October 2000.

Hon, Sin-mi, May, 'Journalists Endorse Self-censorship Fears', *South China Morning Post*, 28 February 2001.

'Focus' section, 'When You Talk Back Too Much', *South China Morning Post*, 16 June 2001.

Schloss, Glenn, 'Pressing Times for the Media', *South China Morning Post*, 6 July 2002.

Ng Kang-chung, 'Majority Believes Government Meddles with the Media', *South China Morning Post*, 22 October 2002.

Chung, Jimmy and Lee, Claudia, 'Panel under Fire over RTHK's Future', *South China Morning Post*, 29 March 2006.

'Editorial', 'Broadcasting Review Can Learn from BBC', *South China Morning Post*, 19 April 2006.

Kwoh, Leslie, and Ng, Michael, 'RTHK Controversy Grows', *The Standard*, 27 April 2006.

Chu Pui-hing, 'End the Confusion in Broadcasting', *South China Morning Post*, 28 June 2006.

Ching, Frank, 'The Future RTHK Takes Shape', *South China Morning Post*, 12 October 2006.

Fung, Fanny and Hung, Denise, 'Public Broadcasting Delay Surprises Lawmakers', *South China Morning Post*, 18 January 2008.

'Why Hong Kong Depends on the Dongjiang Water', *Ming Pao*, 8 August 2010.

'Lai Man-wai's Struggle to Make Documentary on Sun Yat-sen', *Beijing Youth Daily*, 12 August 2011.

Cheung, Gary, 'Into the Lion's Den', *South China Morning Post*, 20 September 2011.

Lau Kit-wai, 'Entertainment Topics', *South China Morning Post*, 19 July 2012.

Chow, Vivienne. 'See the Bigger Picture on the Film Industry', *South China Morning Post*, 17 June 2013.

Li, Raymond, 'Politburo Boss Urged to Stick to Party's Line on Socialism', *South China Morning Post*, 27 June 2013.

Luk, Eddie, '"Whistle-blower" Left Out as RTHK Reshuffles Deck', *The Standard*, 28 June 2013.

PRIMARY SOURCES CITED (CHRONOLOGICAL)

HKRS 41-1-1603, 'Notes on Organisation of an Information Office', 14 November 1946.

Public Relations Office 'Annual Report' (Hong Kong Government Publications, 1951).

HKRS PRO 204, 6/516/52, Murray, Letter to Carstairs, 19 March 1952.

HKRS 160/1/23, 'Reorganisation of the Public Relations Office', PRO 1/2, Murray, Letter to S. H. Evans, CO, London, 19 January 1955.

HKRS 160, 5/7C, PRO Staff - General, Murray, 'Government Publicity in Hong Kong: A Report by the Public Relations Officer', November 1958.

HKRS 'GIS Press', 70-6-580 (i) 1961–73, 'Film on Hong Kong makes Impact on London Cinema Audiences. Hong Kong's Sea Festival enters Sixth Week of World premiere, General Release throughout Britain', 23 February 1963.

HKRS 'GIS Press', 70-6-580 (i) 1961–73, 'Five Hundred Films Available for Lending at Government Library', 29 October 1963.

ISD 5/7/1C, Watt, Nigel, Draft Executive Council Paper: 'Government Information Policy', 11 December 1967.

HKRS 'GIS Press', 70-6-580 (i) 1961–73, 'Film Unit Produces Series of Newsreels on Hong Kong to Keep Public Informed of Interesting Local Happenings', 5 April 1968.

HKRS TC 211/68, 'Notes of a Meeting on Radio Bulletins held in DC's Office at 11.30 am', 72f. 1, 23 November 1968.

HKRS 160-3-13, 'HK Government Film Unit Staff Costs 1970–1971', ISD 1/64 (CR).

HKRS 72 4-1, 'Government Television Unit', 12 March 1970.

HKRS, 'Memorandum', 7 July 1971.

HKRS 70-6-580 (1) 1961–73, 'GIS Press', 'Film Record of Changes in Fishing Industry, GIS Film Unit starts Production', 30 September 1971.

HKRS RHK (A) 1/3/68 (C) 'Memo', Director of Broadcasting to Hon. Colonial Secretary, 23 June 1972.

HKRS 670-1-9, ISD 4/60 (CR), Director of Information Services to Deputy Colonial Secretary, 'Radio News', 5 October 1972.

HKRS 'Memorandum', 8 January 1973.

HKRS 72-4-1, Colonial Secretariat, General Circular no.19/73, 'Government Publicity by Means of Television', 24 May 1973.

Commonwealth Broadcasting Association, *Commonwealth Broadcasting Association Handbook* (1981–2).

Draft Agreement Between the Government of Great Britain and Northern Ireland and the Government of the People's Republic of China on the Future of Hong Kong (known informally as the Joint Declaration), Annex I Paragraph I: 'Elaboration of the People's Republic of China of its Basic Policies Regarding Hong Kong' (1984).

RTHK Programme Staff Union Newsletter, vol. 1 (1987).

CB (C8) 4/9/3 (92) pt. 22, Government Secretariat, letter to RTHK Programme Staff Union, 18 January 1992.

Choi, K. C. 'A Brief History of Hong Kong Independent Film and Video Making', unpublished conference paper, 2003.

Clayton, David, '"Water Famished Hong Kong": The International Political Economy of Water Supplies in Hong Kong. 1960–64', pp. 12–13, unpublished research paper by Dr David Clayton of the University of Bath, presented to Ian Aitken, May 2013.

Index